EXAM✓CRAM

VCP4
VMware Certified Professional,
Second Edition

Elias Khnaser

VCP4 Exam Cram: VMware Certified Professional, Second Edition

ISBN-13: 978-0-7897-4056-4
ISBN-10: 0-7897-4056-7

Library of Congress Cataloging-in-Publication data is on file.

Printed in the United States of America

First Printing: January 2011

Trademarks

All terms mentioned in this book that are known to be trademarks or service marks have been appropriately capitalized. Pearson cannot attest to the accuracy of this information. Use of a term in this book should not be regarded as affecting the validity of any trademark or service mark.

Warning and Disclaimer

Bulk Sales

Pearson offers excellent discounts on this book when ordered in quantity for bulk purchases or special sales. For more information, please contact

U.S. Corporate and Government Sales
1-800-382-3419
corpsales@pearsontechgroup.com

For sales outside of the U.S., please contact

International Sales
international@pearson.com

Associate Publisher
David Dusthimer

Acquisitions Editor
Betsy Brown

Development Editor
Andrew Cupp

Managing Editor
Sandra Schroeder

Senior Project Editor
Tonya Simpson

Copy Editor
Geneil Breeze

Indexer
Brad Herriman

Proofreader
Sheri Cain

Technical Editors
Brian Atkinson
Gabrie van Zanten

Publishing Coordinator
Vanessa Evans

Media Producer
Dan Scherf

Book Designer
Gary Adair

Compositor
TnT Design, Inc.

Contents at a Glance

Table of Contents

Preface

Virtualization is one of the hottest topics in the tech industry today. The leader in the virtualization space at the present time is without a doubt VMware with its virtual infrastructure offering. As VMware software began to take its place in the data center and demand respect in the industry, the need for a certification path became clear. Such a certification separates those who have studied the technology and can apply it at a professional level from those who have just installed it and started messing with it. I am a big believer that there is no alternative to studying a technology thoroughly. There is only so much you can learn from installing it and using it in only a few specific circumstances, because that exposes you only to limited features and obscures you from harnessing the full potential of the software by leveraging features you probably never knew existed. For this reason and many more, I am a strong believer that you should study the software, learn it, and then use it hands on as much as possible. It is by doing this that you truly master the software.

When you have studied and understand a software, taking a certification exam becomes relatively easy. For example, if you've thoroughly studied, you know that the maximum amount of physical memory that ESX/ESXi 4.1 supports is 1TB. However, someone who just installs the software and starts using it may not know this because the software installation does not require this knowledge at the time of installation.

This book aims to present the information you need to recap and reinforce your existing knowledge of VMware vSphere 4 and properly prepare you to confidently take the VCP-410 exam. The book is structured in a way to help you with your final exam preparation and contains enough information to make it a true test preparation book, but in a concise manner.

About the Author

Elias Khnaser is an author, speaker, and IT consultant specializing in Microsoft, Citrix, and VMware virtualization technologies. With more than 14 years of experience, Elias is one of the world's leading experts on virtualization and cloud computing and is a recipient of the VMware vExpert award.

Elias is the practice manager for virtualization and cloud computing at Artemis Technology and is well known for his ability to relate highly technical concepts to align IT with business needs.

Elias is a highly sought-after and top-rated speaker for live and recorded events. He is a frequent contributor to *Forbes* and *InformationWeek*. He has written hundreds of white papers and countless articles. Elias has authored and co-authored many books and computer-based training products for EliasKhnaser.com and TrainSignal.com.

Elias has designed and deployed some of the largest Citrix and VMware implementations in the world.

His other publications and accomplishments include

- ▶ VMware vSphere 4 Training DVD at EliasKhnaser.com (May 2010)
- ▶ *VCP VMware Certified Professional Exam Cram* by Que Publishing, ISBN: 0-7897-3805-8 (December 2008)
- ▶ VMware VI3: ESX Server 3.5 & Virtual Center 2.5 Training DVD at EliasKhnaser.com (April 2008)
- ▶ "VMware ESX Server 3.0 CBT" at EliasKhnaser.com
- ▶ "Citrix MetaFrame XP CBT" at CBTnuggets.com

He is the co-author of three published books:

- ▶ *Citrix CCA MetaFrame Presentation Server 3.0 and 4.0 (Exams 223/256)* (Exam Cram) by Que Publishing, ISBN: 9780789732460
- ▶ *MCSE Designing Security for a Windows Server 2003 Network: Exam 70-298 Study Guide and DVD Training System* by Syngress Publishing
- ▶ *Citrix MetaFrame XP Including Feature Release 1* by Syngress Publishing

He has been a contributing author at

- ▶ Forbes.com
- ▶ InformationWeek.com
- ▶ Dabcc.com

About the Technical Editors

Brian Atkinson is a senior systems engineer with 14 years of experience in the IT field. For the past five years, he has focused on virtualization, storage, and virtualization evangelism. Brian holds both the VCP 3 and VCP 4 certifications and has been awarded the VMware vExpert designation from VMware for both 2009 and 2010. He is a VMware Technology Network (VMTN) Moderator and active contributor. He also maintains his personal blog in the VMTN communities at http://communities.vmware.com/blogs/vmroyale/.

Gabrie van Zanten is a virtualization specialist. As a consultant, he designs and implements virtual infrastructures for customers. Besides being a consultant, Gabrie runs one of the top 10 ranked blogs on VMware at http://www.GabesVirtualWorld.com. He writes about VMware and helps his readers get in-depth understanding on how VMware products work. His blogging activities, the presentations he gives, and the effort he puts into helping members of the VMware community have earned him the VMware vExpert award in 2009 and 2010.

Dedication

*To Maya and Peter, my gorgeous niece and nephew,
for all the joys you bring to our family.*

Acknowledgments

No book would ever come to fruition without the incredible work done by everyone behind the scenes, and as such, I must extend a huge thank you to all the people at Pearson for their amazing work. To Dave Dusthimer, associate publisher, for his immediate interest and excitement about this book, thank you for trusting me on this one. To Betsy Brown, acquisitions editor extraordinaire, thank you so much for your promptness and patience. I'm very thankful to have had you on this project (honestly, it's true!). You're a pleasure to work with. To Drew Cupp, development editor, I can only imagine what you had to put up with to get this done. I enjoyed working with you again and thank you for everything. To Tonya Simpson and Geneil Breeze, thanks for correcting my shoddy grammar, pointing out the obvious mistakes, and tirelessly ensuring that I'm actually saying what I think I'm saying. Special thanks to all the production staff who silently (at least silently from my perspective) work to put everything together. As always, it looks fantastic! And finally, thanks to the great work of our technical editors, Gabrie van Zanten and Brian Atkinson, who provided excellent insight, suggestions, and corrections to my work. Of course, any errors or omissions are strictly my doing. These guys can't be expected to find everything!

And special thanks to the friends and family who had to once again endure the pressures and pains of book writing. They'll get used to it someday....

Happy reading, and good luck!

We Want to Hear from You!

As the reader of this book, *you* are our most important critic and commentator. We value your opinion and want to know what we're doing right, what we could do better, what areas you'd like to see us publish in, and any other words of wisdom you're willing to pass our way.

As an associate publisher for Pearson IT Certification, I welcome your comments. You can email or write me directly to let me know what you did or didn't like about this book—as well as what we can do to make our books better.

Please note that I cannot help you with technical problems related to the topic of this book. We do have a User Services group, however, where I will forward specific technical questions related to the book.

When you write, please be sure to include this book's title and author as well as your name, email address, and phone number. I will carefully review your comments and share them with the author and editors who worked on the book.

Email: feedback@pearsonitcertification.com

Mail: David Dusthimer
Associate Publisher
Pearson IT Certification
800 East 96th Street
Indianapolis, IN 46240 USA

Reader Services

Visit our website and register this book at pearsonitcertification.com for convenient access to any updates, downloads, or errata that might be available for this book.

Introduction

Welcome to the *VCP4 Exam Cram*. The purpose of this book is to properly prepare you and equip you with the needed knowledge to successfully sit and pass the VCP-410 exam. This introduction provides a general overview of the VMware certification program and the exam and covers how this *Exam Cram* book will help you reach your goals of becoming certified.

This book, as with its predecessors in the *Exam Cram* family of certification books, concentrates on reinforcing your knowledge of the subject matter at hand and preparing you to sit the exam. That being said, this book will not teach you everything there is to know about the technology because this is not its primary purpose. As a late-stage exam preparation resource, it concentrates on testing and reinforcing your knowledge of material that is most likely to appear on the exam.

Although reading a book is an excellent way of learning, I strongly recommend that you take the knowledge you acquire from book learning and use it to install and configure VMware ESX/ESXi and vCenter. Hands-on experience is imperative not only to your successful completion of the exam, but also to your successful endeavors in properly implementing and maintaining a vSphere infrastructure.

About the VMware VCP Program

The VMware VCP program was designed to allow candidates to demonstrate their expertise with the software by completing certain requirements and passing an exam. The program is open to any individual who completes the requirements. There are many advantages to becoming VCP certified. For some, it is for career advancement; for others, it is to become VMware partners, and so on.

The requirements set forth by VMware on becoming a VCP are as follows:

- ▶ Attend a VMware authorized course. These instructor-led courses provide a great learning method and hands-on exposure to the product.

- ▶ Gain hands-on experience with the product.

- ▶ Sit and pass the VCP-410 exam to demonstrate your expertise on the matter.

VMware also provides various documents on its website that help you gain a better understanding of the topics that you will be challenged on during the exam. I would like to single out the vSphere 4 Exam blueprint as a great reference for the exam, located here: http://mylearn.vmware.com/lcms/mL_faq/2726/VCPonvSphere4ExamBlueprint.pdf.

About the VCP Exam

Attending a VMware-authorized training class is one of the requirements from VMware Education to become a VMware Certified Professional (VCP). After you have attended the VMware-authorized class and have completed your preparations for taking the exam, you need to register at a VMware testing center in your area. Currently, all VMware certification exams are administered by Pearson VUE. You can register online at http://www.pearsonvue.com/vmware or by calling 1-800-676-2797 in the United States and Canada. Outside the Americas, please consult the Pearson VUE website for contact information in your region of the world.

The VCP-410 exam costs $175 USD and must be booked at least 24 hours in advance. You may reschedule your exam up to 24 hours before the date you intend on taking it. Cancellation may be subject to a fee, so please consult the Pearson VUE website for more details on the policy.

In the test room, the administrator logs you in to your exam, verifying that your user ID and exam number are correct. After you review the introduction information, the exam begins.

The VCP-410 VMware Certification exam has 75 questions, and native English speakers have 105 minutes to complete the exam. Non-English speakers have an additional 30 minutes, for a total of 135 minutes. The testing application is Windows based and presents a single question per screen. On the top right, you find the time and number of questions remaining.

Questions are typically multiple choice, and the difficulty level varies from question to question. You can expect the following:

▶ **Select the correct answer:** With these types of multiple-choice questions, you are asked to choose the one correct answer that most appropriately answers the given question. In some situations, different answers may be correct under slightly different configurations, so make sure you read the question carefully and answer it according to what is asked in the specific question.

▶ **Select all that apply (or don't apply):** These types of questions ask you to select all the answers listed that correctly apply to the question given. None of the answers to all of them may apply, so be sure to read these types of questions carefully. In many cases, subtle wording has been purposely used to trip up those who aren't paying attention. Partial credit is not given for these types of questions. Unless the correct answer is given, you receive no credit for the question.

▶ **True or false:** These types of questions present you with the option to agree with the statement in the question or refuse it. Read the question carefully and choose true or false.

When your test is scored, no added penalty is given for a wrong answer compared to giving no answer at all, so answering every question asked is worthwhile even if you are not sure and must guess. VMware has attempted to make the questions as fair as possible and to ensure that all questions have a single correct answer. Of course, mistakes do happen, and a "poor" question may find its way onto your test, presenting you with a poorly worded or ambiguous question that may not have a clearly correct answer. In this situation, the best thing to do is to answer the question to the best of your knowledge.

After you complete the exam, the testing software responds with your score and informs you whether you have passed or failed. The VCP-410 exam requires a minimum passing score of 75%.

If you don't pass the exam, the key point is not to become discouraged. We have all had days when things just didn't quite go as well as we had hoped. The best method in this situation is to return as soon as possible to the study process and brush up on your weak areas in preparation for another exam attempt. You can reschedule a new test through Pearson VUE as soon as available if you so choose. We recommend that you schedule time sooner rather than later so that material that you have already studied is still fresh in your mind. You are required to pay the full fee to take the test again.

Exam Topics

Table I.1 lists the exam topics covered in this book and indicates the chapter where each is covered.

TABLE I.1 **Exam Cram VCP4 Exam Topics**

Exam Topic	Chapter
VMkernel	1
Service Console (SC)	
vCenter Database Design	
vCenter Preinstallation	
Update Manager	
VMware Symmetric Multi-Processing (SMP)	
vMotion	
Distributed Resource Scheduler (DRS)	
Virtual Machine File System (VMFS)	
VMware Consolidated Backup (VCB)	
High Availability (HA)	
Encapsulation	
Simulation	
Emulation	
Storage vMotion	
ESX Disk Partitions	2
Windows & Linux Filesystems	
ESX/ESXi System Requirements	
Load Drivers	
Creating Datastores	
Lockdown Mode	
SSH Access	
vSphere Client Access	
Configure NTP Client	
Port Trunking	3
802.1Q VLAN Tagging	
vNetwork Distributed Switches	
Virtual Ports	
Virtual Port Groups	
VMDirectPath	
Internal vSwitch	
Single Adapter vSwitch	
Multiple Adapter vSwitch	
Standard Virtual Switches (vSS)	
Physical Switches	
VMkernel	

TABLE I.1 **continued**

Exam Topic	Chapter
VMware vCenter Clustering	
VMware vCenter Heartbeat	
Cold Migrations	6
Snapshots	
Guided Consolidation	
Virtual Appliances	
vApps	
Templates	
Open Virtualization Format (OVF)	
VMware Tools	
Virtual Disk	
VMware Converter	
Capacity Planner	
Virtual Hardware	
Virtual Machine Files	
Virtual Machine Maximums	
Roles	7
Privileges	
Permissions	
vpxuser	
Web Access	
Virtual Machine Shortcut	
WebAccess Tasks	
WebAccess Requirements	
Resource Pools	8
Clusters	
Shares	
Limit	
Reservation	
Expandable Reservation	
vMotion	
Storage vMotion	
Eagerzeroed	
Distributed Resource Scheduler (DRS) Cluster	
VMware EVC	
Affinity Rules	

Exam Topic	Chapter
Hyper-Threading	9
Hardware Execution Context (HEC)	
Transparent Memory Page Sharing	
Balloon-driver	
Hypervisor Swap	
Memory Compression	
Alarms	
Virtual CPU	
Virtual Memory	
CPU	
Memory	
Disk	
VMware Consolidated Backup (VCB)	10
High Availability (HA)	
Admission Control	
Host Backup	
Cluster-in-a-Box	
Cluster-across-Boxes	
Physical-to-Virtual Cluster	
Fault Tolerance	
Data Recovery	
MSCS Clustering	
Host Isolation	

The Ideal VCP Candidate

Before you attempt to take the VCP-410 exam and try to become a VMware Certified Professional (VCP), it is imperative that you know considerable information about VMware vSphere 4 and all its suite components.

To complete the VCP certification, you have to be a well-rounded ESX/ESXi Server-aware individual. The VCP certification is meaningful and maps closely to the everyday virtualization work environment found in the real world. With that said, you will also likely find this particular exam quite challenging to complete successfully.

The exam requires you to have at least a base level of knowledge about the entire vSphere suite. You need to know how ESX/ESXi 4 networking works, including the concept of virtual networking within a virtual infrastructure. You need to be intimately familiar with storage in a vSphere environment, including what types of storage are supported and how to best configure this storage for optimal performance of the virtual machines. Backup is no small task in any environment, and knowing how to safeguard your VMs and recover them when necessary is crucial to VCP certification. Monitoring and resource management are other areas where you will be tested without a doubt. And all these text topics are certainly not to dismiss vCenter in all its intricacies.

Increasing numbers of people are becoming VCPs, so the goal is within reach. If you're willing to tackle the process seriously and do what it takes to obtain the necessary experience and knowledge, you can take—and pass—the exam involved in obtaining a VCP certification.

Just to give you some idea of what an ideal candidate is like, here is some relevant information about the background and experience such an individual should have:

▶ Training or significant on-the-job experience in network theory, concepts, and operations is helpful. This includes everything from networking media and transmission techniques through network operating systems, services, and applications.

▶ Experience with any UNIX operating system is a plus to any candidate. Because the Service Console operating system is Linux based, knowing Linux in particular or UNIX in general will help you navigate better and use common UNIX commands in daily tasks.

▶ Training or significant on-the-job experience in storage technologies including Fiber Channel and iSCSI is a huge plus, but this book covers these concepts to the extent they are tested on the VCP exam. However, knowledge of these technologies will make you more comfortable with the material.

▶ A thorough understanding of how to install operating systems is required because these virtual machines require an OS installation.

How to Prepare for the Exam

Preparing for the VCP exam, as with any other technical exam, requires that you dedicate time to both acquiring and studying material directly related to the VCP-410 exam. To pass this exam, you are expected to know the different components and technologies that make up the VMware vSphere 4 suite, which includes intimate knowledge of both ESX/ESXi 4.1 and vCenter 4.1.

> **Note**
>
> There is significant information to absorb and go through that is required for you to pass the VCP-410 exam. Therefore, if your plan is to study the night before or a few days before the exam, don't expect to be fully prepared on the day of the exam.

The following is a general list of material that can be helpful in preparing you for the VCP-410 exam:

- This *Exam Cram* book, which provides you with a concise and thorough review of the material considered vital to your exam-taking success. This book serves as a supplement to reinforce your knowledge of the technology.

- VMware vSphere 4 evaluation kits from VMware. By acquiring an evaluation of the software, installing it, and getting intimately familiar with it, you are training yourself hands on, and this knowledge is extremely valuable as you learn better as you do things. This step also takes you from the theoretical to the practical.

- VMware-authorized training course. The instructor-led four-day class enables you to focus your training on a mixture of lecture and hands-on labs. The instructor-led class is filled with valuable information and helpful labs and is sure to prime you for the VCP exam in addition to its being a requirement for fulfilling the VCP requirements.

- VMware vSphere 4 Training DVD from http://www.eliaskhnaser.com is a great way to learn, reinforce existing knowledge, or simply have handy as a reference any time you need it. The DVD is filled with information and goes beyond the VCP-410 requirements. It is a study-at-your-own-pace training course.

▶ Exam preparation tests from respectable vendors. Getting accustomed to the types of questions that are asked on the VCP exam is extremely helpful; you will find that VMware has some sample questions on its website. You may also find certification exam vendors that sell respectable preparation tests.

▶ VMware vSphere 4 documentation is an imperative part of your testing preparation. We would like to highlight the Configuration Maximums for vSphere 4 and 4.1, and the vSphere 4 Resource Management Guide, all of which are available via the vSphere 4 documentation page: http://www.vmware.com/support/pubs/vs_pages/vsp_pubs_esxi41_i_vc41.html.

How to Use This Book and CD

vSphere 4 is a large topic, and covering it in technical detail is an immense task. What we did in this book is laser focus on the topics and technical details that you need to know to pass the exam. This book should be used to reinforce your knowledge and help you prepare. The accompanying CD holds practice exams and a digital copy of the tear-out cram sheet available in the beginning of the book.

Chapter Format and Conventions

Every Exam Cram chapter follows a standard structure and contains graphical clues about important information. The structure of each chapter includes the following:

▶ **Opening topics list:** This defines the exam topics to be covered in the chapter.

▶ **Cram Saver questions:** At the beginning of each section is a quiz. Take the quiz to assess how well versed you are in that section's topics. From there, you can read the section or move on to the Exam Alerts and questions at the end.

▶ **Topical coverage:** The heart of the chapter. Explains the topics from a hands-on and a theory-based standpoint. This includes in-depth descriptions, tables, and figures that are geared to build your knowledge so that you can pass the exam.

▶ **Exam Alerts:** These are interspersed throughout the book. Watch out for them!

ExamAlert

This is what an Exam Alert looks like. Normally, an alert stresses concepts, terms, hardware, software, or activities that are likely to relate to one or more certification test questions.

▸ **Cram Quiz questions:** At the end of each section is a quiz. The Cram Quizzes, and ensuing explanations, gauge your knowledge of the subjects. If the answers to the questions don't come readily to you, consider reviewing the section.

Additional Elements and CD

Beyond the chapters, two more tools help you prepare for the exam:

▸ **Practice exams:** There are two practice exams, consisting of 75 questions each. One is located in the printed book, and the other is in the exam engine on the CD.

▸ **Cram Sheet:** The tear out Cram Sheet is located right in the beginning of the book. This is designed to jam some of the most important facts you need to know for the exam into one small sheet, allowing for easy memorization.

Onward, Through the Fog!

After you've assessed your readiness, undertaken the right background studies, obtained the hands-on experience that will help you understand the products and technologies at work, and reviewed the many sources of information to help you prepare for a test, you'll be ready to take a round of practice tests. When your scores come back positive enough to get you through the exam, you're ready to go after the real thing. If you follow this regimen, you'll know not only what you need to study, but also when you're ready to take the exam. Good luck!

CHAPTER 1

Introducing vSphere 4

This chapter covers the following VCP exam topics:

- ▶ VMkernel
- ▶ Service Console (SC)
- ▶ vCenter Database Design
- ▶ vCenter Preinstallation
- ▶ Update Manager
- ▶ VMware Symmetric Multi-Processing (SMP)
- ▶ vMotion
- ▶ Distributed Resource Scheduler (DRS)
- ▶ Virtual Machine File System (VMFS)
- ▶ VMware Consolidated Backup (VCB)
- ▶ High Availability (HA)
- ▶ Encapsulation
- ▶ Simulation
- ▶ Emulation
- ▶ Storage vMotion

(For more information on the VCP exam topics, see "About the VCP Exam" in the introduction.)

This chapter digs in and starts talking about virtualization in general and progresses to a discussion of vSphere 4 specifically. The word *virtualization* gets thrown around a lot these days, and in most cases it's used to imply server virtualization. But because virtualization is so much more than just server virtualization, this chapter discusses the different types of virtualization technologies that are at your disposal today.

It will be imperative that you, as a virtualization professional, can identify and distinguish between types of virtualization solutions. After you have reinforced your knowledge of the types of virtualization, this chapter moves on to a virtual machine overview and provides an understanding of the different components of a *virtual machine (VM)* and how a VM compares to a physical machine.

The chapter wraps up with an introduction to vSphere 4, which is the subject of this book and the topic of your exam. This chapter breaks down the main components of the vSphere suite—identifying and explaining its main architectural features.

What Is Virtualization?

▶ **VMkernel**

▶ **vCenter Database Design**

▶ **vCenter Preinstallation**

Cram**Saver**

If you can correctly answer these questions before going through this section, save time by skimming the Exam Alerts in this section and then completing the Cram Quiz at the end of the section.

1. Consider a scenario in which ESX Servers are separated from a vCenter Server by a firewall. What port would you need to open to allow authentication communications?

   ○ **A.** 902
   ○ **B.** 903
   ○ **C.** 904
   ○ **D.** 906

2. True or false: You can create a database for vCenter on a dedicated database server using the setup wizard during the installation of vCenter.

   ○ **A.** True
   ○ **B.** False

Answers

1. **A** is correct. Port 902 needs to be open when ESX/ESXi hosts and vCenter Server are separated by a firewall for authentication communications to flow back and forth.

2. **B**, False, is correct. The vCenter database cannot be created by the setup wizard during the installation of vCenter if the database server is a dedicated remote server. In this case the database must be created prior to the installation of vCenter. However, you can use SQL Express for small environments, which has the added benefit of automatically creating the database during installation.

When you think of the concept of virtualization and realize that it has been around for quite some time now, you might ask what happened to suddenly make this technology so attractive that it has penetrated every data center in the world one way or another and even requires its own professional certification. Virtualization in its purest form is the separation of the physical hardware from the software that is installed on it by adding a layer of software between them. This layer is known as the *hypervisor* and is typically installed on bare metal.

The hypervisor enables you to install multiple instances of the same or different operating systems on the same physical machine. It virtualizes the hardware components of the machine it is installed on and presents virtual hardware to the operating system to facilitate the installation. The hypervisor then acts as the "maestro," or the regulator, that organizes how these operating system instances (referred to as virtual machines) have access to the hardware.

Why You Need Virtualization

To understand why you need virtualization, first take a quick look at the data center today without virtualization. The first things you will notice in any data center are siloed servers and applications; in other words, there is a one-to-one relationship between the server and the application that resides on it. Examples include servers that are dedicated for Microsoft Exchange or SQL or Internet Information Services (IIS) or Citrix; there are servers that are just domain controllers, domain name system (DNS) servers, or print servers. This practice leaves servers that are underutilized as far as resources are concerned. So if you have a dual-socket, dual-core server acting as a domain controller or an IIS server, for example, a closer look at these servers will reveal that their resource utilization as far as CPU is concerned is probably no more than 15–20%.

So underutilized hardware and crowded data centers that require a lot of cooling and power are the main denominators at any data center. This is where virtualization shines. By virtualizing, you are taking advantage of the best of both worlds: You can have multiple server instances on the same hardware, preserving the one-to-one, server-to-application siloing you have been accustomed to for stability and separation reasons, while now taking better advantage of resources and reducing the amount of cooling and power needed. As the amount of physical hardware shrinks, this allows for more efficient usage of energy, leading to "Green IT."

Types of Virtualization

There are different types of virtualization. The most common and most popular as of this writing is operating system virtualization, which is what vSphere 4 does. Server virtualization is the process of separating the physical hardware from the operating system software.

The different forms of virtualization can be categorized as follows:

▶ *Hypervisor type-1 virtualization* is what ESX and ESXi are. This type of operating system virtualization installs a thin layer of software known as the hypervisor, or the virtualization layer, on bare metal.

▶ With *hypervisor type-2 virtualization*, you have an underlying operating system loaded on the physical machine and then you install software that allows virtual machines to be created and run. Examples include VMware Workstation, VMware Server, Microsoft Virtual PC, and Microsoft Virtual Servers. This type of virtualization is less efficient because it carries the additional resource burden of an underlying operating system and also relies on this operating system to remain stable for the VM loaded on it to function properly. The advantage of a type-2 hypervisor is that a wider range of hardware is supported, because it leverages the operating system's support of hardware, and since Type-2 installs on an existing operating system, by reciprocity it is able to support the same hardware profile.

> **ExamAlert**
>
> As a VMware Certified Professional, you are expected to know the difference between host-based and bare metal hypervisors. The exam will surely touch on this subject.

▶ *Application virtualization* is the process of separating the application from being installed on the operating system. What you end up with here is a bunch of files that make up the virtual application. The virtual application is then run on the operating system as if it were installed on it but without actually installing. This eliminates any potential for application conflicts and shared DLL problems because the application is not installed and is not sharing the Registry or the DLLs. All the files and Registry settings it needs to run are encapsulated within the files of the virtual application.

▶ *Storage virtualization* is the process of presenting virtual storage to the hosts. This virtual storage can be a combination of different physical technologies and can reside in different places on the network, but is presented to the host as a single storage capacity.

Cram Quiz

Answer these questions. The answers follow the last question. If you cannot answer these questions correctly, consider reading the section again.

1. True or false: vCenter 4.0 is supported on both 32-bit and 64-bit operating systems.

   ○ **A.** True

   ○ **B.** False

2. True or false: It is recommended that vCenter 4.1 server and the license server be installed on the same server.

   ○ **A.** True

   ○ **B.** False

Cram Quiz Answers

1. **A** is correct. vCenter 4.0 is supported on 32- and 64-bit operating systems, whereas v*Center 4.1 is supported only on 64-bit operating systems.

2. Answer **B**, False, is correct. As of the release of vSphere 4, a license server is not a component of the virtual infrastructure suite anymore. The only time a license server would still be required is in the event that you want to extend support to ESX/ESXi hosts that are pre-ESX/ESXi 4, as they would need a license server for proper licensing.

Virtual Machine Overview

▶ **Encapsulation**

▶ **Simulation**

▶ **Emulation**

Cram**Saver**

If you can correctly answer these questions before going through this section, save time by skimming the Exam Alerts in this section and then completing the Cram Quiz at the end of the section.

1. One of the benefits of virtual machines is that if one of them crashes, it does not affect the others. What is the correct term for this benefit?

   ○ **A.** Hardware independence

   ○ **B.** Compatibility

   ○ **C.** Isolation

   ○ **D.** Encapsulation

2. Select three benefits of virtual machines.

   ○ **A.** Isolation

   ○ **B.** Encapsulation

   ○ **C.** Hardware Bound

   ○ **D.** Compatibility

Answers

1. **C** is correct. Although hardware independence, compatibility, and encapsulation are all benefits of VMs, isolation is the correct answer here. With isolation, if a VM crashes, it has no effect on other VMs. Hardware independence means that VMs do not detect and are not aware of the actual physical hardware. Encapsulation means that VMs are a collection of files. Compatibility means they share identical hardware based on x86 standard architecture.

2. **A, B**, and **D** are correct. Virtual machines are not hardware bound; they are actually hardware independent. That is one of the advantages of VMs because they use "identical hardware."

Virtual machines are similar to physical machines in terms of what they are made up of and what constitutes them. The only difference is that physical machines obviously use physical hardware, whereas virtual machines use virtual hardware. In virtual machines, you find all the usual components that make up a physical machine, such as a virtual CPU, virtual memory, virtual hard drive, and a virtual network interface card (NIC). Similar to physical machines where you can add additional physical components like small computer system interface (SCSI) adapters or serial ports, virtual machines enable you to add virtual components on the fly, whether they are SCSI adapters, serial ports, or parallel ports.

In essence, a virtual machine creates an x86 or x64 platform that allocates all the needed virtual components to allow for an operating system installation. Virtual machines are also very portable because they are made up of a collection of files, which means at any given time you can back up these files, move them, copy them to your USB drive, and take them anywhere.

Virtual machines using VMware technology have two main file extensions:

> **.vmx:** This file contains all the configurations that make up a particular VM, such as how many virtual processors are allocated, how much memory is reserved, the path to the hard drive, and any additional components that are configured for this VM.

> **.vmdk:** This file is the physical hard drive equivalent. It holds the file system, the operating system, and any applications or software loaded on this VM.

Note

VMware's file extension for VMs is known as VMDK, whereas Microsoft and Citrix for instance have the file extension as VHD. Hopefully one day, an industry standard will emerge, which would then allow for VMs to be run on any hypervisor.

Virtual machine benefits are numerous, but the following are the fundamental benefits:

> **Isolation:** Because virtual machines run independently of one another and are not dependent on one another to function, the failure of one VM is completely isolated to that VM and in no way affects other VMs running on the same ESX host.

> **Encapsulation:** Virtual machines are encapsulated in a series of files and are thus very portable and easy to work with.

> **Hardware independence:** Virtual machines running on ESX hosts are unaware of the underlying hardware and don't care about it. They interact with physical hardware resources through the virtualization layer.

▶ **Compatibility:** All virtual machines are presented with a standard x86 or x64 hardware architecture, thereby ensuring proper compatibility and stability between the virtualized hardware and the operating system.

Simulation and Emulation

A common mistake that people not familiar with virtualization make is that they think virtualization is similar to emulation or simulation. In fact, virtualization is neither emulation nor simulation, because with virtualization you install the actual operating system on virtual hardware. You go through the same steps, and the operating system itself does not know that it is being installed on virtualized hardware. Furthermore, virtualization requires no custom development or programming of any sort, whereas simulation and emulation do.

That being said, it's important to understand what simulation and emulation are so you have a clearer understanding of why they are not virtualization. A simulation is a preconfigured environment in which limited functionality is available, and as such you are limited to this preconfigured environment. For example, you can develop a fighting simulation based on certain rules and programming languages to mimic real conflict, without there being actual fighting. You do this for training purposes mainly. A flight simulator is a common example of using a simulator for training—computers can mimic the complications of flight without the trainee having to take the risk of flight.

Emulation, on the other hand, is the process of taking a piece of hardware and trying to port it to software. For example, to emulate a router (hardware), you need to create software that performs the functions of the router. You basically need to program the commands that you want to emulate and make sure they respond the same way they would on the real hardware.

In both simulation and emulation, a significant programming and development process takes place to re-create something, whereas that is not the case with virtualization.

> **ExamAlert**
>
> Part of VMware's virtualization marketing strategy is to emphasize that virtualization is not simulation or emulation. It would be a safe assumption that this topic will be covered on the exam.

Virtual and Physical Machine Comparison

One of the main advantages to using VMs over physical machines is that VMs use VMware standardized virtual hardware, and what we mean by that is VMs will always run on the same type of virtual motherboard with all the same components. Whether you are loading Linux or Windows, the VM sees the same standardized hardware. This capability is great because if you are running your ESX/ESXi host on an HP and decide to move your VMs to an IBM or Dell, they are not affected because they don't know the difference and in no way rely on the underlying hardware of the host.

They all see the same x86 standard hardware presented to them. This capability is critical for the stability of the system; historically, blue screens and other instability factors were in most cases related to hardware and software not coexisting—incompatible drivers, firmware issues, and so on. However, by standardizing the virtual hardware, you have now stabilized the system and chopped off a significant factor that used to lead to instability.

Physical machines have the following limitations compared to virtual machines:

▶ Underutilize resources

▶ Are bound to the hardware

▶ Require complicated process to be copied, cloned, or moved

On the other hand, virtual machines have the following benefits:

▶ No binding to a particular set of hardware

▶ Standard x86 architecture

▶ Collection of files can be easily moved around, copied, or backed up

ExamAlert

Because one of the main reasons to virtualize is to replace physical machines with virtual machines, this topic will surely make the VCP exam.

Why vSphere 4?

Virtualization has been around for many years. The reason it is now one of the most needed and most sought after solutions on the market is that VMware developed this technology with the enterprise in mind. You can now do virtualization on an enterprise level. vSphere has many features that make it attractive—all of which are discussed in different chapters in this book. These features include *vMotion*, which allows you to move a virtual machine from one host to another without powering it down, and *Distributed Resource Scheduler (DRS)*, which automatically moves virtual machines from one host to another if it determines that a host is running low on resources where another host has plenty available.

vSphere has made the provisioning of a server a quick and easy process, as well as a portable process.

Cram Quiz

Answer these questions. The answers follow the last question. If you cannot answer these questions correctly, consider reading the section again.

1. True or false: VMware ESX is an application that gets installed on top of an existing operating system such as Microsoft Windows or Linux.

   ○ **A.** True

   ○ **B.** False

2. True or false: VMware ESX/ESXi allows virtual machines to have some direct access to physical resources.

   ○ **A.** True

   ○ **B.** False

Cram Quiz Answers

1. **B**, False, is correct. VMware ESX Server is a bare metal install that does not rely on an underlying operating system to run.

2. **A**, True, is correct. In general, VMware ESX/ESXi does not allow VMs direct access to physical resources. However, as of vSphere 4, you can now assign a physical PCI adapter directly into a VM, thereby giving VMs direct access to certain hardware. This feature is known as VMDirectPath.

vSphere 4 Suite

▶ **Update Manager**

▶ **Storage vMotion**

▶ **VMkernel**

▶ **Service Console (SC)**

▶ **VMware Symmetric Multi-Processing (SMP)**

▶ **vMotion**

▶ **Distributed Resource Scheduler (DRS)**

▶ **Virtual Machine File System (VMFS)**

▶ **VMware Consolidated Backup (VCB)**

▶ **High Availability (HA)**

Cram**Saver**

If you can correctly answer these questions before going through this section, save time by skimming the Exam Alerts in this section and then completing the Cram Quiz at the end of the section.

1. Which VMware product is used to migrate physical machines to virtual machines with vCenter?

○ **A.** VMware P2V Assistant

○ **B.** VMware vCenter Converter

○ **C.** Virtual Center Clone

○ **D.** VMware vMigrator

2. Which file system does VMware ESX/ESXi use to run virtual machines?

○ **A.** EXT3

○ **B.** VFS

○ **C.** VMFS

○ **D.** VMDK

Answers

1. **B** is correct. Although P2V Assistant is a correct answer for earlier versions, the question is which product to use with vCenter. In this case, the only correct answer is **VMware Converter**.

2. **C** is correct. EXT3 is a Linux file system, VFS does not exist, and VMDK is the file extension given to the files that hold the VM virtual hard drive.

vSphere 4 is a suite of applications that collectively make enterprise class virtualization possible. The vSphere components are organized as follows:

- **VMware ESX or ESXi:** The platform upon which VMs run. The main difference between ESX and ESXi is that ESX uses a *Service Console (SC)* as its management arm, whereas ESXi has no Service Console and has a smaller footprint of just 32MB. We discuss this in broader detail in later chapters.

- **VMware Virtual Symmetric Multi-Processing (SMP):** The VMware-developed technology that allows virtual machines to have more than one virtual CPU (vCPU). SMP allows VMs to have up to 8 vCPUs and thus be able to virtualize those applications that are resource hungry.

- **VMware vCenter:** A Windows-based application that centrally manages your enterprise deployment of ESX Servers. From vCenter, you can control all your ESX hosts, configure resource optimization, and take advantage of all the enterprise-class tools available with ESX.

- **vMotion:** The technology that allows you to move VMs between hosts without interruption to the user or downtime.

- **Storage vMotion:** A new feature introduced with vCenter that allows you to migrate the virtual machine files from one shared storage to another with no interruption to the user or loss of data.

- **Update Manager:** A feature that allows for the automatic download and patching of ESX Server and its Windows and Linux VMs. Think of it as the Windows Update equivalent.

- **VMware vCenter Converter:** The tool that allows you to convert physical machines to virtual machines, a process otherwise known as P2V. It also allows you to convert non-ESX VMs to ESX-compatible VMs, a process otherwise known as V2V.

- **High Availability (HA):** A technology that automatically restarts VMs on a different ESX/ESXi host in the event that the original host should experience failures. HA ensures the VMs are brought back online as quickly as possible.

- **Distributed Resource Scheduler (DRS):** A technology that allows for the balancing of ESX host resources. In the event that an ESX host is running low on system resources on CPU or memory, DRS will migrate VMs from this host to another ESX host that is not experiencing a lack of resource allocation.

▶ **VMware Consolidated Backup (VCB):** A backup framework that allows third-party backup software to plug in and back up VMs in a centralized fashion.

▶ **Data Recovery:** A Linux based appliance that is dedicated for backup and recovery of VMs. It is best suited for small to medium sized environments.

▶ **vStorage APIs for Array Integration (VAAI):** A new feature introduced with vSphere 4.1 that allows storage arrays to hook into the ESX/ESXi hypervisor and offload certain storage related tasks to the array. Think of VAAI as hardware assist for VMs, in essence it makes the storage arrays VM-aware.

> ### Exam**Alert**
> It is important to know that while VCB is still supported by VMware, it has been officially replaced with Data Recovery.

You might have noticed how feature rich the vSphere suite is, and what makes it even more compelling and powerful is the fact that it is self-contained. You can run a *virtual infrastructure* without needing any other tools. This is not to say that you will not need third-party tools that can render many tasks easier and less complicated, but in the final analysis, the vSphere suite can run on its own. VMware recognized that the suite it is offering will need an optimal environment to run in and therefore created the Virtual Machine File System, the vSphere suite's playground.

VMware View

VMware View is to physical desktops what vSphere is to servers. It is an enterprise product that facilitates the virtualization of desktops. VMware View is a virtual desktop infrastructure (VDI) solution that leverages vSphere as its virtual infrastructure.

VMware vCenter Site Recovery Manager (SRM)

Business continuity and disaster recovery are important cornerstones of any IT strategy. VMware vCenter SRM enables organization that built their virtual infrastructures using vSphere to automate the failover and failback of virtual systems between two sites. It also automates the run book and allows for testing of your failover and failback plans without interruption to production systems.

VMware vCenter Lab Manager

VMware vCenter Lab Manager is the natural evolution of the virtual infrastructure into a more automated and more orchestrated environment. Lab Manager provides self-service portals, isolated environments, a library of available VMs for checkout, and the capability to build environments that mimic production without creating a conflict.

What Is VMFS?

Virtual Machine File System (VMFS) is a VMware-developed file system designed solely to run virtual machines. VMFS is a lightweight file system in that it does not have all the overhead that the other file systems have, making it an ideal environment for VMs to run in.

The VMkernel

The *VMkernel*, also known as the hypervisor, is the software installed on the bare metal hardware and thus creates the virtualization layer. The VMkernel is the regulator that manages access to the physical hardware.

It is imperative to note that the VMkernel is a proprietary kernel that was developed by VMware. (See the "Is VMware ESX Based on UNIX or Linux?" sidebar.)

ExamAlert

It is highly possible that one of the questions on the exam will ask whether VMkernel is a proprietary kernel developed by VMware.

Is VMware ESX Based on UNIX or Linux?

Many people are confused about whether VMware ESX Server is based on UNIX or Linux, and the reason is simple: They see Linux in the commands and in the boot process; therefore, they automatically conclude that ESX is just another modified version of Linux. The VMkernel itself is proprietary, and VMware makes that point very clear, so there should be no confusion here. The confusion comes into play with the relationship the Service Console has with the VMkernel. Many people believe that because the SC facilitates the ESX boot process, it is relying on Linux and cannot boot on its own and thus is derived in some form from Linux. VMware clearly answers those arguments with the introduction of ESXi, which does not rely on the SC for booting, and as such the VMkernel boots on its own and is not a modified version of Linux or UNIX. It does, however, use BusyBox, which is a modified version of Linux, as its command-line interface with some useful tools.

Furthermore, for those interested in the origins of VMkernel, check out the biographies of the founders of VMware—people like Dr. Mendel Rosenblum, chief scientist; Edouard Bugnion; and Scott Devine, principal engineer—and you will notice that they all worked together at Stanford University and developed the Hive operating system, the SimOS machine simulator, and the Disco virtual machine monitor. So it would be safe to assume that ESX Server is based on the latter.

The Service Console

Think of the Service Console as the first VM on the ESX host. It is used to manage ESX Server, but it is also used to help the VMkernel during its boot process. The Service Console operating system is a 64-bit, 2.6 based Linux kernel, compatible with Red Hat Linux Enterprise 5.2, CentOS 5.2, and equivalent Linux systems. The Service Console also provides the following services:

▸ Apache Tomcat Web Server

▸ Firewall

▸ Secure Shell (SSH) access

▸ SNMP agents

ExamAlert

The VCP exam is sure to test your knowledge of the Linux distributions that the Service Console is compatible with.

The vSphere Client

The vSphere client is a Windows-based application used to provide a GUI to connect to either an ESX/ESXi host directly or to vCenter. Using the vSphere client, you can configure different features on the ESX/ESXi host or via vCenter.

Cram Quiz

Answer these questions. The answers follow the last question. If you cannot answer these questions correctly, consider reading the section again.

1. Which feature of the vSphere 4 family allows a running virtual machine to be migrated to another host without interruption?

    ○ **A.** Distributed Resource Scheduler (DRS)
    ○ **B.** Storage vMotion
    ○ **C.** vMotion
    ○ **D.** VMware Converter

2. Which Virtual Infrastructure technology allows VMs to have more than one virtual CPU?

    ○ **A.** High Availability
    ○ **B.** Symmetric Multi-Processing
    ○ **C.** Virtualization Technology (VT)
    ○ **D.** vCenter

3. What is the maximum number of virtual processors you can allocate to a virtual machine?

    ○ **A.** 4
    ○ **B.** 6
    ○ **C.** 8
    ○ **D.** 2

Cram Quiz Answers

1. **C** is correct. DRS is a feature that distributes the resource load between ESX hosts and organizes resource pools. Storage vMotion moves a running VM's files from one shared storage to another. VMware Converter converts a physical machine into a virtual machine or converts a virtual machine into another virtual machine. vMotion is the technology that moves a running VM between ESX hosts with no interruption.

2. **B** is correct. High Availability is a feature that allows VMs from a failed host to be started on another host and does not allow for multiprocessing on VMs. VT is an Intel technology that is enabled in the BIOS of a system and is required for running vSphere. vCenter is an enterprise management tool.

3. **C** is correct. VMware SMP currently supports a maximum of 8 vCPUs per VM.

CHAPTER 2

Planning, Installing, and Configuring ESX/ESXi 4.1

This chapter covers the following VCP exam topics:

- ▶ ESX Disk Partitions
- ▶ Windows and Linux File Systems
- ▶ ESX/ESXi System Requirements
- ▶ Load Drivers
- ▶ Creating Datastores
- ▶ Lockdown Mode
- ▶ SSH Access
- ▶ vSphere Client Access
- ▶ Configure NTP Client

(For more information on the VCP exam topics, see "About the VCP Exam" in the introduction.)

One of the basic tasks you need to perform as a VMware Certified Professional is properly installing ESX/ESXi 4.1 and also knowing the different methods available for installing it. In this chapter, we look at the prerequisites and different methodologies of installing ESX.

32

CHAPTER 2: Planning, Installing, and Configuring ESX/ESXi 4.1 .

ESX 4.1 Minimum Hardware Requirements

▶ **ESX Disk Partitions**

▶ **Windows and Linux File Systems**

▶ **ESX/ESXi System Requirements**

Cram**Saver**

If you can correctly answer these questions before going through this section, save time by skimming the Exam Alerts in this section and then completing the Cram Quiz at the end of the section.

1. What is the default size of the /var/log partition?

   ○ **A.** 500MB

   ○ **B.** 2.00GB

   ○ **C.** 5,000MB

   ○ **D.** Varies

2. True or false: By default, ESX Server's Service Console does not allow root access via an SSH client.

   ○ **A.** True

   ○ **B.** False

3. What is the default amount of memory allocated to the Service Console?

   ○ **A.** 272

   ○ **B.** 300

   ○ **C.** 800

   ○ **D.** 1600

   ○ **E.** Varies depending on host physical memory

4. What is the default size of the swap partition?

   ○ **A.** 544–572

   ○ **B.** 600–1600

   ○ **C.** 574–594

   ○ **D.** 576–596

Answers

1. **B** is correct. By default, setup suggests that the /var/log partition have a 2.00GB size.

2. **A**, True, is correct. By default, the Service Console does not allow root access via SSH.

3. **B** and **E** are correct. The SC memory default settings are dictated by the amount of physical memory installed on the ESX host and therefore varies accordingly. That being said, answer B is correct because it is a valid and very common SC minimum memory setting. Answer E is also correct because SC memory varies. Answer A is incorrect because it is an ESX 3.5 minimum requirement that is no longer valid. All other answers are incorrect.

4. **B** is correct. The default size of the swap partition is twice the size of the default memory allocated to the SC. Because, by default, the SC is allocated 300, the correct size is 600.

Before we dig deep into the steps of installing ESX 4.1, let's look at the minimum hardware requirements needed to install the software. Keep in mind, this is only the *minimum* you need to install the software; this is by no means a recommended hardware configuration. ESX servers in the real world are beefy servers, which is what allows them to host so many virtual machines. The requirements are as follows:

▶ Intel or AMD 64-bit x86 processors

ExamAlert

ESX/ESXi 4.1 now requires a 64-bit x86 processor. The VCP exam is sure to challenge your knowledge on the minimum system requirements, so make sure you know them well.

▶ 2GB of physical memory or RAM

ExamAlert

If you are upgrading an ESX/ESXi host that is managed by vCenter, the minimum RAM requirement changes to 3GB. Watch out for this type of question.

▶ 1 gigabit network interface card (NIC)

▶ 1 RAID LUN, Fiber Channel LUN, SCSI LUN, or SCSI disk with at least 9.5GB of free space

With ESX 4.1, you can install and boot from the following disks:

- SCSI disk

- IDE disk

- SATA disk

- Storage Area Networks (SANs)

Tip

Before purchasing or installing ESX/ESXi 4.1, consult "Systems Compatibility Guide for ESX and ESXi" at http://www.vmware.com/resources/guides.html.

Note

ESX/ESXi 4.1 supports 10GB Ethernet cards; make sure you check the compatibility guides for the models supported and the vendors.

Disk Partitioning ESX 4.1

As with any operating system deployment, disk partitioning is critical with ESX 4.1. Knowing how to partition the disk to best fit the operating system is just as important. Now because ESX 4.1 has a console operating system based on Red Hat Linux, familiarity with the Linux file system is necessary.

The Linux file system is a single hierarchy file system where everything is mounted under the root represented by /. This means that if you were adding a new partition, this partition would show up in a directory under the root and is known as a *mount point*. This differs from a typical Windows file system where every new partition is its own root represented by a letter, for example, C:\ or D:\. With Windows, every drive letter is the equivalent of the root in Linux. Figure 2.1 shows a comparison between a Windows file system and a Linux file system hierarchy.

Also note that an x86 disk can have a total of four primary partitions, which is a limitation because you need more partitions to satisfy the different operating system architectures. That being said, if you take the fourth partition and make it into an extended partition rather than a primary, you now have more partitions and are no longer limited. You do this at no sacrifice to performance. It is also important to note here that IDE disks can have a maximum of 63 partitions, whereas SCSI disks can have a maximum of 15 partitions.

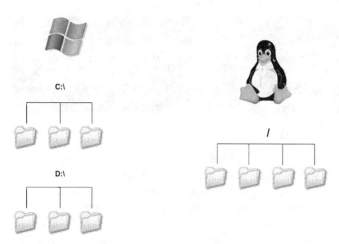

FIGURE 2.1   Windows and Linux file systems.

Table 2.1 lists the different partition configurations, their types, and what they do.

TABLE 2.1   **ESX Disk Partitions**

Mount Point	Type	Size	Function
/boot	ext3	1100MB	This is the place where ESX Server stores all the files it needs to boot.
/	ext3	5GB	This is the root of the Service Console operating system.
none	swap	600MB	This is the swap file of the Service Console. The recommended minimum requirement is 600MB, and the maximum is 1600MB.
/var/log	ext3	2GB	This is the place where all the logs are stored. It is also used to patch management. The default size is 2GB, but best practice calls for an increase in disk space allocation.
none	VMFS-3	Varies	This is the place where all the VMs will live; you can also store images here. The size varies here, but by default VMFS-3 is equal to the disk size minus all the sizes of all the other partitions.
none	VMFS3	1.2GB	This is the location where the Service Console will be installed on each host. The SC needs to reside on a VMFS partition. It is stored in a file called esxconsole.vmdk with a size of 1200MB or 1.2GB.
none	vmkcore	100MB	This is the place where ESX Server writes its dump information in the event of a system crash or a Purple Screen of Death (PSOD).

ExamAlert

Pay attention to the boot disk. The minimum boot disk requirement is 1.25GB of free disk space. It includes two partitions: /boot partition with a minimum free disk requirement of 1100MB or 1.1GB and a vmkcore partition with a minimum free disk space requirement of 100MB. Be careful of questions that might focus on that.

Note

The Service Console can be allocated a maximum of 800MB of memory. Therefore, the swap partition should not be allocated more than 1600MB of disk space. Otherwise, you would be wasting disk space. The swap file is calculated based on the Service Console memory allocation.

Cram Quiz

Answer these questions. The answers follow the last question. If you cannot answer these questions correctly, consider reading the section again.

1. Choose the five partitions that are required for ESX Server installation.

- ○ **A.** /boot
- ○ **B.** /var
- ○ **C.** /etc
- ○ **D.** swap
- ○ **E.** /
- ○ **F.** vmfs
- ○ **G.** vmkcore

2. Choose the correct partition type of the swap partition.

- ○ **A.** none
- ○ **B.** ext3
- ○ **C.** vmfs
- ○ **D.** swap

3. True or false: The vmkcore partition has a mount point of /vmkcore.

- ○ **A.** True
- ○ **B.** False

Cram Quiz Answers

1. **A, D, E, F,** and **G** are correct. The partitions that are required for an ESX 4.1 installation are /boot, swap, /, vmfs, and vmkcore. All other partitions are not required for the installation.

2. **D** is correct. Swap's partition type is swap; therefore, all other answers are incorrect.

3. **B** is correct. Vmkcore does not need a mount point.

Installing ESX 4.1 and ESXi 4.1

▶ **Load Drivers**

▶ **Lockdown Mode**

▶ **Creating Datastores**

Cram**Saver**

If you can correctly answer these questions before going through this section, save time by skimming the Exam Alerts in this section and then completing the Cram Quiz at the end of the section.

1. True or false: ESX does not support the loading of third-party drivers.

   ○ **A.** False

   ○ **B.** True

2. What is the default root password that you should use upon first login to ESXi 4.1?

   ○ **A.** vmware

   ○ **B.** VMWARE

   ○ **C.** There is no password.

   ○ **D.** You will be prompted to enter a password on first login.

Answers

1. **A** is correct. ESX supports the loading of third-party drivers and allows you to do that as part of the setup wizard.

2. **C** is correct. There is no password. Upon first login to ESXi, you can use the console to set your root password.

There are many ways by which you can install ESX 4.1 and ESXi 4.1; however, the setup wizard once initiated prompts you for the same information. In this section we go over the installation of both ESX 4.1 and ESXi 4.1 from CD-ROM.

Installing ESX 4.1 Using a CD-ROM

To begin the installation, you need to configure the server to boot from a CD-ROM. Pop in the VMware ESX 4.1 CD, and the first screen should look similar to the one in Figure 2.2.

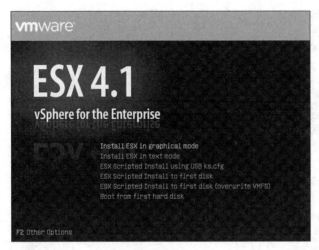

FIGURE 2.2 **Installation mode.**

The first choice you need to make is one of the following:

▶ *Graphical mode*, as its name suggests, guides you through the installation with a graphical user interface in which you can use your mouse. This is the default mode.

▶ *Text mode* is a lightweight installation method that skips on the rich and colorful graphics and relies solely on a text-based installation, which also means you will not have the use of the mouse. This method is ideal for ESX installations over slow networks.

For the purposes of this demonstration, choose the graphical mode. Up next, you are presented with the welcome screen similar to that shown in Figure 2.3, which prompts you to start the installation process. Click Next to continue with the installation.

Up next is the license agreement. Feel free to read through it, and when you are ready, accept the terms and click on Next to move to the next step. The next screen prompts you to select the type of keyboard that you have. We elect to stay with the default selection for this prompt.

This next step in the installation process gives you the option to load any third-party drivers you may need to extend support for new features or hardware. Your options are No or Yes. As shown in Figure 2.4, we opted to stay with the default setting of No. After you have made your choice, click Next to move forward with the installation. You are immediately prompted with a window to load the system drivers; click on Yes to continue. At this point, setup loads all the necessary system drivers. When finished you are required to click Next to resume the installation process.

FIGURE 2.3 **Welcome screen.**

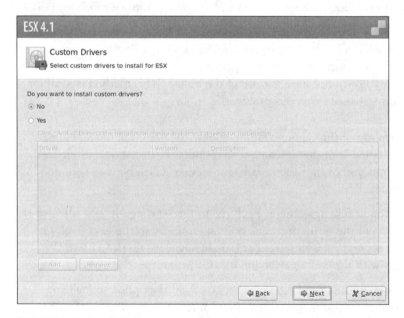

FIGURE 2.4 **Load drivers.**

The installation wizard now prompts you to enter the license serial number for your product. If you are ready to do so, you may enter it at this point. If you are not, you can choose to do so later. For the purposes of this demo, we opted to enter the serial number later. Click Next to move on.

> **Tip**
>
> If you intend to let vCenter manage licenses, you can choose to enter the serial number later and then use vCenter to assign serial numbers from a pool of available licenses.

We now need to choose the network interface card that we want to associate with the management console. From the drop-down menu, select the physical adapter you want to use. This is your opportunity to also configure a VLAN ID if applicable. Once you are ready, click Next to continue. Keep in mind, typically in an ESX host, you have multiple adapters, so make sure you are selecting the one you have cabled for the management console. This is important because this is the method by which you will connect to your ESX host once the installation is complete.

The setup now prompts you to assign the server network settings, as shown in Figure 2.5. You need to supply an IP address, a subnet mask, a default gateway, primary and secondary DNS entries, and a hostname in the form of a fully qualified domain name (FQDN) for this server. Enter the appropriate values and click Next to continue.

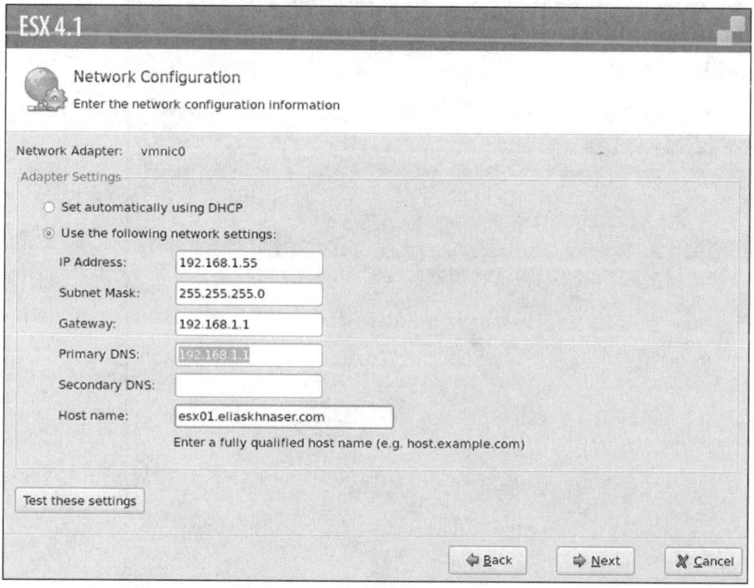

FIGURE 2.5 **Network settings.**

Setup now needs to know what type of installation you want to run. You have two options: Standard and Advanced. The Standard option uses defaults settings to set up ESX as a single drive. The Advanced option allows you to modify the partition tables and add partitions. For the purposes of this example, we chose Advanced.

> **Tip**
>
> If you want to select the first physical NIC on the server, as in NIC 0, make note of the MAC addresses of the physical NICs during post. This will ensure you have the right NIC.

> **Caution**
>
> Selecting the wrong physical NIC will result in your server being inaccessible, so make sure that the device you select is the correct one that you want to use for the Service Console.

The next screen, shown in Figure 2.6, prompts you to choose the device that will hold the datastore to be used to install ESX. Select the appropriate device and click Next. This next step is important because you have to be cautious not to initialize a device that might hold data. This means that if you have more than one device connected to the server, such as a SAN LUN, you should select Cancel for this prompt. Otherwise, you will lose all data on this device.

FIGURE 2.6   **Disk initialization.**

For the purposes of this example, click Ok and continue the installation.

Our installation now brings us to Figure 2.7. You are now tasked with creating a datastore. Make the appropriate selections, give your datastore a name, and move on with the installation. This part of the setup wizard allows you to make any changes necessary to the partition tables before they are committed.

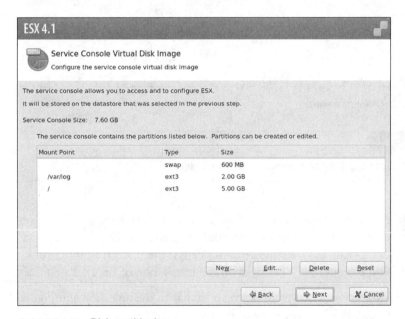

FIGURE 2.7   **Disk partitioning.**

Time zone selection is next. Make sure you choose the time zone in which your server resides and click Next to continue. At the next screen you can adjust the date and time and click Next to move forward.

As you can see in Figure 2.8, you are now prompted to enter a password for the root account, which is the administrator account on the ESX host. Enter a strong password. This screen also allows you to create additional users that can manage ESX, which is important to be able to log on remotely. The root user remote logon is disabled by default; therefore, creating a user at this step of the installation will make remote access easier later. Once you are satisfied with your selections, click Next to continue.

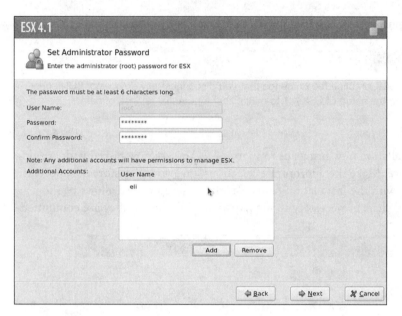

FIGURE 2.8   **Root password.**

> **Note**
>
> The root password must be a minimum of six characters.

You are one step away from the end of the journey. This is the place where you are provided with a summary of all the settings you chose during the setup wizard's run to the install. Go over the settings one last time, and if all looks correct, click Next to continue. This kicks off the installation of ESX 4.1.

When the installation is complete, a screen similar to the one shown in Figure 2.9 is displayed. Click Finish to reboot ESX 4.1.

After the server reboots, you are provided with information that you need to remotely connect to the ESX Server, as shown in Figure 2.10.

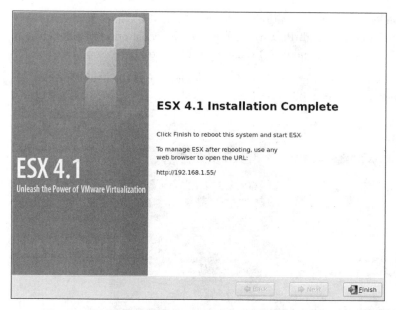

FIGURE 2.9   **Installation complete.**

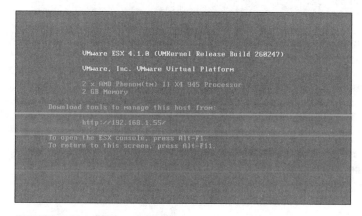

FIGURE 2.10   **ESX console screen.**

Installing ESXi 4.1

The installation of ESXi is much simpler and takes a fraction of the time to complete. ESXi is a light software install that takes up less than 100MB of space. Many server manufacturers ship their servers with chipsets that run ESXi, so all you have to do is power on the server and configure it, an extremely elegant turnkey solution. ESXi, however, also comes as an installable version that is straightforward with no configurable options other than accepting a license agreement and selecting the disk to install it on.

The majority of the configuration in ESXi happens after the installation of the hypervisor and through a user interface as shown in Figure 2.11.

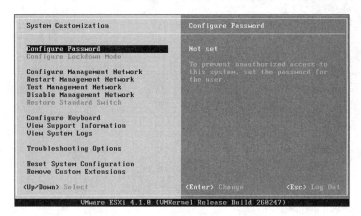

FIGURE 2.11 **ESXi console.**

To log in to the management interface from the console, press F2 to customize the system. You are prompted to authenticate; enter username root. The initial password is blank, which means just press Enter to bypass the password.

> **Tip**
>
> Make sure you change the password on first login to a more complex password in accordance with best practices. A blank password to the console of the hypervisor is a serious security vulnerability.

Once you have logged in, you are presented with a screen similar to the one shown in Figure 2.11. The local console allows you to configure the following settings:

▶ Change Password allows you to change the root password.

▶ Configure Lockdown Mode allows you to tighten security around the use of local accounts including root. If enabled, no local user will be able to log in directly to the ESXi host via the vSphere client or CLI, and all management would have to be done through vCenter. This feature is initially grayed out and disabled and can only be enabled and manipulated after the server has been added to vCenter.

ExamAlert

vSphere 4.1 disables all local user access once lockdown mode is enabled, as opposed to vSphere 4.0, which disabled only the root user when lockdown mode is enabled and allowed other local user accounts to log in. The test might challenge your knowledge on this.

▶ Configure Management Network allows you to edit and configure the networking stack. It also allows you to select the physical network adapter you want to associate with the management network and add a VLAN ID if necessary.

▶ Restart Management Network allows you to restart the management network as a troubleshooting measure or to force into effect certain changes you may have made that require the restarting of these services.

▶ Test Management Network gives you access to troubleshooting tools that allow you to use ping and try to resolve FQDN, which would help in identifying whether you are having name resolution issues.

▶ Disable Management Network as the name implies allows you to disable the management network.

▶ Restore Standard Switch allows you to restore standard switch functionality if you have migrated to vNetwork Distributed Switch and want to switch back.

▶ Configure Keyboard allows you to configure the keyboard layout.

▶ View Support Information displays support information, such as the license serial number and other relevant support information.

▶ View System Logs allows you to view system logs for messages, config, and management agent.

▶ Troubleshooting Options allows you to restart management agents and enable local or remote tech support.

▶ Reset System Configuration restores all the system defaults. You will lose all configurations.

▶ Remove System Extensions removes all system extensions that have been installed and requires a reboot for the changes to take effect.

> **Exam Alert**
>
> VMware has announced that ESX is now end of life and as such will no longer have an upgrade path. All future versions of vSphere or its successor will be built around ESXi.

> **Tip**
>
> When planning the installation of vSphere, you should always plan on installing ESXi unless there is a compelling reason for choosing ESX. This will make future upgrades less of a hassle.

Aside from these configurations, all aspects of managing ESXi happen through the vSphere client. ESXi can be managed independently or added to vCenter and managed centrally.

Cram Quiz

Answer these questions. The answers follow the last question. If you cannot answer these questions correctly, consider reading the section again.

1. What is the minimum password complexity requirement for the root user?

   ○ **A.** 6 characters

   ○ **B.** 6 character alpha-numeric

   ○ **C.** 8 characters

   ○ **D.** 8 character alpha-numeric

2. How do you enable lockdown mode?

   ○ **A.** By accessing the ESXi from the vSphere client

   ○ **B.** By adding the ESXi host to vCenter

   ○ **C.** By enabling it using CLI first

   ○ **D.** By enabling it using the local console

Cram Quiz Answers

1. **A** is correct. The password should be 6 characters long and does not have to be alpha-numeric.

2. **B** is correct. You would need to add ESXi to vCenter before you can enable lockdown mode.

ESX 4.1 Post-Installation Configurations

▸ **SSH Access**

▸ **vSphere Client Access**

▸ **Configure NTP Client**

Cram**Saver**

If you can correctly answer these questions before going through this section, save time by skimming the Exam Alerts in this section and then completing the Cram Quiz at the end of the section.

1. Can you SSH into an ESX host as root by default?

    ○ **A.** Yes

    ○ **B.** No

2. What Service Console firewall port is open when you enable the NTP client?

    ○ **A.** UDP 124

    ○ **B.** UDP 123

    ○ **C.** TCP 123

    ○ **D.** TCP 124

3. Which file needs to be edited to allow root access via SSH to an ESX host?

    ○ **A.** /etc/ssh/ssh_config

    ○ **B.** /etc/sshd/ssh_config

    ○ **C.** /etc/ssh/sshd_config

    ○ **D.** /etc/ssh/sshp_config

Answers

1. **B** is correct. You cannot access an ESX host via SSH as root by default.

2. **B** is correct. When you enable the NTP client, UDP port 123 is automatically opened on the Service Console firewall.

3. **C** is correct. The correct file is /etc/ssh/sshd_config.

When ESX 4.1 is up and running, you need to complete a few post-installation configurations before you begin further advanced configurations or prior to putting the server in full production. We cover the following:

▶ Accessing ESX using the vSphere client

▶ Accessing ESX using SSH

▶ Modifying Service Console memory allocation

▶ Configuring NTP client on ESX

Accessing ESX Using the vSphere Client

You can download the vSphere client from any ESX Server by opening a supported Internet browser such as Internet Explorer or Firefox and pointing to the IP address or FQDN of the server. This leads you to a screen similar to the one shown in Figure 2.12. From here, you can click Download VMware Infrastructure Client. This prompts you to download or run the setup package. Go ahead and install it now.

> ## ExamAlert
>
> At the time of this writing, the vSphere client is a 32-bit application. Make sure you double-check this point prior to taking the exam just in case VMware releases a 64-bit version and happens to put a question on the exam in this regard.

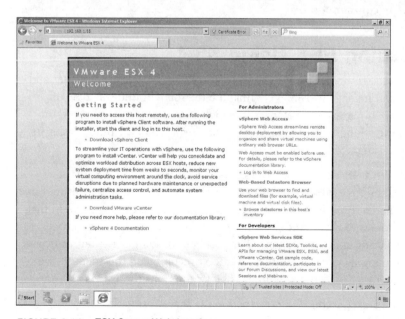

FIGURE 2.12   **ESX Server Web interface.**

After you install the vSphere client, you can run it, which brings you to a screen similar to the one shown in Figure 2.13. Enter the IP address or FQDN of your ESX Server host. Enter **root** for username and the password you assigned during setup. Click Login.

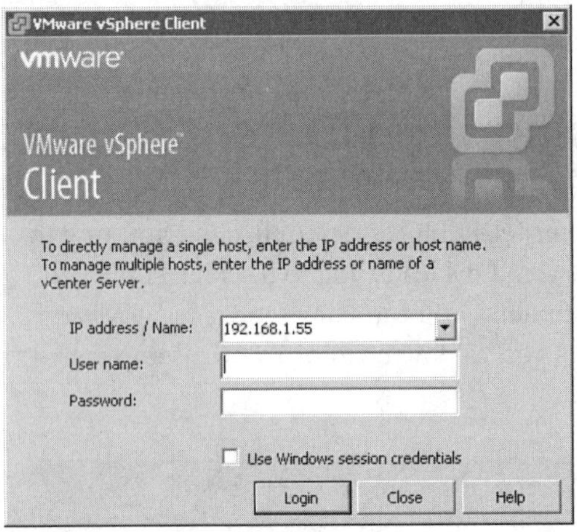

FIGURE 2.13   **vSphere client.**

The vSphere client is your graphical user interface into ESX/ESXi's hardware and software configuration.

Accessing ESX Using SSH

Secure Shell (SSH) access allows you to remotely access your ESX Server and configure and manage it from a command line. You will find this type of access useful in many circumstances in which you need advanced configurations that the vSphere client does not provide or it would be much easier to accomplish using SSH.

By default, ESX 4.1 denies SSH access to the root user. This security best practice measure is enabled to deny hackers the ability to perform a brute force attack on the server. It is recommended that you create a generic account that you use to log in to the server using SSH and then switch the user to root, thereby acquiring root permissions. That being said, some may want to bypass this step and log in as root. Although we don't recommend this method, we demonstrate how you can configure it. The two options for SSH access are

▶ Create a user account that can access the server using SSH.

▶ Enable SSH root access.

Creating a User Account That Can Access the Server Using SSH

Creating a user account on the ESX Server is easy. Remember that the Service Console that manages ESX runs a modified version of Linux; therefore, ESX host user accounts are Linux accounts and can be created in the same manner as you would a Linux account. For the purposes of this example, use the VMware vSphere client to create the account, even though you can create it through the command line using Linux commands. The following steps show how to accomplish this:

1. Launch the vSphere client and log in.

2. Click the Local Users & Groups tab.

3. In the Users pane, right-click and select Add.

4. When the Add New User dialog is displayed, fill in the information.

5. Check Grant Shell Access to This User.

6. Click OK. The user you created should show up in the Users pane.

Enabling SSH Root Access

To enable SSH access using root, you need to have console access to the ESX 4.1 Server and follow these steps:

1. Type vi /etc/ssh/sshd_config. This command launches the vi editor in Linux and allows you to edit the file sshd_config.

2. Change the parameter PermitRootLogin no to PermitRootLogin yes.

3. Press the Esc button, and then type :wq, so the command should look like Esc :wq, which saves the files and exits the editor.

4. At the command prompt, type service sshd restart, which restarts the SSHD service.

5. Using your SSH client, try logging in using root.

ExamAlert

It is highly possible that one of the questions on the exam will revolve around security best practices and why the root account is disabled. Make sure you are aware of this and are well prepared to answer it.

Modifying Service Console Memory Allocation

After the installation of ESX 4.1, you should modify the value of the Service Console memory. By default, it is allocated the minimum memory requirement, which varies depending on the host's installed physical memory. It is calculated as follows:

- ESX Host 8GB installed RAM defaults the SC to 300MB of RAM.

- ESX Host 16GB installed RAM defaults the SC to 400MB of RAM.

- ESX Host 32GB installed RAM defaults the SC to 500MB of RAM.

- ESX Host 64GB installed RAM defaults the SC to 602MB of RAM.

- ESX Host 96GB installed RAM defaults the SC to 661MB of RAM.

- ESX Host 128GB installed RAM defaults the SC to 703MB of RAM.

Best practice calls for the increase of this memory, especially if you will be using third-party applications, because this will eat away from the SC memory. The maximum memory you can allocate to the SC is 800MB, and the minimum is 300. To modify the SC memory, follow these steps:

1. Launch the vSphere client and log in to the ESX Server.

2. In the right pane, select the Configuration tab.

3. Under the Hardware menu, select the Memory link.

4. Click Properties.

5. Enter a value between 300 and 800.

6. Click OK.

7. For your changes to take effect, you must restart your ESX Server.

Configuring NTP Client on ESX Server

Time is of the essence in ESX Server. It is a critical component to configure and should be a top priority because time synchronization issues can affect backups, authentication, performance charting, SSH key expiration, and more. To avoid all these nuisances, follow these steps to configure the Network Time Protocol (NTP) client:

1. Launch the vSphere client and log in to the ESX Server.

2. In the right pane, select the Configuration tab.

3. Click the Time Configuration link.

4. Click Properties.

5. Check NTP Client Enabled.

6. Click Options.

7. Select NTP Settings in the left pane.

8. Click Add and add the hostname or IP address of your NTP server.

9. Check the Restart NTP Service box to apply the changes.

10. Click OK.

11. Verify the NTP Client is running and the correct NTP servers are configured.

ExamAlert

When you enable the NTP client, you are opening UDP port 123 on the SC firewall. The VCP loves to quiz you on port numbers, so keep this one in mind.

Troubleshooting ESX 4.1 Installation

The reality is that issues may come up with installation. Knowing how to properly deal with them and what tools are at your disposal makes the troubleshooting process a little bit easier. In this section we tackle common issues, covering what to look for and what to do in certain circumstances.

Hardware Issues and Misconfigurations

If this is a new ESX Server installation that is experiencing problems after installation, the most likely cause is hardware. Hardware issues can be a combination of things, including

▶ The hardware you are using is not compatible with ESX 4. Check the compatibility guide and make sure your hardware is compatible.

▶ Hardware problems can also be caused by a faulty CPU, for example, or a bad memory module, so make sure that the hardware you are using is healthy and is not faulting. Do so by testing the hardware and software configuration for a few days prior to putting the server in production.

Misconfigurations are also an issue that you need to examine carefully because they may cause problems. For example, if you did not properly configure the correct physical NIC during installation, the server will be rendered inaccessible because there will be no communication with it. Therefore, checking your existing configuration should be your second step.

Purple Screen of Death

Microsoft has its infamous Blue Screen of Death, and VMware has its Purple Screen of Death (PSOD). If a PSOD occurs, that is bad, and the server console will go, as you might have guessed, purplish. Two of the most common reasons for PSOD are

- ▶ CPU problems

- ▶ Memory problems

When a PSOD occurs, memory and runtime logs are dumped to the vmkcore partition. After ESX/ESXi reboots, the contents of the vmkcore partition are collected and zipped in a file named vmkernel-zdump-<*datestamp*> which is then saved in the /root or /var/core, depending on whether you are using ESX or ESXi. This dump file, as with any other, can be sent to VMware support for analysis and advanced troubleshooting.

Diagnostic Data Collection

In the event of a server crash, you need to go through the normal steps of troubleshooting the problem. For example, determine whether anything changed recently that could cause the server to crash. Variables can include hardware changes. Has anything changed in the environment where ESX is hosted, has the temperature changed, have you had a power loss? You also need to check whether any external devices such as LUNs have been disconnected, and finally make sure you take a screen capture of any console errors that may appear because this will help VMware support staff as they troubleshoot the problem.

Finally, using the vSphere client, you can export *diagnostic data* that you can send to VMware support. To do this, follow these steps:

1. Launch and log in to the ESX Server.

2. From the File menu, select File > Export > Export System Logs.

3. Choose a folder where you want to save the data.

4. The diagnostic data is stored in a folder called VMware VirtualCenter-support-date@time and contains the following:

- ▶ A folder named viclient-support-date@time.tgz, which contains vSphere Client's log files

- ▶ A file named esx-support-date@time.tgz, which contains ESX Server diagnostic data

> **Tip**
>
> You can generate the diagnostic data file by initiating the command vm-support from an SSH command prompt.

Cram Quiz

Answer these questions. The answers follow the last question. If you cannot answer these questions correctly, consider reading the section again.

1. How much time does best practice dictate for hardware burn in?
    - ○ **A.** 24 hours
    - ○ **B.** 36 hours
    - ○ **C.** 48 hours
    - ○ **D.** 72 hours

2. Why should the ESX log files be stored on a different partition?
    - ○ **A.** For better performance.
    - ○ **B.** To prevent the / from being filled.
    - ○ **C.** Easier access to the files.
    - ○ **D.** Partition will be shared with other hosts.

Cram Quiz Answers

1. **D** is correct. Best practice dictates 72 hours for hardware burn in.

2. **B** is correct. The logs are stored on a separate partition to prevent them from taking up all the disk space available for the root file system and thereby halting the service console.

CHAPTER 3
vNetworking Operations

Just as physical machines connect to physical networks, virtual machines connect to virtual networks. In turn, virtual networks connect to the physical network. Virtual networking is the bridge by which physical connectivity is made possible to virtual machines. Similar to physical machines that require an entire networking infrastructure and framework to connect different devices and create different environments, virtual networking mimics physical networking by creating a virtual environment and a virtual framework for virtual machines.

In this chapter, we discuss all the components that make up virtual networking and how it facilitates communications for virtual machines.

What Are Virtual Switches?

▶ **802.1Q VLAN Tagging**

▶ **vSwitch Maximum Ports**

▶ **vSwitch Connection Types**

CramSaver

If you can correctly answer these questions before going through this section, save time by skimming the Exam Alerts in this section and then completing the Cram Quiz at the end of the section.

1. How does 802.1Q help virtual switches?

   ○ **A.** It allows VMs to join VLANs.

   ○ **B.** It allows a virtual switch to identify packets destined for a specific VM.

   ○ **C.** It is port trunking on the physical NICs.

   ○ **D.** It allows physical NICs to join VLANs.

2. What is the maximum number of ports that a standard virtual switch can support?

   ○ **A.** 4086

   ○ **B.** 4087

   ○ **C.** 4088

   ○ **D.** 4089

3. How many different connection types does a virtual switch have?

   ○ **A.** 2

   ○ **B.** 3

   ○ **C.** 4

   ○ **D.** Unlimited

Answers

1. **B** is correct. 802.1Q is configured at the port group level and allows the virtual switch to pass packets to the corresponding VM in the right port group.

2. **C** is correct. The maximum number of ports that are supported with a standard virtual switch is 4088.

3. **B** is correct. A virtual switch has 3 connection types: VMkernel, Service Console, and virtual machine.

Virtual switches (vSwitches) are the inevitable route that all communications inbound to or outbound from an ESX/ESXi host must go through. Virtual switches make up the networking backbone of an ESX/ESXi deployment. Whether you are seeking to implement IP storage or simply connect virtual machines to virtual machines, communications must pass through a virtual switch.

You can quickly see how virtual switches are the beating heart of the infrastructure, and it is by leveraging them that you are able to create different scenarios. For example, you could create an isolated environment where VMs can communicate only with other VMs on the same ESX host, you could create a DMZ-like environment, or you could provide fault tolerance through virtual switches. There are two types of virtual switches, Standard Virtual Switches (vSS) and vNetwork Distributed Switches (vDS) . Virtual switches have the following characteristics:

▶ Standard virtual switches are software objects that reside on the VMkernel of every ESX/ESXi host.

▶ vNetwork distributed switches are also software objects that are centrally managed at the vCenter server level and provide networking for the entire datacenter.

▶ Standard virtual switches in ESX/ESXi can have a minimum of 8 ports and a maximum of 4,088 ports. Similar to physical switches that have available ports on them for physical devices to connect to, virtual switches also have that functionality. The advantage with virtual switches is the port density is much higher, and you can customize your virtual switches with the port capacity you need. With physical switches, that is not easy; you would have to swap out the switch for another. Virtual switches give you the flexibility to add or remove ports as needed.

▶ Standard virtual switches can be serviced by zero, one, or more physical NICs. More NICs provide fault tolerance and more, as you see throughout this chapter.

▶ Virtual NICs that connect to port groups have unique MAC addresses just like every physical network interface card (NIC) has its own unique MAC address.

▶ Virtual switches support 802.1q (known as VLAN tagging), which allows VMs connected to a virtual switch to communicate with different VLANs in your network infrastructure. This topic is covered in greater detail in the "VLANs in Virtual Networking" section in this chapter.

▶ Virtual switches also support different port groups or connection types that outline the communication of this virtual switch, such as Service Console, VMkernel, or virtual machine communications.

Exam**Alert**

By default, when you are creating a virtual switch, and unless you manually change it, the first virtual switch is created with 56 ports. Since ESX 4.1, extra virtual switches have 120 ports when created.

Note

Virtual switches operate at layer 2 of the OSI model and are capable of providing segregation, security, and checksums.

Cram Quiz

Answer these questions. The answers follow the last question. If you cannot answer these questions correctly, consider reading the section again.

1. How many physical NICs does a standard virtual switch need to communicate with the physical network?

   ○ **A.** 1

   ○ **B.** 2

   ○ **C.** 3

   ○ **D.** None

2. True or false: Virtual NICs require dedicated MAC addresses.

   ○ **A.** True

   ○ **B.** False

Cram Quiz Answers

1. **A** is correct. A standard virtual switch requires a minimum of one physical NIC to communicate with the physical network.

2. **A**, True, is correct. Each virtual NIC requires a dedicated virtual MAC addresses that enables it to properly communicate with the rest of the physical and virtual network.

Comparing Physical and Virtual Switches

▶ **Standard Virtual Switches (vSS)**

▶ **Physical Switches**

Cram**Saver**

If you can correctly answer these questions before going through this section, save time by skimming the Exam Alerts in this section and then completing the Cram Quiz at the end of the section.

1. How many standard virtual switches can be interconnected?

- ○ **A.** 2
- ○ **B.** 3
- ○ **C.** Unlimited
- ○ **D.** None

2. Which of the following is dissimilarity between physical and virtual switches?

- ○ **A.** Virtual switches maintain MAC address tables.
- ○ **B.** Virtual switches check each frame's MAC address upon receipt.
- ○ **C.** Virtual switches' forwarding data table is unique to each virtual switch.
- ○ **D.** Virtual switches forward frames.

Answers

1. D is correct. Standard virtual switches cannot be interconnected.

2. C is correct. Virtual switches' forwarding data table is unique to each virtual switch. Choices A, B, and D are all features that are similar between virtual and physical switches.

Virtual switches (vSS and vDS) are to virtual machines what physical switches are to physical devices. The virtual switches concept was created in the image of physical switches, so they share many similarities. However, they do differ somewhat in functionality and capability. Let's start off by examining the similarities between physical and virtual switches:

▶ They both maintain MAC address tables.

▶ They both check each frame's MAC address destination upon receiving it.

▶ They both forward frames to one or more ports.

▶ They both avoid unnecessary deliveries.

Now that you recognize the similarities, let's outline the differences:

▶ Virtual switches (vSS and vDS) do not require or support the Spanning Tree Protocol.

▶ Standard virtual switches cannot be stacked to one another the same way physical switches can be. You can connect VMs to a virtual switch, but you cannot connect another virtual switch.

▶ A standard virtual switch's forwarding data table is unique to each virtual switch.

▶ Standard virtual switch isolation prevents loops in the switch configuration.

ExamAlert

As VMware makes the case for virtualization, you can be assured that the VCP exam will challenge your knowledge of the advantages and disadvantages of virtual versus physical switches.

Cram Quiz

Answer these questions. The answers follow the last question. If you cannot answer these questions correctly, consider reading the section again.

1. True or false: Virtual switches support spanning tree.

   ○ **A.** True

   ○ **B.** False

2. True or false: Virtual switches can forward packets to multiple ports.

   ○ **A.** True

   ○ **B.** False

Cram Quiz Answers

1. **B** is correct. Virtual switches do not support spanning tree.

2. **B** is correct. Virtual switches like physical switches cannot forward packets to multiple ports.

Standard Virtual Switches (vSS) and Port Group Types

▶ **Internal vSwitch**

▶ **Single Adapter vSwitch**

▶ **Multiple Adapter vSwitch**

▶ **VMkernel**

▶ **Service Console**

▶ **Virtual Machine**

Cram**Saver**

If you can correctly answer these questions before going through this section, save time by skimming the Exam Alerts in this section and then completing the Cram Quiz at the end of the section.

1. What is a characteristic of an internal vSwitch?

   ○ **A.** It is a vSwitch with no physical NIC adapters.

   ○ **B.** It is a virtual switch that can communicate with all vSwitches on the same host.

   ○ **C.** It is a virtual switch that can communicate with other vSwitches in the same datacenter.

   ○ **D.** It is a vSwitch internal to the vCenter Server.

2. If you want to use iSCSI, what type of port group would you need to configure on a virtual switch?

   ○ **A.** Virtual Machine

   ○ **B.** Service Console

   ○ **C.** VMkernel

   ○ **D.** vSwitch

Answers

1. **A** is correct. An internal only vSwitch is a vSwitch that has no physical NICs and no communication with the rest of the network. Virtual machines on the same internal vSwitch can communicate with one another.

2. **C** is correct. To configure iSCSI, you need to create a port group on your virtual switch that is of type VMkernel.

Types of Virtual Switches

There are three different types of virtual switches that you can configure, depending on the case or scenario that you need to implement. Within the framework of these three virtual switch types, you can create isolated environments, a DMZ, and fault tolerance, and you can maximize throughput for optimal performance and for those bandwidth-hungry applications. In the following sections, we discuss the following three virtual switch types and their usage scenarios:

▸ Internal virtual switch

▸ Single adapter virtual switch

▸ Multiple adapter virtual switch, also known as NIC teaming

Internal Virtual Switch

An internal virtual switch is used to provide communication to virtual machines that are on a single ESX host. In other words, when you deploy an internal virtual switch, virtual machines on the ESX host can communicate with one another but are completely isolated from the rest of the network and cannot communicate with other VMs on other ESX hosts or any other devices on the network. Figure 3.1 shows a sample of this configuration. A possible usage scenario for this type of virtual switch is isolating a single application for testing purposes where you build a series of VMs on a single ESX host that are required by this application, and then you test against this application before allowing to communicate with the rest of the production network.

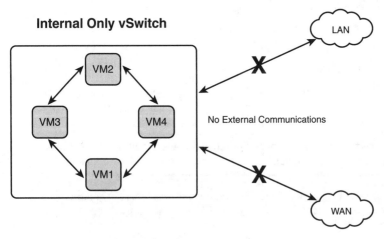

FIGURE 3.1 **Internal only vSwitch.**

Single Adapter Virtual Switch

A single adapter virtual switch is one that is supported or serviced by a single *physical* NIC. This NIC is what allows the virtual switch and the VMs access to the rest of the network. Figure 3.2 shows an example of how this can be implemented.

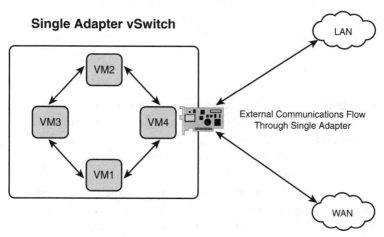

FIGURE 3.2   Single NIC vSwitch.

Multiple Adapter Virtual Switch

NIC teaming, or a multiple adapter virtual switch, is a virtual switch supported by two or more NICs. This type of virtual switch allows for fault tolerance. This is a typical scenario for mission-critical applications that you want to make sure have the maximum resources available to them and built-in failover and packet distribution. Figure 3.3 shows a sample configuration.

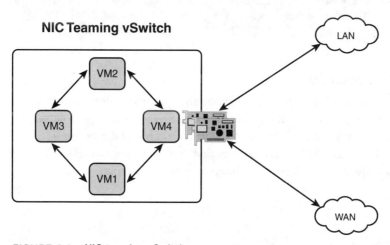

FIGURE 3.3   NIC teaming vSwitch.

Types of Virtual Switch Port Groups

Now that we have covered the types of virtual switches, let's get down to the virtual switch ports. Ports on a virtual switch can be configured to handle different connection types as follows:

▶ Service Console

▶ VMkernel

▶ Virtual machine

This capability is helpful and allows the virtual switch to be a multifunction object rather than an object that does just one static task. To make things easier for you from a management standpoint, you have at your disposal *port groups*. A port group is a collection of ports on the vSwitch that all have the same configuration. So, instead of configuring each port individually on the vSwitch, you group them and give them a particular configuration. A port group specifies port configuration options such as bandwidth limitations and VLAN tagging policies for each member port. Network services connect to vSwitches through port groups. Port groups define how a connection is made through the vSwitch to the network. In typical use, one or more port groups is associated with a single vSwitch.

In the following sections, we explore the different port groups that can be configured and their usage scenarios.

> **ExamAlert**
>
> The virtual switch port types touch on many aspects of virtualization with ESX, from networking to the different kinds of storage. For this reason, the exam will focus on the port types, so make sure you understand when each is used.

Service Console

The Service Console connection type allows for communication to and from the Service Console. During the installation of ESX, a Service Console port labeled vswif0 is automatically associated with vSwitch0, as illustrated in Figure 3.4. The Service Console requires that you configure the IP stack, including a dedicated IP address, a subnet mask, and a default gateway.

vSwitch Name

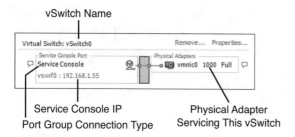

Service Console IP

Port Group Connection Type

Physical Adapter
Servicing This vSwitch

FIGURE 3.4   **Service Console port group.**

Note

Additional Service Console ports enumerate as vswif1, vswif2, vswif3, and so on.

Because the Service Console is a critical component, you might want to think of providing some redundancy, and as such, two scenarios exist to help facilitate that, as follows:

▶ **Multiple Service Console ports:** Create a Service Console port group on two different virtual switches that are serviced by two different physical NICs and assign each service console a different IP address. This creates a redundant second entry point into your ESX host should the primary fail. Figure 3.5 illustrates this scenario.

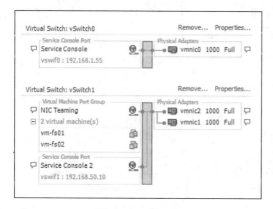

FIGURE 3.5   **Multiple SC port groups.**

▶ **Service Console NIC team:** Add a second physical NIC to the same virtual switch where the original Service Console port groups reside, and therefore, you create redundancy at the physical level. If a NIC fails, the second one picks up seamlessly. In this scenario, you do not need a second IP address because it is being shared. Figure 3.6 illustrates this scenario clearly.

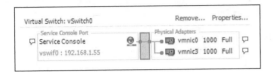

FIGURE 3.6 **SC NIC team.**

VMkernel

A VMkernel port group connection type allows you to configure communication for technologies like vMotion, iSCSI, and NAS/NFS. This connection type requires you to configure the IP stack. The reason behind this is that these technologies will more than likely be connecting to different VLANs or different networks altogether. Figure 3.7 gives an example of how this works.

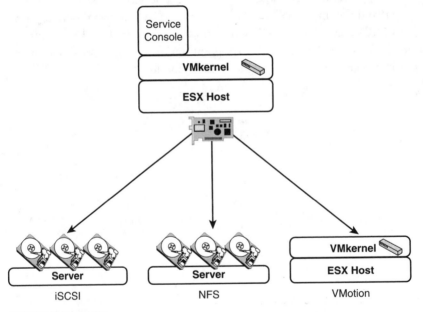

FIGURE 3.7 **VLANs.**

Virtual Machine

A virtual machine (VM) port group opens communication between the VMs configured on the virtual switch and the rest of the physical network by connecting the virtual switch to the physical switch by way of the NIC or NICs configured to support the virtual switch. Figure 3.8 shows this configuration scenario.

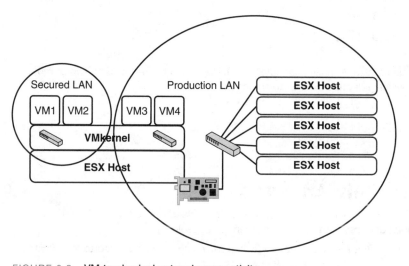

FIGURE 3.8   **VM to physical network connectivity.**

Note

Virtual machine port groups do not need the IP stack configured. Your network administrator should configure the physical port that the physical NIC is plugged into to see the networks and VLANs that need to be accessed by the VMs on this virtual switch.

Cram Quiz

Answer these questions. The answers follow the last question. If you cannot answer these questions correctly, consider reading the section again.

1. Why is Service Console redundancy necessary?

   O **A.** To allow for a secondary method of accessing the management console.

   O **B.** To allow for clustering of the host.

   O **C.** ESX requires at least two entry points into the host.

   O **D.** For load balancing purposes

2. True or false: A single adapter vSwitch allows the switch to communicate with any device on the network.

   O **A.** True

   O **B.** False

3. True or false: A multiple adapter vSwitch is a vSwitch serviced by two or more physical adapters for fault tolerance purposes.

   O **A.** True

   O **B.** False

Cram Quiz Answers

1. **A** is correct. Service Console redundancy is needed to allow for a secondary point of access to the ESX management console.

2. **A** is correct. A single adapter vSwitch allows any VM connected to the vSwitch to communicate with any other device on the network.

3. **A**, True, is correct. vSwitches that are serviced by two or more physical NICs are fault tolerance resistant.

VLANs in Virtual Networking

- ▶ **Trunk Ports**
- ▶ **Port Trunking**
- ▶ **Private VLANs**
- ▶ **802.1Q VLAN Tagging**

Cram**Saver**

If you can correctly answer these questions before going through this section, save time by skimming the Exam Alerts in this section and then completing the Cram Quiz at the end of the section.

1. Private VLANS are a feature of _____.

- ○ **A.** Standard virtual switches.
- ○ **B.** Distributed virtual switches.
- ○ **C.** All virtual switches.
- ○ **D.** Private VLANs are only available with physical switches.

2. What is a port trunk?

-   **A.** A port that spans multiple virtual switches
-   **B.** A port that spans multiple physical switches
-   **C.** A port that spans multiple hosts
-   **D.** A port that has access to multiple VLANs

Answers

1. B is correct. Private VLANs are only available with the Distributed Virtual Switch.

2. D is correct. A trunk port is a port that has visibility to multiple VLANs and can therefore pass traffic to these VLANs based on VLAN ID.

A virtual local area network (VLAN) is a logical grouping of several different LANs. Traditionally, a LAN spans a single segment, whereas a VLAN, being a logical entity represented in software, is capable of breaking this barrier and extending beyond the single segment limitation of a LAN by grouping different LANs together.

Using VLANs allows you to dictate which ports on the switch are connected to which IP segment, thereby reducing the need for additional hardware. You are now capable of allocating different ports on the switch to different subnets. Figure 3.9 further clears up this issue.

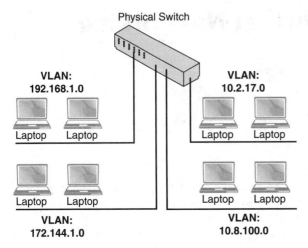

Physical Switch

**VLAN:
192.168.1.0**

Laptop   Laptop

Laptop   Laptop

**VLAN:
172.144.1.0**

**VLAN:
10.2.17.0**

Laptop   Laptop

Laptop   Laptop

**VLAN:
10.8.100.0**

FIGURE 3.9   **VLAN connectivity to different LANs.**

Trunk Ports

A trunk port is a port on the physical switch that you configure to be aware of other VLANs that exist on other switches. Anything that plugs into this port can pass IP communications to all the visible VLANs. Traditionally, a switch could see and give access only to a single IP segment or subnet. With *port trunking*, you can now configure multiple ports on multiple switches to be part of the same VLAN. This characteristic helps overcome geographic limitations and eases management. Figure 3.10 illustrates trunk ports.

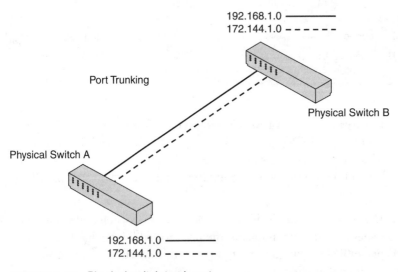

192.168.1.0 ─────────
172.144.1.0 ─ ─ ─ ─ ─ ─

Port Trunking

Physical Switch B

Physical Switch A

192.168.1.0 ─────────
172.144.1.0 ─ ─ ─ ─ ─ ─

FIGURE 3.10   **Physical switch trunk port.**

> **ExamAlert**
>
> Understanding how port trunking and VLAN tagging works in vSphere's virtual networking is important if you are taking the test. Focus on understanding what needs to be configured on the physical switches and what needs to be configured on the virtual switch port groups.

802.1Q VLAN Tagging

ESX has built-in support for *802.1Q VLAN tagging*. The first thing you do to get 802.1Q VLAN tagging to work is to connect a physical NIC to a port that is configured as a trunk port on the physical switch. You then assign this NIC to a vSwitch. What you have accomplished so far, then, is making all the VLANs that are configured on that trunked port visible to the vSwitch.

Now you create port groups on this virtual switch. Port groups, as the name implies, are groupings of several ports and are configured to see a particular VLAN by configuring a VLAN ID in the port group that matches the VLAN ID assigned on the physical switch. Now when you try to add virtual machines to these port groups, your VMs are part of the VLAN assigned to that port group. Figure 3.11 illustrates VLAN tagging.

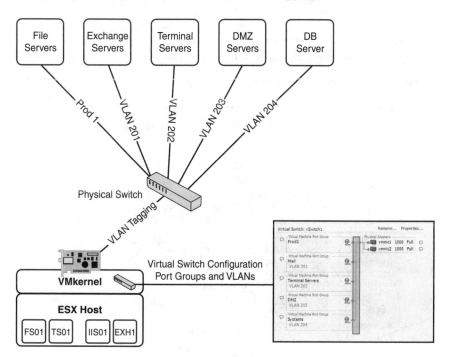

FIGURE 3.11 **VLAN tagging.**

Private VLANs

Private VLANs are a feature available only to vNetwork Distributed Switches and are a way to subdivide an existing VLAN into several different more controlled entities. For example, you can isolate a group of hosts to communicate only among each other even when they are part of a larger VLAN. There are two types of private VLANs:

- **Primary:** The original VLAN that can be subdivided into multiple secondary pVLANs.

- **Secondary:** pVLANs exist only inside the primary VLAN. Each secondary pVLAN has a VLAN ID, which is a subset of the primary VLAN ID. For example, if the primary VLAN ID is 100, the secondary private VLAN ID may be 100.1. Each packet is then associated with a secondary pVLAN ID that identifies its mode. The physical switch can then use this ID to identify the secondary pVLAN mode (promiscuous, Isolated, or Community) and route traffic to it.

Private VLANs Secondary Node Modes

As shown in Figure 3.12, when dealing with secondary private VLANs, there are three modes with which you should be familiar:

- **Promiscuous:** May send and receive packets to any secondary pVLAN. Typically routers are attached to promiscuous ports.

- **Isolated:** May only send and receive packets from the promiscuous pVLAN.

- **Community:** May send and receive packets between any secondary pVLANs that are in community mode. This mode can also communicate with the promiscuous pVLAN mode.

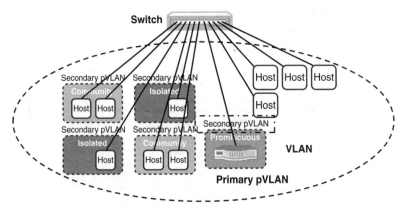

FIGURE 3.12 **Private VLAN architecture.**

Cram Quiz

Answer these questions. The answers follow the last question. If you cannot answer these questions correctly, consider reading the section again.

1. A promiscuous secondary VLAN is typically assigned to _____.

   ○ **A.** Switch

   ○ **B.** Router

   ○ **C.** Virtual switch

   ○ **D.** Security appliance

2. How many modes exist for secondary private VLANs?

   ○ **A.** 1

   ○ **B.** 2

   ○ **C.** 3

   ○ **D.** 4

Cram Quiz Answers

1. **B** is correct. A promiscuous secondary VLAN is typically associated with a router.

2. **C** is correct. A secondary private VLAN has 3 modes: Promiscuous, Isolated, and Community. Answers A, B, and D are incorrect.

Virtual Switch Policies

▶ **Traffic Shaping**

▶ **NIC Teaming**

▶ **Port Blocking**

CramSaver

If you can correctly answer these questions before going through this section, save time by skimming the Exam Alerts in this section and then completing the Cram Quiz at the end of the section.

1. Select the three types of security policies that can be applied to either virtual switches or port groups.

   ○ **A.** IP Hash

   ○ **B.** MAC Address Changes

   ○ **C.** Forged Transmits

   ○ **D.** Promiscuous Mode

2. What are the two circumstances under which physical switches are notified of a change?

   ○ **A.** When a new physical NIC is added to a virtual switch

   ○ **B.** When a new physical NIC is removed from a virtual switch

   ○ **C.** When a physical NIC failover occurs

   ○ **D.** When a virtual NIC failover occurs

Answers

1. **B, C**, and **D** are correct. MAC Address Changes, Promiscuous Mode, and Forged Transmits are the three security policies. IP Hash is a load balancing policy.

2. **A** and **C** are correct. Notify Switches notifies physical switches when a physical NIC failover occurs or when a new physical NIC is added to a virtual switch.

Virtual switches allow you some flexibility to configure them for optimal performance and maximized security. These settings can also be configured for each of the port groups configured on the virtual switch. When closely examining a virtual switch or port group properties, you find the following tabs:

- ► General

- ► Security

- ► Traffic Shaping

- ► NIC Teaming

You can get to these tabs by clicking Properties of a vSwitch in the Networking tab on the ESX host. You can then select the appropriate port group and edit its settings or select the vSwitch and edit its settings.

We examine security, traffic shaping, and NIC teaming in greater detail in the following sections, but first look at Figure 3.13, which shows the contents of the General tab. The General tab is the place where you limit the number of ports you want this virtual switch to have. After you modify the number of ports on the switch, you must restart the system before your changes will take effect.

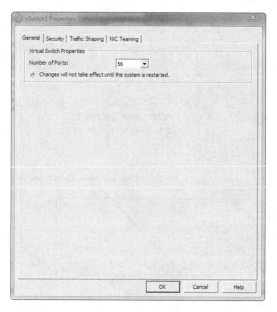

FIGURE 3.13   **vSwitch policies.**

Virtual Switch Security

Three types of Layer 2 security policies can be configured on virtual switches or port groups from the Security tab:

▶ **Promiscuous Mode:** If set to Accept, this setting would pass all the
  unicast frames that pass through the virtual switch to a virtual machine
  connected to that virtual switch. This setting is set to Reject by default
  to prevent frames destined for a particular VM from being read by other
  VMs. You should enable this mode only if you are running troubleshooting tests or running intrusion detection systems that require the
  system to investigate these frames.

▶ **MAC Address Changes:** If set to Reject, this setting would deny
  incoming IP traffic from reaching the VM if the MAC address defined
  in the guest operating system does not match the MAC address listed in
  the VM's configuration file or vmx, as illustrated in Figure 3.14. By
  default, this setting is set to Accept.

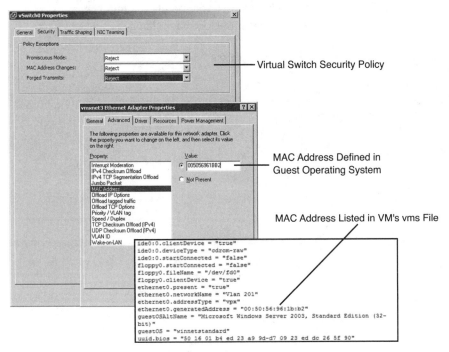

FIGURE 3.14 **VM MAC match configuration file.**

▶ **Forged Transmits:** This setting is the same as the MAC Address
  Changes setting, except it controls the outgoing IP traffic rather than
  the incoming. If set to Reject, this setting would deny outgoing IP traffic from the VM if the MAC address specified in the guest OS does not
  match the MAC address listed in the VM's configuration file or vmx. By
  default, this setting is set to Accept.

> **Tip**
>
> For the highest level of security, set all the values to Reject.

When applying security to a virtual switch or to a port group, you need to understand the policy processing and what takes precedence over what. You can apply the policy as follows:

- ▶ **Virtual switch:** When applying to the virtual switch, the policy propagates to all the port groups configured on this virtual switch.

- ▶ **Port group:** When applied to a port group, a policy overrides the policy applied to the virtual switch and takes precedence over it.

Traffic Shaping

Traffic shaping gives you greater control over the amount of outgoing bandwidth available to virtual machines and enables you to tweak it and prioritize it. Traffic shaping is a great feature and can be useful in some cases in which adding more physical NICs is not permitted. However, given the relatively cheap cost of adding network interface cards, it would be much easier to add more NICs and increase network bandwidth using NIC teaming than it is to tweak bandwidth with traffic-shaping policies.

Traffic shaping is disabled by default; however, should you need to enable it, you have three configurable settings that can help you tweak bandwidth:

- ▶ **Average Bandwidth:** Defines the average bandwidth this virtual switch should handle over time. It basically establishes the normal bandwidth load value for this vSwitch. It measures this in kilobits per second (kbps).

- ▶ **Peak Bandwidth:** Defines the maximum bandwidth that a virtual switch can handle. Packets received after the maximum has been reached are queued and processed as bandwidth is available. If the queue becomes full, any packets after that are bounced. This parameter is also set in kbps.

- ▶ **Burst Size:** Allows you to configure in kilobytes what you want the maximum burst size to be under normal conditions. The burst size also queues packets if the maximum is reached, and if the queue is full, any other packets are dropped.

Physical Switch VLAN

This is a vDS network policy only and allows a virtual network to join in a physical switch configured VLAN.

Port Blocking

Port blocking is another vDS only networking policy. As its name implies port blocking allows you to block communication to a certain port.

NIC Teaming

NIC teaming provides for fault tolerance and load balancing of outgoing traffic from the virtual switch. You can adjust the settings on the NIC Teaming tab of the vSwitch Properties window, as shown in Figure 3.15.

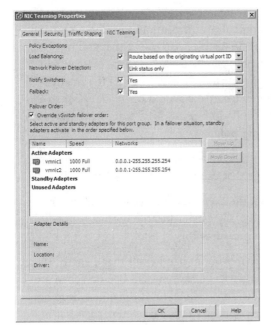

FIGURE 3.15   **NIC teaming.**

Load Balancing

You can select load balancing policies in the Load Balancing drop-down list. There are four load balancing policies that you can configure the virtual switch to take advantage of, as follows:

▶ **Route Based on the Originating Virtual Port ID:** This setting configures communications based on the virtual port where the VM is connected on the virtual switch. In essence, because every VM is configured on a virtual port ID and because this port ID rarely changes, communications are consistent.

> **ExamAlert**
>
> The exam might have a question about whether the port ID will change in the event of a vMotion. The answer is yes because the VM is moving from one vSwitch to another and a completely new host. Keep that in mind.

▶ **Route Based on Source MAC HASH:** This setting configures a communications uplink based on the MAC address of the VM from which the traffic originated. This method has low overhead; however, in this setting, VMs cannot take advantage of multiple physical NICs' bandwidth, and they are limited to the bandwidth of the NIC to which they are connected.

▶ **Route Based on IP Hash:** When this setting is selected, each packet's source and destination IP addresses are hashed, and an uplink communication link is selected based on that hashing. This setting has a higher CPU utilization overhead but provides an advantage by allowing a single VM to take advantage of multiple physical NICs' bandwidth and has better load balancing of traffic across physical NICs. It also requires that the physical switches be configured for EtherChannel or 802.3AD.

▶ **Use Explicit Failover Order:** If this policy is selected, the topmost physical NIC in the list is always used, and if it becomes unavailable, the second NIC on the list takes over.

> **Note**
>
> When you use NIC teaming and add multiple adapters to a virtual switch, you also increase the bandwidth available to the VMs connected to the virtual switch.

Network Failover Detection

ESX/ESXi has built-in capabilities that would notify it when a network failover was detected from one physical NIC to the other, and you can configure this either based on virtual switch or port groups in one of two ways:

- **Link Status:** This method determines if there is a connection by whether a connection is detected on the port. If a cable is connected to the port, it reports the connection as a success; if not, it fails over.

- **Beacon Probing:** In addition to doing Link Status, this method is similar to a heartbeat in that it continuously sends packets between the adapters, and if a heartbeat is missed, it assumes there is an issue and fails over.

Notify Switches

The Notify Switches option is a great performance tweak. When set to Yes, it notifies physical switches of changes such as the following:

- Physical NIC failover occurs where a virtual NIC is now using a different physical NIC to pass its communication.

- A new physical NIC was added to a NIC team.

This feature is especially helpful because, without it, virtual machines would experience latency and slowness as the physical switches update their lookup tables. This is especially helpful after vMotions and, of course, in the event of failovers.

> **Caution**
>
> Do not set the Notify Switches option to Yes if you will be using Microsoft Network load balancing in Unicast mode. Check out the VMware knowledgebase article 1556 for more information. The knowledgebase is located at http://kb.vmware.com.

Failback

The Failback policy determines what happens when a failed physical NIC is functional again. There are two options:

- If this policy is set to Yes, when a failed adapter is restored to a functioning state, it immediately seizes the role of active physical NIC and retires the current active one to standby mode.

- If this policy is set to No, when a failed adapter is restored, it goes into standby mode and does not become active again until the next time a failover occurs.

Explicit Failover Order

When the Explicit Failover Order option is selected, you can manually control what happens in the event of a failover. For example, in the Active adapters, the topmost adapter is always the first one to be used; however, you can control which adapter is on top. The Standby adapters are the ones that are used in the event the active adapter fails; again, you can control which one is used first. The Unused adapters are simply out of commission and should not be used.

Cram Quiz

Answer these questions. The answers follow the last question. If you cannot answer these questions correctly, consider reading the section again.

1. Select the three load balancing methods that can be used.
    - ○ **A.** Route Based on IP Hash
    - ○ **B.** Route Based on the Originating Port ID
    - ○ **C.** NIC teaming
    - ○ **D.** Route Based on Source MAC Hash

2. Which load-balancing method distributes load more efficiently and allows VMs to take advantage of more than a single NIC's available bandwidth?
    - ○ **A.** IP Hash
    - ○ **B.** MAC Hash
    - ○ **C.** Port ID
    - ○ **D.** NIC teaming

3. Which two methods are used to detect a network failure?
    - ○ **A.** Notify Switches
    - ○ **B.** Link Status
    - ○ **C.** Alarm Notification
    - ○ **D.** Beacon Probing

Cram Quiz Answers

1. **A, B,** and **D** are correct. The three types of load balancing methods are Route Based on IP Hash, Route Based on Originating Port ID, and Route Based on Source MAC Hash.

2. **A** is correct. Route Based on IP Hash is the ideal method if you want the most efficient bandwidth load balancing; it also allows VMs to take advantage of multiple physical NICs' bandwidth capabilities. It does, however, add a CPU load and requires the physical switches to be configured for EtherChannel.

3. **B** and **D** are correct. Link Status and Beacon Probing are the two methods by which a network failure is detected.

vNetwork Distributed Switches

▶ **vNetwork Distributed Switches**

▶ **vCenter Object**

▶ **dvPort Groups**

▶ **dvPorts**

Cram**Saver**

If you can correctly answer these questions before going through this section, save time by skimming the Exam Alerts in this section and then completing the Cram Quiz at the end of the section.

1. An Uplink can be allocated from?

    ○ **A.** Any physical NIC on any ESX host.

    ○ **B.** Any vmnic on any ESX host

    ○ **C.** Any physical NICs on vCenter Server.

    ○ **D.** Any vmnics on vCenter Server

2. Which is a function of a vDS switch and not of a vSS?

    ○ **A.** Port Blocking

    ○ **B.** Load Balancing

    ○ **C.** Traffic Shaping

    ○ **D.** Security

3. True or false: A vDS is a virtual switch that spans multiple ESX/ESXi hosts.

    ○ **A.** True

    ○ **B.** False

Answers

1. B is correct. An uplink can be allocated from any vmnic available from any ESX host.

2. A is correct. Port Blocking is a network policy that is only available with vDS.

3. B, False, is correct. vDS does not span multiple hosts, rather it allows multiple hosts to subscribe to it. ESX/ESXi hosts still have a virtual switch that is centrally configured and managed by vDS.

One of the newest and most anticipated features released with vSphere is the vNetwork Distributed Switch (vDS). It allows multiple ESX/ESXi hosts to subscribe to it. It can be managed and configured centrally from vCenter.

A vDS supports all the traditional vNetwork Standard Switch port groups like VMkernel, Service Console, and Virtual Machine.

Advantages of vDS

vDS is only available with the Enterprise Plus version of vSphere and offers all the features of vNetwork Standard Switches. There are, however, several other advantages of using vDS as follows:

▶ Provides a framework for third parties to offer their own version of a vDS

▶ Simplifies datacenter virtual networking administration and configuration by allowing vCenter to centrally control vDS

▶ Provides advanced VLAN features such as private VLANs

▶ Enables networking statistics and policies to migrate with virtual machines during a vMotion

While most of the vDS configuration is owned by vCenter, some aspects are configured at the host level. For example, all the uplinks that are configured for use with vDS are owned and managed at the host level. Similarly, the configuration of the Service Console and VMkernel is also done at the host.

vDS Components and Architecture

The vDS is a component that exists at the vCenter server level and is responsible for network management across the datacenter. The components that make up vDS are as follows:

▶ **Distributed ports or dvPorts:** These are the equivalent of regular ports on a vNetwork Standard Switch and can be configured to allow virtual machine connections, VMkernel interface connections, and Service Console interface connections.

▶ **Distributed port groups:** A logical collection of distributed ports that are grouped together to simplify configuration and management.

▶ **Uplinks:** The equivalent of vmnics used to associate vmnics from multiple hosts to a vDS.

The architecture of vDS consists of two main functions as follows:

- ▶ **Control plane:** This is responsible for the configuration of the vDS, the distributed port groups, the distributed ports, and the uplinks. It is also responsible for coordinating the migration of ports.

- ▶ **I/O plane:** This is a hidden vSwitch that resides in the VMkernel of each ESX host. It is also responsible for forwarding packets and for managing the I/O hardware on each ESX host.

ExamAlert

You should be familiar with the features of the vNetwork Distributed Switches and how they map to Standard Virtual Switches (vSS). You should also be familiar with the differences between vDS and vSS as you are sure to get questions on this subject.

While vDS is a vCenter component, one of its primary functions is to abstract virtual switches that exist on each ESX/ESXi host. This means that you should not think of vDS as single virtual switch that replaces a standard virtual switch and spans multiple hosts. It is not. You should think of it as a template that configures standard virtual switches on each ESX/ESXi host. It then abstracts these virtual switches from all ESX/ESXi hosts and combines them at the vCenter server level so they appear as a single logical entity.

Cram Quiz

Answer these questions. The answers follow the last question. If you cannot answer these questions correctly, consider reading the section again.

1. A vDS is made up of how many architectural planes?

   - ○ **A.** 1
   - ○ **B.** 2
   - ○ **C.** 4
   - ○ **D.** 8

2. True or false: A vDS preserves the network statistics of a migrated port.

   - ○ **A.** True
   - ○ **B.** False

Cram Quiz Answers

1. **B** is correct. A vDS is made up of 2 architectural planes. The Control plane and the I/O plane.

2. **A** is correct. One of the advanced functionality features of a vDS is its capability to preserve network statistics across migrated ports.

Networking Maximums

▶ **Virtual Ports**

▶ **Virtual Port Groups**

▶ **VMDirectPath**

Cram**Saver**

If you can correctly answer these questions before going through this section, save time by skimming the Exam Alerts in this section and then completing the Cram Quiz at the end of the section.

1. What is the maximum VMDirectPath devices supported per host on a standard virtual switch?

   ○ **A.** 4

   ○ **B.** 8

   ○ **C.** 16

   ○ **D.** None

2. If you are using vDS, what is the maximum number of virtual ports that you can have in a single vCenter instance?

   ○ **A.** 4088

   ○ **B.** 8012

   ○ **C.** 16000

   ○ **D.** 20000

Answers

1. **B** is correct. VMDirectPath is supported per host and available with either vSS or vDS with a maximum of 8 devices per host.

2. **D** is correct. The maximum number of virtual ports when using vDS in a single vCenter instance is 20000; therefore, answers A, B, and C are incorrect.

It is inevitable that the VCP exam will include questions regarding networking maximums. Table 3.1 provides these figures to help make sure you are aware of them both for the exam and later for your day-to-day administration and design of ESX environments.

> ## ExamAlert
>
> If you are taking the VCP-410 exam and you have previously taken the VCP-310, pay close attention to the maximum values as they have changed significantly from 3.5 and even from 4.0 to 4.1.

TABLE 3.1 **Networking Maximums**

Component	Standard vSwitch	vDS
Virtual switches	248	32 / vCenter
Virtual ports	4088	20000 / vCenter
Port groups	512	5000 / vCenter
E100 NICs (PCI-e)	24	24
E1000 NICs (PCI-x)	32	32
Active ports	1016 / host	1016 / host
NIC teams	32	32
Hosts per vDS		350
VMDirectPath per host	8	8

Cram Quiz

Answer these questions. The answers follow the last question. If you cannot answer these questions correctly, consider reading the section again.

1. What is the maximum number of vSS supported?
   - ○ **A.** 127
   - ○ **B.** 248
   - ○ **C.** 512
   - ○ **D.** 1016

2. What is the maximum number of E1000 (PCI-x) NICs that are supported?
   - ○ **A.** 16
   - ○ **B.** 32
   - ○ **C.** 64
   - ○ **D.** 128

Cram Quiz Answers

1. **B** is correct. 248 is the maximum number of standard virtual switches supported.
2. **B** is correct. 32 is the maximum number of E1000 PCI-x NICs that are supported.

CHAPTER 4

vStorage Operations

This chapter covers the following VCP exam topics:

- ▶ Fiber Channel Architectural Components
- ▶ Fiber Channel Addressing
- ▶ Internet Small Computer System Interface (iSCSI)
- ▶ iSCSI Addressing
- ▶ iSCSI Targets Discovery
- ▶ Pluggable Storage Architecture (PSA)
- ▶ Network File System (NFS)
- ▶ NFS Features on ESX
- ▶ Configuring NFS
- ▶ Multipathing
- ▶ Extending a VMFS
- ▶ VMFS Volume Growth
- ▶ Zoning
- ▶ Thin Provisioning in vSphere
- ▶ Types of Virtual Disks

(For more information on the VCP exam topics, see "About the VCP Exam" in the introduction.)

When you are planning a VMware Infrastructure deployment on an enterprise level or even on a small- or medium-size level, storage considerations occupy a large percentage of the discussion. Storage is an integral part of the deployment that unlocks features such as VMotion, High Availability, and Distributed Resource Scheduler. Storage also has a significant positive or negative impact on performance of the virtual machines loaded on the ESX hosts. For all those reasons and many more, being intimately familiar and comfortable with all the storage operations in a virtual infrastructure will be the deciding factor between a successful implementation and a mediocre one.

Storage in vSphere 4

Storage as a general subject is so large and vast that it would probably take a book to cover all the options and technologies available. This chapter discusses the different storage technologies that VMware vSphere 4 supports and leaves the vendor selection to your planning phase when you decide to evaluate which solution fits your environment the best. The aim here is to pour a solid storage foundation upon which you can build sharp decision making when the time comes. vSphere 4 presents four different storage architectures to choose from for your deployments:

- ▸ Local Storage

- ▸ Fiber Channel Storage

- ▸ iSCSI Storage

- ▸ Network Attached Storage (NAS)

These architectures, like anything else, have their pros and cons, and your selection depends on the deployment at hand, but that's not to say you cannot mix and match technologies. The importance of storage lies in the enterprise features that require the ESX hosts to see shared storage to allow for technologies like VMotion, Storage VMotion, HA, DRS, and others to work together. Without shared storage between ESX/ESXi hosts, there would be no way of enabling these features because the hosts would not be able to see the VMs that reside on other storage disks to manipulate them in any way. That being said, these technologies also require a certain level of robustness to allow for these live migrations or recoveries to take place in a timely manner that is acceptable.

> **Tip**
>
> Prior to committing to buy any hardware in general for a virtual infrastructure, but before committing to any storage solutions in particular, make sure you check the VMware compatibility guide at http://www.vmware.com/resources/compatibility/ search.php?action=base&deviceCategory=san.

While we are on the subject of performance, you should become intimately familiar with the two types of data transfer that are available:

▶ **Block-level transfer:** The storage area network (SAN) administrator carves up and presents a block of storage to a host. In this scenario, the host treats this storage as if it were local storage on the host. This is typically the case with Fiber Channel (FC) and iSCSI SANs. In this scenario, you can format the storage with the file system that is appropriate to the environment for which it is being deployed.

▶ **File-level transfer:** The host is presented with a logical pointer to a block of disk; a perfect example of this is a network drive letter in Windows. Windows sees the disk as a drive letter but does not have lock capabilities on the disk to format it. Windows sees only the storage and can use it but cannot claim ownership over it.

Exam Alert

Storage is a fundamental building block of the vSphere infrastructure. The difference between file-level transfer and block-level transfer is essential knowledge that you should master before sitting the exam.

Based on the storage solution you choose, file level or block level, performance will vary. For example, block-level transfer in the forms of Fiber Channel and iSCSI render superior data transfer speeds than you would get using file-level transfer with NAS.

Fiber Channel

▶ **Zoning**

▶ **Fiber Channel Addressing**

▶ **Fiber Channel Architectural Components**

Cram**Saver**

If you can correctly answer these questions before going through this section, save time by skimming the Exam Alerts in this section and then completing the Cram Quiz at the end of the section.

1. What is a World Wide Name (WWN)?

  ○ **A.** It is a Unique 16-bit address assigned to an HBA.

  ○ **B.** It is a Unique 32-bit address assigned to an HBA

  ○ **C.** It is a Unique 64-bit address assigned to an HBA.

  ○ **D.** It is a Unique 128-bit address assigned to an HBA.

2. What is the difference between Hard and Soft Zoning?

  ○ **A.** Hard Zoning is meant to obscure while Soft Zoning is meant to prevent access to a device.

  ○ **B.** Soft Zoning is meant to obscure while Hard Zoning is meant to prevent access to a device.

  ○ **C.** Hard Zoning is implemented at the Fabric level.

  ○ **D.** Soft Zoning is implemented at the host level.

3. What is an FC Logical Unit Number (LUN)? (Choose two answers.)

  ○ **A.** It is block-level storage.

  ○ **B.** It is file-level storage.

  ○ **C.** It is a physical collection of disks.

  ○ **D.** It is a logical grouping of disks.

Answers

1. C is correct. A World Wide Name consists of a 64-bit alpha-numeric address that is assigned to an HBA.

2. B is correct. Soft Zoning is meant to obscure access to devices in a zone while Hard Zoning is meant limit access to devices in a zone and prevent access to devices from outside a zone.

3. A and **D** are correct. A Fiber Channel LUN is block-level storage made up of a collection of disks logically grouped.

Fiber Channel storage area networks are the most efficient, most reliable, and best performing of all the other solutions. They are also the most expensive of them all. However, depending on your enterprise's needs and the types of applications that you plan to deploy, Fiber Channel may be the best solution, and thus, performance and reliability become the deciding factor over cost.

A Fiber Channel SAN is a high-speed transport protocol that moves SCSI commands between two nodes at speeds of up to 8GB.

Knowing how a Fiber Channel SAN works with ESX is critical if you plan on deploying ESX in that environment. FC SANs extend the following options to ESX:

- **SAN Boot ESX:** Allows you to configure the ESX Server's BIOS to point to the right LUN where ESX was installed and therefore boot from that LUN.

- **Create VMFS Datastores:** Allows you to create VMFS partitions and take advantage of a robust foundation where VMs run at an optimal level. This option also provides for a location where you can store VM templates and ISO images.

- **Enable Enterprise Features:** FC SANs allow for features like VMotion, Storage VMotion, DRS, and HA to have a shared disk or common playground that allows for these technologies to function properly.

- **Allow VMs Access to Raw LUNs:** Allows you to configure a VM to have access to a raw LUN; this is the same concept as attaching a LUN to a physical server and then allowing this physical server to use this LUN as if it were a local disk. The same applies to a VM: You are presenting this LUN to it, and the VM treats this as a local disk and manages it according to the operating system installed on it.

vSphere 4.1 supports 256 LUNs that range from 0–255, 0 being the first LUN. These LUNs are identified by the VMkernel during the boot process. However, many times you will find yourself adding a SAN LUN to ESX/ESXi and wanting it to see it without having to reboot the server; this is where the rescan option, shown in Figure 4.1, can be a very handy tool. You can access the rescan tool by going to the Configuration tab of the ESX host and then choosing Storage Adapters.

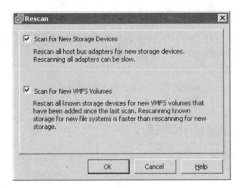

FIGURE 4.1 **Rescan LUNs.**

ESX/ESXi 4.1 can see a maximum of 256 LUNs with four paths each.

FC SAN Architecture

Familiarizing yourself with the different components that make up the Fiber Channel architecture is imperative in your virtual infrastructure deployment. The following sections cover the different components that make up the FC network:

- Host bus adapters

- Fiber Channel switches

- Logical Unit Numbers

- Storage systems

- Storage processor

Host Bus Adapters

A host bus adapter (HBA) is a physical device that is typically installed in a server and is similar to the network interface card (NIC) except it uses a different protocol and different type of cable. It is used to connect the host to a Fiber Channel network.

Every HBA is assigned a unique 64-bit address known as the World Wide Name (WWN), which identifies this device on the Fiber Channel network. The WWN is similar in functionality to a MAC address that is found on NICs. Figure 4.2 shows a typical WWN as noted from an ESX 4 host.

FC HBA WWN

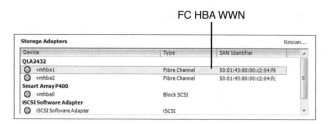

FIGURE 4.2   **World Wide Name.**

Fiber Channel Switches

A Fiber Channel switch, also known as the "fabric," is similar in functionality to an Ethernet switch except it supports FC ports, FC cables, and a different protocol. FC switches create the framework by which Fiber Channel devices can communicate with one another in a secure, optimal way.

Logical Unit Numbers

A Logical Unit Number (LUN) is a logical grouping of physical disks, sometimes referred to as Just a Bunch Of Disks (JBOD), or storage containers that are JBOD with the added advantage of RAID for fault tolerance. A Logical Unit (LU) can be a JBOD, a storage container, or part of a JBOD or storage container.

Storage Systems

A storage system is the collection of actual physical hard drives that are available in their rawest format and ready to be carved up into LUNs.

Storage Processor

A storage processor, also referred to as a controller, is the actual maestro or brain that creates the LUNs, implements security, and controls and regulates route access to the LUNs from the hosts.

Masking

LUN masking is the process of obscuring or hiding specific LUNs from being visible to hosts. LUN masking is implemented at the HBA or SCSI controller level. LUN masking should not be viewed as a secure way of preventing access to LUNs but rather an administrative measure to prevent operating systems from corrupting each other's LUNs. An example would be a Windows operating system: If you don't hide LUNs from a Windows operating system, it attempts to write a signature on all the visible disks, thereby corrupting some LUNs that were not its own to begin with. LUN masking prevents such nuisances by hiding these LUNs and limiting visibility only to the host's operating system.

> **Note**
>
> The reason LUN masking should not be considered a strong security measure is that an HBA WWN can be spoofed or forged.

Zoning

Zoning in a Fiber Channel SAN is the logical grouping of physical devices that are allowed to communicate together. Zoning is the compartmentalization of the fabric to break it down into smaller, more secure, and optimally managed subsets with controlled interference. The devices that are connected to the Fiber Channel fabric should not be allowed to freely interact with one another. Zoning regulates which devices should be communicating. There are two primary types of zoning in a Fiber Channel SAN:

▶ **Hard Zoning:** Implemented at the Fiber Channel switch level. It prevents physical access to any device that is not a member of the zone, thus making this type of zoning a more secure one.

▶ **Soft Zoning:** Also implemented at the Fiber Channel switch level. It is the method of obscuring ports so that they are not visible to devices outside their native zone. Therefore, what you can't see, you can't access. That being said, the security risk in this scenario lies in the fact that if you can discover the physical address of the device, you can still contact it and communicate with it.

> **Note**
>
> In most Fiber Channel deployments, seasoned SAN administrators always use a combination of hard and soft zoning to better manage the SAN.

FC Addressing

Addressing, as its name implies, is a method of providing a unique identifier that allows an ESX host to reach a LUN or partition. Just like your home address allows others to reach you, the VMkernel also has an address scheme that connects an ESX host's HBA to the drives. Figure 4.3 breaks down the addressing scheme.

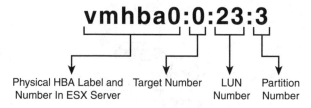

FIGURE 4.3 **Addressing scheme.**

The addressing scheme components are as follows:

▶ **Physical HBA label and number in ESX Server:** A default label that identifies the device as an HBA. The label is "vmhba." A number is appended to this label that distinguishes the HBAs that are installed in the host. So if you have two or three HBAs, you can identify them by the appended number.

▶ **Target number:** The path or route that the storage processor presents to reach the SCSI disks. If you have two storage processors, depending on which SP will be used to route your request, the SP's number is appended to the target.

▶ **LUN number:** The number identifying the LUN.

▶ **Partition number:** The number of the target partition where traffic is destined. If you are trying to reach partition 3, 3 is appended.

Figure 4.4 illustrates a sample address that is destined to a LUN and also a sample address that is destined to a partition. The figure also shows how the traffic flows from the ESX host to its destination. Taking a closer look at what is going on in Figure 4.4, you can see that the top scenario is that of an ESX host that has two HBAs that are single ports. vmhba0 is trying to get to partition 3 on LUN 23 via storage processor 0, and thus, the address would be vmhba0:0:23:3; while vmhba1 is trying to get to LUN 24 via storage processor 1, and its address translates into vmhba1:1:24.

In the bottom scenario in Figure 4.4, an ESX host has two dual-port HBAs connecting to two dual-port storage processors. vmhba0 is again trying to access partition 3 on LUN 23; however, this time it is configured to have two paths to this partition:

▶ **vmhba0:0:23:3**

This path uses storage processor 0 to get to partition 3.

▶ **vmhba0:1:23:3**

This path uses storage processor 1 to get to partition 3.

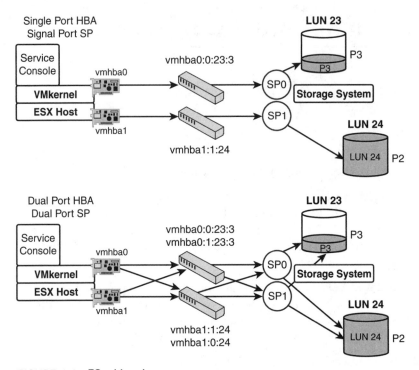

FIGURE 4.4 **FC addressing.**

Similarly, vmhba1 is trying to get to LUN 24 in two different paths:

▶ **vmhba1:0:24**

   This path uses storage processor 0 to get to LUN 24.

▶ **vmhba1:1:24**

   This path uses storage processor 1 to get to LUN 24.

Exam Alert

Fiber Channel Addressing is an important concept that is critical to any enterprise class vSphere deployment that uses Fiber Channel SAN. It is very likely that the VCP-410 exam will test your knowledge on these concepts, so make sure you master them.

Cram Quiz

Answer these questions. The answers follow the last question. If you cannot answer these questions correctly, consider reading the section again.

1. What is the method of hiding or obscuring LUNs on a per host basis known as?

- ○ **A.** Hard zoning
- ○ **B.** Soft zoning
- ○ **C.** LUN masking
- ○ **D.** Storage processor zoning

2. Identify the LUN number from vmhba0:2:3:4.

- ○ **A.** 0
- ○ **B.** 2
- ○ **C.** 3
- ○ **D.** 4

Cram Quiz Answers

1. **C** is correct. LUN masking is the method of obscuring LUNs on a per host basis.

2. **C** is correct. vmhba0 identifies the HBA adapter number in the ESX host. The second number, which is 2 in this example, identifies the target. The third number, which is 3, identifies the LUN number. The fourth number, which is 4, identifies the partition number.

iSCSI

▶ **Internet Small Computer System Interface (iSCSI)**

▶ **iSCSI Addressing**

▶ **iSCSI Targets Discovery**

CramSaver

If you can correctly answer these questions before going through this section, save time by skimming the Exam Alerts in this section and then completing the Cram Quiz at the end of the section.

1. Which command-line interface (CLI) directs the iSCSI Software initiator to use a specific vmkNIC?

   ○ **A.** esxcli swiscsi nic add.

   ○ **B.** esxcfg swiscsi nic add.

   ○ **C.** esxcli iscsi nic add.

   ○ **D.** esxcfg iscsi nic add.

2. How many types of target discovery are there?

   ○ **A.** Two Types

   ○ **B.** Three Types

   ○ **C.** Four Types

   ○ **D.** Six Types

Answers

1. **A** is correct. The CLI command that allows you to direct the Software Initiator to use a specific vmkNIC is **esxcli swiscsi nic add**. All other answers are incorrect.

2. **A** is correct. There are two types of target discovery: Static Discovery and Dynamic Discovery.

Internet Small Computer System Interface (iSCSI) is an IP-based storage networking architecture that is capable of transmitting SCSI commands over your existing Ethernet infrastructure. This option is attractive to some organizations because the cost of deploying an iSCSI-based SAN is much cheaper than that of deploying a Fiber Channel SAN, and the performance benchmarks of iSCSI are impressive and yield excellent results. Fiber Channel remains a more robust solution, but with advancement and the availability of 10GB Ethernet, iSCSI will continue to yield impressive performance benchmarks.

Another reason iSCSI is attractive is that you can use your existing Ethernet architecture, and you do not need to deploy special switches or cabling to support it. iSCSI can be deployed over your LAN, WAN, or even over the Internet.

ESX Server supports iSCSI and extends the same support and feature capabilities as it does the Fiber Channel solution, as follows:

▶ **SAN Boot ESX:** Allows you to configure the ESX Server's BIOS to point to the right LUN where ESX was installed and therefore boot from that LUN. This option is supported only if you are using the hardware initiator. The reason behind that is the software initiator is software based and the driver does not load before ESX Server; therefore, the option is not available.

▶ **Create VMFS Datastores:** Allows you to create VMFS datastores on iSCSI LUNs.

▶ **Enable Enterprise Features:** iSCSI LUNs support enterprise features like VMotion, Storage VMotion, HA, and DRS.

▶ **Allow VMs Access to Raw LUNs:** Allows you to assign a raw iSCSI LUN directly to a VM the same way you can assign a raw LUN directly to a physical machine.

iSCSI Addressing

iSCSI, like Fiber Channel, also has a unique way of assigning addresses to initiators and targets for them to quickly, easily, and accurately route packets to one another. The iSCSI addressing scheme consists of the following:

▶ **iqn:** iqn, which stands for iSCSI Qualified Name, is a standard label affixed at the beginning of the naming convention.

▶ **Date:** This string specifies the year and the month in which the organization registered a valid domain or subdomain.

▶ **Reversed domain:** The organizational naming authority basically consists of the domain name of the organization presented backward—for example, .com.vmware.

▶ **Alias:** This optional string is represented by a colon (:) and is appended at the end of the name string followed by the friendly name or alias given.

When you break it down, the iSCSI naming convention looks something like this:

iqn.2007-02.com.eliaskhnaser:ipstor

Software Initiator

The software initiator is a technique that renders the NIC in the ESX server a multifunction NIC that is capable of connecting an ESX host to a storage system over a traditional IP network without needing to add anymore hardware components.

The software initiator requires a VMkernel port group on a vSwitch on your ESX host to function properly. It is the responsibility of this VMkernel port to handle iSCSI session initiation, security, authentication, and input/output (I/O) traffic.

You can also configure multipathing thereby adding a layer of redundancy for ESX host accessibility to the Storage Area Network (SAN). This is particularly important because of a vSphere environment relies heavily on the SAN, and eliminating a single point of failure is particularly important to allow for continuous uninterrupted access to the storage subsystem.

> **ExamAlert**
>
> In vSphere 4, you no longer need a Service Console port for iSCSI to function properly.

Enabling the Software Initiator

The *iSCSI software initiator*, being software based, needs to be enabled before the existing NICs can be set in multifunction mode. Enabling the software initiator is a two-step process:

1. First open TCP port 3260 on the SC firewall. To do this, you need to edit the Security Profile, which is located under the Configuration tab. Check the box next to Software iSCSI Client. See Figure 4.5 for an example.

2. Edit the properties of the iSCSI software initiator in the Storage Adapters link under the Configuration tab. Select Configure and then Enable.

> **ExamAlert**
>
> Although there are two steps to enable the software initiator, the process does not work properly without your configuring a VMkernel port group and configuring the IP stack.

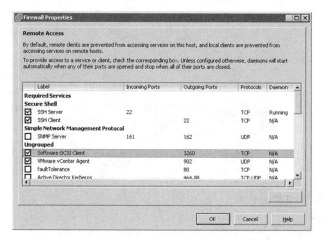

FIGURE 4.5   **Enable iSCSI.**

Setting Up Software iSCSI Port Group

Before we can use iSCSI, we need to set it up, and the first step in that process is to create a port group on a vSwitch configured for iSCSI. This is an easy task that involves either creating a new vSwitch or selecting an existing vSwitch and adding a VMkernel port group and associating that port group with a physical NIC. You need to configure the IP stack for this NIC by assigning it an IP, Subnet, and Gateway.

Configuring Multipathing

Multipathing for iSCSI enables the ESX host to have more than one physical connection to the iSCSI storage. It allows the ESX host to be aware of multiple paths to this storage. There are two methods by which you can architect a multipathing solution:

- ▶ **Single vSwitch, multiple port groups:** In this scenario, you have a single vSwitch with multiple VMkernel port groups. The trick is that each VMkernel port group is associated with a physical NIC, as shown in Figure 4.6.

- ▶ **Multiple vSwitches, single port group:** This is a straightforward scenario in which you have multiple vSwitches with a single VMkernel port associated with a physical NIC, as shown in Figure 4.6.

Multipathing Scenarios

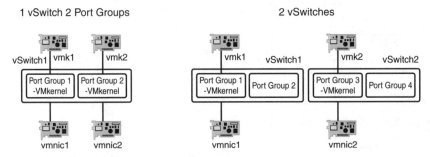

FIGURE 4.6 **iSCSI multipathing scenarios.**

If you decide to go with the single vSwitch option, you need to perform the following tasks:

1. Associate an additional physical NIC with the vSwitch you intend on setting up for multipathing.

2. Create multiple VMkernel port groups on the same vSwitch.

3. Associate each VMkernel port group with a physical NIC by editing the properties of the port group and overriding the vSwitch failover order under the NIC Teaming tab, as shown in Figure 4.7.

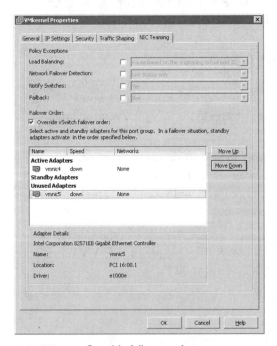

FIGURE 4.7 **Override failover order.**

For detailed step-by-step configuration, check out the VMware document iSCSI SAN Configuration Guide located here: http://www.vmware.com/pdf/vsphere4/r40/vsp_40_iscsi_san_cfg.pdf#page=30.

Enabling Multipathing

So far, all we have done is configure or properly lay down the physical architecture for iSCSI connectivity by creating the port groups and associating them with physical NICs. Now we need to tell the software initiator how to use our newly created infrastructure. Remember the iSCSI Initiator we are discussing here is software based, so we need to configure it. The following need to be completed for the software iSCSI to be properly set up and ready for use:

1. Identify the vmkNICs assigned to the VMkernel iSCSI ports. These are the ESX vmNICs that are assigned to physical adapters. Using the vSphere client you can easily identify the vmkNICs by going to the networking tab, as shown in Figure 4.8.

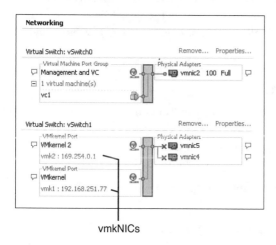

FIGURE 4.8   iSCSI software adapter.

2. From a CLI, direct the software initiator to use the appropriate vmkNICs by initiating the following command:

   esxcli swiscsi nic add -n *<port_name>* **-d** *<vmhba>*

3. If you don't know the vmhba name, you can easily find that from the vSphere client; navigate to the Configuration tab in Storage Adapters and you will see it under iSCSI Software Adapters, as shown in Figure 4.9.

vmhba name

Storage Adapters		
Device	Type	WWN
iSCSI Software Adapter		
⊙ vmhba33	iSCSI	iqn.1998-01.com.vmware:esx01-3d723770:
631xESB/632xESB IDE Controller		
⊙ vmhba2	Block SCSI	
⊙ vmhba32	Block SCSI	
ISP2432-based 4Gb Fibre Channel to PCI Express HBA		
⊙ vmhba1	Fibre Channel	50:01:43:80:00:c1:fd:99 50:01:43:80:00:c1:fd:98

FIGURE 4.9   **vmhba name lookup.**

Once you have successfully completed these steps, you should end up with multiple paths to your storage.

Dynamic Discovery

The second tab on the properties of the iSCSI Software Initiator is the Dynamic Discovery tab. Here, you can configure the iSCSI server's IP address with the associated port that can be queried for available targets. This method is also known as the SendTargets method because it establishes a discovery session with the SendTargets Server, also known as the iSCSI Server, and the server responds back with a list of all the available targets that you can connect to.

CHAP Authentication

Using the CHAP button in the General tab, you can configure CHAP authentication. As shown in Figure 4.10, two sections can be configured, CHAP (Target Authenticates Host) and Mutual CHAP. Under the CHAP (Target Authenticates Host) section, you have the following options:

▶ **Do Not Use CHAP:** As the name implies, this option will disable CHAP.

▶ **Do Not Use CHAP Unless Required by Target:** If the target requires CHAP authentication then credentials are provided, but the host will not use CHAP unless prompted by the target.

▶ **Use CHAP Unless Prohibited by Target:** CHAP is used unless the target specifically refuses it.

▶ **Use CHAP**

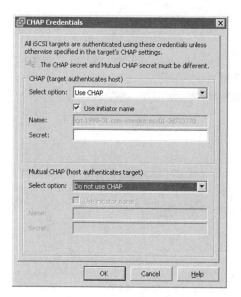

Figure 4.10   CHAP authentication.

With the exception of Do Not Use CHAP, all other options require you to enter a CHAP name. To make your name selection easy, you can use the software initiator name, if you choose, by selecting that option, as shown in Figure 4.10. You are then prompted to enter the CHAP secret. The CHAP secret that you enter must match the secret on the destination device that you are establishing communications with.

Under the Mutual CHAP section of this dialog box, the only time the Use CHAP option will be available is if you selected Use CHAP in the previous section CHAP (Target Authenticates Host).

Hardware Initiator

The hardware initiator has all the benefits of the software initiator described previously but also has better performance metrics. You can see when using a software initiator that you put a strain on the ESX host's CPU because it is used to process all the TCP packets. By using a hardware initiator, you offload the CPU processing burden from the host's CPU to the hardware initiator, thereby increasing performance. The hardware initiator also has two main advantages over the software initiator:

▶ The hardware initiator allows ESX to boot from a SAN LUN.

▶ The hardware initiator uses Static Discovery.

Static Discovery is a tab on the iSCSI initiator properties that allows you to manually specify the IP address of targets that you know ESX can access.

Cram Quiz

Answer these questions. The answers follow the last question. If you cannot answer these questions correctly, consider reading the section again.

1. Choose the two iSCSI discovery methods that ESX 4 supports.

   ○ **A.** Dynamic Discovery

   ○ **B.** Static Discovery

   ○ **C.** SendTargets

   ○ **D.** Fixed Targets

2. What is the default authentication method for iSCSI?

   ○ **A.** Kerberos

   ○ **B.** CHAP

   ○ **C.** NTLM

   ○ **D.** Radius

3. True or false: VMware best practice calls for separating iSCSI traffic on its own network.

   ○ **A.** True

   ○ **B.** False

4. What does IQN Stand for?

   ○ **A.** iSCSI Quiesced Name

   ○ **B.** iSCSI Quiesced Node

   ○ **C.** iSCSI Qualified Name

   ○ **D.** iSCSI Qualified Node

Cram Quiz Answers

1. **A** and **B** are correct. The two iSCSI methods supported by ESX are Static Configuration and SendTargets.

2. **B** is correct. iSCSI uses CHAP as the default method of authentication.

3. **A**, True, is correct. VMware best practices recommend that iSCSI be separated on its own network.

4. **C** is correct. IQN stands for iSCSI Qualified Name. All other answers are incorrect.

Network Attached Storage

▶ Network File System (NFS)

▶ NFS Features on ESX

▶ Configuring NFS

CramSaver

If you can correctly answer these questions before going through this section, save time by skimming the Exam Alerts in this section and then completing the Cram Quiz at the end of the section.

1. Is VMotion Supported on NFS?

   ○ A. Yes.

   ○ B. No

2. Is Raw Device Mapping a supported feature with NFS?

   ○ A. Yes

   ○ B. No

Answers

1. A is correct. VMotion is a supported feature when using NFS.

2. B is correct. Raw Device Mapping (RDM) is not a supported feature of NFS.

Network Attached Storage (NAS) is a self-sufficient storage system—an entity on its own that can be attached via Ethernet to the traditional network. NAS is different from SAN in that, with the NAS system, a complete entity is attached to the network, whereas a SAN is a network on its own that allows connections from storage devices to gain access to storage systems.

Note

It is possible to have NAS devices also attached to the Fiber Channel network; however, one of the main reasons for using NAS is the capability to attach to the existing Ethernet network.

NAS is less expensive than both Fiber Channel and iSCSI-based SANs but also yields lower performance benchmarks when compared to FC or iSCSI SANs. NAS, however, is easier to manage and maintain.

Whereas NAS supports different types of protocols, such as *Network File System (NFS)* and *Common Internet File System (CIFS)*, which is also known as Server Message Block (SMB), ESX 4 supports only NFS and more specifically NFS 3.

> **Note**
>
> NAS disk drives have traditionally been SCSI, but you can build NAS on almost any type of disk, including ATA.

ESX Features on NFS Datastores

ESX supports NFS datastores; therefore, you are able to store VM files, templates, and ISO images on NFS datastores just as you would on FC or iSCSI datastores. ESX trusts NFS datastores to perform the following tasks:

- ▶ VMotion
- ▶ DRS
- ▶ HA
- ▶ VCB

Table 4.1 puts forth the features that are supported by ESX on the different storage types to make it easier for you to identify what is supported where.

TABLE 4.1 **Storage Systems Feature Support on ESX**

Feature	Local	NFS	iSCSI	Fiber Channel
VMFS	✓	X	✓	✓
RDM (Raw Disk Mapping)	✓	X	✓	✓
VMotion	X	✓	✓	✓
HA	X	✓	✓	✓
VCB	✓	✓	✓	✓
DRS	X	✓	✓	✓
MSCS (Microsoft Cluster Server)	X	X	X	✓

> **ExamAlert**
>
> The VCP-410 exam is sure to challenge your knowledge on the feature limitation of NAS/NFS when compared to iSCSI or FC. Make sure you know these differences well.

Configuring NFS Datastores

When configuring an NFS datastore for use with ESX, you need to know a few points that will make it easier for you to complete the configuration in a successful manner. Aside from the GUI portion of creating an NFS datastore, you should familiarize yourself with some of the syntax in `/etc/exports` because this file defines which system can access the shares on the NAS device. The syntax is as follows:

- **Share name:** This is the name of the directory that will be shared on the NAS device.

- **Subnet:** This defines which subnet is allowed to access this share.

- **sync:** This ensures the completion of a write request before accepting additional requests.

- **rw:** This enables read and write requests on the NAS device.

- **no_root_squash:** This enables the root user or UID0 to access NFS with extended privileges.

NFS addressing is in the form of an IP address followed by the share name. When configuring it in ESX, you need to create a dedicated VMkernel port group on a vSwitch that is separate from that of the Service Console because it requires an IP address differentiation between it and the Service Console.

Cram Quiz

Answer these questions. The answers follow the last question. If you cannot answer these questions correctly, consider reading the section again.

1. What is the **no_root_squash** option used for?

   ○ **A.** Enable Root access to NFS

   ○ **B.** Enable Root extended privilege access to NFS

   ○ **C.** Disable Root access to NFS

   ○ **D.** Enable limited Root access to NFS

2. True or false: NFS requires a VMkernel port group and a Service Console port group to allow for proper network communication.

   ○ **A.** True

   ○ **B.** False

Cram Quiz Answers

1. **B** is the correct response. **No_root_squash** enables the root user or UID extended privilege access to NFS.

2. **B**, False, is the correct response. NFS only requires a VMkernel port group to allow IP communication to the storage.

Virtual Machine File System

- ▶ **Multipathing**
- ▶ **Extending a VMFS**
- ▶ **VMFS Volume Growth**
- ▶ **Pluggable Storage Architecture (PSA)**

Cram**Saver**

If you can correctly answer these questions before going through this section, save time by skimming the Exam Alerts in this section and then completing the Cram Quiz at the end of the section.

1. How many multipathing options does vSphere offer by default?
   - ○ **A.** 1
   - ○ **B.** 2
   - ○ **C.** 3
   - ○ **D.** 4

2. What is the maximum number of extents that a VMFS can have?
   - ○ **A.** 16
   - ○ **B.** 32
   - ○ **C.** 64
   - ○ **D.** 128

Answers

1. **C** is correct. By default you have 3 multipathing options. Fixed, Most Recently Used, and Round Robin.

2. **B** is correct. A VMFS volume can have a maximum of 32 extents.

So far in this chapter, we have looked at the different hardware storage solutions. Now let's focus our attention on what file system (software) leverages the hardware solutions we discussed previously. This brings us to the topic of the Virtual Machine File System (VMFS).

VMFS is a VMware proprietary file system that was designed and optimized to host virtual machine files, templates, and iso images. VMFS is a lightweight file system with little overhead. Unlike other file systems such as Windows NTFS, which allows only a single host access to the file system at one time, VMware's VMFS allows multiple hosts access at the same time without stepping on each other. This process is handled by the metadata file, a file that keeps track of the different changes that each attached host makes to the file system.

ExamAlert

The metadata files present on every VMFS volume are represented by files with the .fs extension.

Another reason VMware chose to build its own file system rather than use an existing file system like NTFS or ext is that it wanted a file system with the least overhead. For example, VMFS does not have any of the overhead that NTFS requires for security. Therefore, VMFS has one purpose only, and that is to provide VMs with a superior, well-optimized space to operate and accelerate.

But how, you might ask, does VMFS allow multiple hosts to lock the volume to write to it? VMFS uses file-level locks rather than entire volume-level locks, so by locking only the file being used, it allows other hosts to access other files on the partition and write to them at the same time. The only time a lock is placed on the entire partition is when the metadata file is being accessed; this is why, during the planning of your storage solution, LUN sizing is critical, because you don't want to put so much disk I/O on your LUNs that it slows down performance.

Performance is affected when hosts are queued to write to the metadata file. You therefore should be very cautious to design LUNs that can perform without having to wait for locks on the metadata to be released so that they can lock the metadata and write to it.

When working with VMFS, a common challenge is datastore size and capacity. vSphere gives you the flexibility to manage the size of the VMFS datastore to satisfy your storage needs. If you originally provisioned a VMFS volume and want to increase its size, you have two options to accomplish this task:

▶ Extent Volume enables you to dynamically add more storage to an existing VMFS thereby increasing its size past its maximum allowable capacity.

▶ Volume Grow allows you to expand the existing volume up to the maximum VMFS capacity.

In both instances, you are allowed to perform these tasks without downtime and while VMs are in production. However, you should always take the necessary precautionary measures, such as having a good recent backup of all VMs running on the VMFS volume in question.

Extending a VMFS

vSphere allows you the flexibility of extending a VMFS volume to address space limitations on existing volumes. Extent Grow allows you to dynamically extend a VMFS volume, which means you can add more space without interrupting productivity. To add more space, your storage administrator will provision additional LUNs, which you will then attach to the VMFS volume you want to grow. Once you have attached them, the system logically groups them together and presents them as a single entity. The maximum size that you can allocate to a VMFS is 2TB–512 bytes. You can dynamically grow a VMFS volume that is less than 2TB up to the maximum using Volume Grow; however, should you need to get around this limitation, you can add extents to an existing VMFS volume. The maximum size of an extent is also 2TB, but you can add up to 32 extents to a single VMFS.

> ## ExamAlert
>
> A VMFS volume with extents can be as large as 64TB. The maximum number of extents that can be added to a single VMFS is 32, and the maximum size of each extent is 2TB (32 * 2 = 64TB).

So if you want an 8TB VMFS datastore, you create the VMFS datastore at 2TB in size and then add three extents, each 2TB in size, which totals 8TB. We strongly recommend that you carefully scale out your VMFS to avoid taking a performance hit. Even though you can get an 8TB VMFS, it does not necessarily mean you should. As we discussed before, every VMFS volume has a metadata file that gets locked by a different host when it is making updates to the volume. The larger the volume, the longer hosts have to wait to lock and write to the metadata file and the more performance suffers.

> ## Caution
>
> When using multiple extents, you should be aware that the first extent in the set is the one that hosts the metadata. Loss or corruption of the first extent leads to data loss on the other extents.

When an extent has been assigned to a datastore, you cannot remove that extent without destroying the entire datastore and the contents on it. So, although adding an extent is relatively easy, the capability to remove an extent and preserve the datastore is not supported at this time. Figure 4.11 illustrates a VMFS with several extents that form the extent set or extent group.

FIGURE 4.11   **VMFS extents.**

Growing a VMFS

Volume Grow is another method of increasing the size of a VMFS datastore. With Volume Grow, you are able to expand the current VMFS volume size provided that disk capacity is immediately available adjacent to the current partition it is located on. Volume Grow allows you to expand the size of the existing VMFS so that it grows in size and has no dependency on an extent. It's as if you had originally created it with this size.

At first read, it would appear that Volume Grow is a better technology. Although that may be true in some cases, in other cases extending a VMFS volume is your only choice. For example, Volume Grow still suffers from the same limitation as Extent Grow, which is a VMFS volume cannot be more than 2TB in size. If you want to create a VMFS larger than 2TB, it is mandatory that you use Extent Grow. Another example of using an Extent Grow would be in the event that disk space is not immediately available adjacent to the volume you want to grow.

Multipathing

Multipathing is a concept that allows the ESX host to have more than one path to the storage systems configured for this host. This method is used to ensure continuous uninterrupted access to this storage by configuring the different ports on the HBAs in the ESX host to be aware of more than one way to reach the storage systems. So, in essence, it is designed to provide High Availability in the event of a hardware failure.

Pluggable Storage Architecture

vSphere 4 introduced the Pluggable Storage Architecture, which is a framework that manages simultaneous Multiple Multipathing Plugins (MPP) (see Figure 4.12). The idea here is in addition to the MPP that VMware provides, third-party software developers, especially storage manufacturers, can write their own MPPs that can easily be plugged in and used for multipathing.

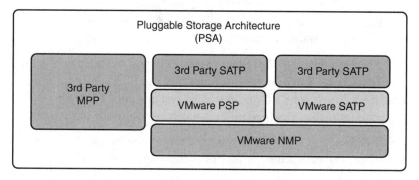

FIGURE 4.12 **Pluggable Storage Architecture.**

VMware provides by default an MPP called the Native Multipathing Plugin (NMP), which supports all the storage arrays listed in the VMware Hardware Compatibility List (HCL). The NMP in turn has two submodules, Storage Array Type Plugins (SATPs) and Path Selection Plugins (PSPs).

SATP

All operations relating to the storage array are assigned to the SATP, and an SATP exists for every type of array that is supported by VMware. SATPs can be organized in three categories, Active/Active, Active/Passive, and direct attached storage (Local storage). Every SATP takes advantage of the different options available to a particular storage array and leverages these options to determine a path state or to activate an inactive path. An SATP is responsible for the following tasks:

▶ Monitors and reports state changes in each path

▶ Storage array failover tasks such as activate a passive path

PSP

The PSP as its name implies is responsible for path selection of I/O requests. Once an SATP has been associated with a storage array, the NMP then assigns the appropriate PSP that matches the capabilities of that particular storage array. By default the following PSPs are supported:

- **Fixed:** The default method of access used with Active/Active storage. It dictates that the ESX Server use the preferred path to the storage systems. In the event that this path is not available for any reason, it automatically reverts to the alternate paths.

- **Most Recently Used (MRU):** The default method of access used with Active/Passive storage devices. It dictates that the ESX server continue to use the most recent path to the storage systems until this path becomes unavailable, at which point it reverts to using the other path.

- **Round Robin:** this type of access is used mostly for load balancing purposes where the path selection rotates to maintain a balanced load.

Managing your paths in ESX Server is relatively easy and straightforward. Navigate to the Configuration tab. Choose Storage and then Properties (storage system of your choice). Click Manage Paths. Then select the device for which you want to configure pathing, as shown in Figure 4.13 you can select the path algorithm you want to use from the drop-down menu. You may also Enable or Disable a particular path by right-clicking it and selecting appropriately.

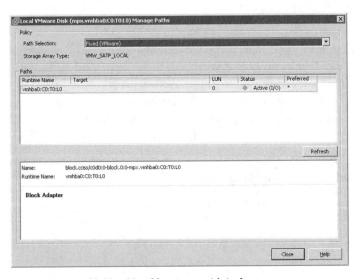

FIGURE 4.13 **Multipathing Management Interface.**

In some cases, you may want to disable a certain path to the storage devices for maintenance purposes or if you are reconfiguring your SAN. If you choose Enabled, this path actively participates in load balancing and failover. Disabled, of course, completely disables the path so that it cannot be used as an access route to the storage devices.

Note

You can use preferred paths only with the fixed policy.

Although multipathing in a SAN environment requires some configuration and has some configuration options to consider, with iSCSI, it is built in and utilizes the underlying IP network to achieve this. In a routed network, if a specific path to a device is not available, another route is provided to ensure the packet reaches the destination. To achieve multipathing with iSCSI, you really just have to do NIC teaming. By adding a second physical NIC to the vSwitch where iSCSI is configured, you achieve multipathing.

Cram Quiz

Answer these questions. The answers follow the last question. If you cannot answer these questions correctly, consider reading the section again.

1. What is the maximum VMFS datastore size?
   - ○ **A.** 2TB—512 bytes
   - ○ **B.** 4TB—1024 bytes
   - ○ **C.** 6TB—512 bytes
   - ○ **D.** 8TB—1024 bytes

2. Can you grow a VMFS volume?
   - ○ **A.** Yes, but only if there is adjacent space available.
   - ○ **B.** Yes, but only if there is space on the same volume.
   - ○ **C.** Yes, by allocating space from any volume.
   - ○ **D.** No.

3. How many submodules does the Pluggable Storage Architecture have?
   - ○ **A.** 2.
   - ○ **B.** 3.
   - ○ **C.** 4.
   - ○ **D.** 6.

Cram Quiz Answers

1. **A** is the correct response. A VMFS datastore can have a maximum of 2TB—512 bytes without extents.

2. **B** is the best response. You can grow a VMFS volume but only if there is adjacent space available.

3. **A** is correct. The Pluggable Storage Architecture has two submodules, the SATP and the PSP.

Thin Provisioning

▶ **Thin Provisioning in vSphere**

▶ **Types of Virtual Disks**

Cram**Saver**

If you can correctly answer these questions before going through this section, save time by skimming the Exam Alerts in this section and then completing the Cram Quiz at the end of the section.

1. At what level can you do thin provisioning in vSphere 4?

    ○ **A.** At the array level

    ○ **B.** At the vSphere level

    ○ **C.** At the SAN level

    ○ **D.** None of the above

2. How many types of virtual disks does vSphere offer?

    ○ **A.** 2

    ○ **B.** 3

    ○ **C.** 4

    ○ **D.** 5

Answers

1. **A** and **B** are correct. In vSphere 4, you can do thin provisioning at both the array and the vSphere levels.

2. **B** is correct. There are three types of virtual disks: Thin, Thick, and Eagerzeroedthick.

Thin Provisioning is the process of allocating space on an as-needed basis. Traditionally, IT professionals estimated how much a particular server would need in terms of storage and preallocated this storage up front. This methodology commits the space to a particular device. Therefore, the end result in most cases is always an overprovisioned storage capacity as the system does not use nearly the available space allocated to it. There are other cases where the system does use the space, but it does so over an extended period of time where this space could have been used elsewhere in the meantime and provisioned to this system when it needed it. This is not to say that we always overprovision storage. In deployments where storage is calculated and measured, such as an Exchange or SQL deployment, wasted storage space is much less.

The issue of overprovisioning storage is particularly obvious in virtualized environments where we have templates with preallocated space or where we assign virtual disks with large disk capacity. How many times has someone asked for a server and you gave them a 17GB C:\ and a 30GB D:\? I am willing to bet you that D:\ is 50% unused. This habit of just giving a system a lot of disk comes from the days where we had local disk that was cheap, and we had a lot of it in our servers that we could use. Once we make the move to virtualize and are now using a shared storage system of some sort, space becomes a bit more expensive and more complex to manage.

Thin provisioning significantly reduces the overprovisioning of storage. It allows you to assign a system as much space as it needs or you think it will need, but it does not commit this space until it actually gets used. This is great because it allows you to promise space that you may not necessarily have yet. You would obviously have to monitor your storage more closely now to make sure that as space becomes scarce you can provision more. Remember, the system does not know that the space it has is not available, as far as it is concerned that space is there and it expects to use it when it needs it.

Thin Provisioning in vSphere 4

Traditionally, thin provisioning was done at the array level, but with the introduction of vSphere 4, you can now do thin provisioning at the virtual disk level. This is particularly helpful for organizations where thin provisioning is not available with their particular storage array. The question then becomes, if I have thin provisioning at the array level, can I use vSphere thin provisioning and what are my advantages? The answer is yes, you can use thin provisioning on both the array level and from within vSphere. The downside to that is now you would have to monitor both your vSphere datastore storage and your array storage. And since you really get no benefit from this scenario, why do it at all?

How Does It Work?

In vSphere, you enable thin provisioning by selecting the virtual disk type you assign to a virtual machine. You have three choices: Thin, Thick (zeroedthick), and Eagerzeroedthick, all of which are explained in detail in the following sections. ESX 3.5 also had these types of disk except you had to use the command-line tool VMKFSTOOLS to control them.

Both vSphere and ESX 3.5 automatically default to zeroedthick for VMFS datastores and thin for NFS datastores. The difference, however, is that with vSphere we can control these settings using a GUI, and vSphere has seen a significant performance enhancement over ESX 3.5 in that when deploying from template it does not automatically get an Eagerzeroedthick disk. This was the behavior in ESX 3.5; with vSphere we can now control that, which allows for a more efficient use of thin provisioning.

Thin

A thin virtual disk shows up in the datastore as consuming exactly the amount of space that is currently being used by the guest operating system, and thereby the VMDK file is the same size as the virtual disk capacity. For example, a 100GB Thin VMDK file that has only 20GB of used space will show up in the datastore as a 20GB VMDK (see Figure 4.14). As space is needed, the VMkernel zeroes it out and makes it available for the guest. The VMkernel also automatically grows the VMDK file accordingly. This is how vSphere does thin provisioning.

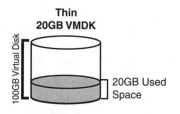

Virtual Disk Types

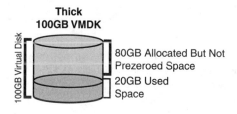

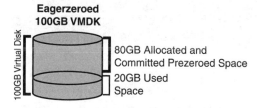

FIGURE 4.14 **Virtual disk types.**

> **Note**
>
> Using this method, you have to constantly monitor the datastore because the used space automatically changes as the thin VMDK files are grown. It is imperative that you do not run out of disk space to avoid performance and system instability.

> **Exam Alert**
>
> Thin virtual disks are the default method allocated when using a NAS datastore.

Thick (Zeroedthick)

Thick, or otherwise known as zeroedthick, virtual disk is meant for thin provisioning at the array level. When you look at a thick virtual disk from the datastore perspective, it is consuming the entire capacity of the disk. For example, if you have a 100GB virtual disk of which only 20GB is being used, the datastore shows a 100GB VMDK file. The difference is the VMkernel only zeroes out what is being used, so in this case it zeroes out 20GB. As the VM needs more space, the VMkernel zeroes out more space inside the VMDK, but the size of the VMDK never changes as far as the datastore is concerned. This method allows you to move the management of thinly provisioning space to the storage array.

> **Note**
>
> You could see how if you had thin virtual disks and were running thin provisioning on the array you would have to monitor both the array storage availability and the datastore storage availability.

> **Exam Alert**
>
> Thick (zeroedthick) is the default method of creating new virtual disks in vSphere 4.

Eagerzeroedthick

An Eagerzeroedthick virtual disk is a true thick disk where the entire space is committed or zeroed, thereby no thin provisioning could take place. For example, if you have a 100GB virtual disk with only 20GB used space, you see a 100GB VMDK file in the datastore, and that space is preallocated whether it is being used or not (refer to Figure 4.14).

In ESX 3.5, whenever you cloned a VM or deployed an image from template, it would automatically be assigned an Eagerzeroedthick VMDK. That is why cloning or deploying from template always took longer, while creating a new disk did not because it defaulted to zeroedthick.

In vSphere 4, you are now given the option during cloning or deploying from template to choose the type of disk to assign the VM, which significantly improves provisioning time. You can choose Thin, Thick (Eagerzeroed), or same as source (see Figure 4.15).

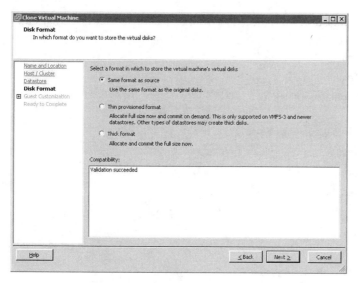

FIGURE 4.15 **Virtual Disk Wizard.**

Cram Quiz

Answer these questions. The answers follow the last question. If you cannot answer these questions correctly, consider reading the section again.

1. What is the default virtual disk type?

   ○ **A.** Thin

   ○ **B.** Thick

   ○ **C.** Eagerzeroedthick

2. What is the virtual disk type required for VMware Fault Tolerance and Clustering in general?

   ○ **A.** Thin

   ○ **B.** Thick

   ○ **C.** Eagerzeroedthick

3. Can you change virtual disk types?

   ○ **A.** Yes.

   ○ **B.** No.

   ○ **C.** Yes, but only from Thin to Thick.

   ○ **D.** Yes, but only from thin to Eagerzeroedthick.

Cram Quiz Answers

1. **B** is correct. By default, virtual disks are created with the Thick type.

2. **C** is correct. For any type of clustering, the Eagerzeroedthick virtual disk type must be selected, which would zero out all the space on that virtual disk and is a requirement for clustering to function properly.

3. **A** is the best response. You can change the virtual disk type using a number of different ways including Storage VMotion, cloning, or even inflating the disk and forcing the writes of zeroes across all free space.

CHAPTER 5

Administration with vCenter

vCenter is the one fundamental piece of the VMware Infrastructure suite that enhances the value for the enterprise. vCenter unlocks all the enterprise features that make the VMware Infrastructure so valuable; features such as vMotion, High Availability, and others are all managed by vCenter. It is the backbone of the infrastructure that can make ESX/ESXi hosts aware of each other and make them work together in resource pools, for example. This chapter covers installation of vCenter, design of a functional VC inventory, and administration with VC.

Planning and Installing vCenter

▶ **vCenter Blueprint**

▶ **vCenter Database Design**

▶ **vCenter Preinstallation**

Cram**Saver**

If you can correctly answer these questions before going through this section, save time by skimming the Exam Alerts in this section and then completing the Cram Quiz at the end of the section.

1. Choose the port that is responsible for vMotion incoming requests.

   ○ **A.** 902

   ○ **B.** 903

   ○ **C.** 3260

   ○ **D.** 8000

2. What is the maximum recommended number of ESX/ESXi hosts and VMs that you can have if you are using SQL Server Express as your vCenter database?

   ○ **A.** 5 hosts and 50 VMs

   ○ **B.** 5 hosts and 100 VMs

   ○ **C.** 10 hosts and 50 VMs

   ○ **D.** 10 hosts and 100 VMs

Answers

1. **D** is correct. Port 8000 needs to be open to accept incoming vMotion requests.

2. **A** is correct. If you are using the Microsoft SQL Express Edition, the maximum number of recommended ESX/ESXi hosts is 5, and the total number of VMs is 50.

vCenter is a Windows-based application that allows you to control both ESX/ESXi hosts and their virtual machines. It is also the application that allows you to use enterprise technologies such as vMotion, High Availability, and Distributed Resource Scheduler. vCenter also introduces the following new technologies to complement and enhance its other features:

▶ **VMware Update Manager:** An automated tool used for patch management of ESX/ESXi hosts and virtual machines.

▶ **VMware vCenter Converter:** A conversion tool that allows you to perform physical to virtual machine migration in addition to virtual machine to virtual machine migrations into the vSphere infrastructure.

▶ **VMware vCenter Guided Consolidation:** Toned-down version of VMware Capacity Planner, a tool used to analyze a physical server infrastructure and recommend physical machines that are good candidates for conversion to virtual machines.

vCenter is a framework that requires several elements to be functioning to make the entire suite work properly. Depending on the deployment scenario of your vCenter Server and its different elements, sometimes ports need to be open to allow the flow of communications to take its proper course. Table 5.1 shows ports and their use in the VC deployment.

TABLE 5.1 **VC Port Matrix**

Flow (From -> To)	Port
vCenter to License Server	27000 and 27010
vCenter to Oracle DB	1521
vCenter to SQL DB	1433
Web Access and SDK Clients to VC	80 and 443
vCenter to ESX Hosts	902
vSphere Client to vCenter and ESX Hosts	443
ESX/ESXi to ESX/ESXi	902
VM Remote Console Traffic	903
NFS Transactions	2049
iSCSI Transactions	3260
vMotion Incoming Requests	8000

vCenter Blueprint

Understanding the architecture behind vCenter greatly impacts the level of understanding you possess of the technology. vCenter is not complicated software; on the contrary, it is cleanly built and well defined. Figure 5.1 illustrates how the vCenter blueprint is laid out.

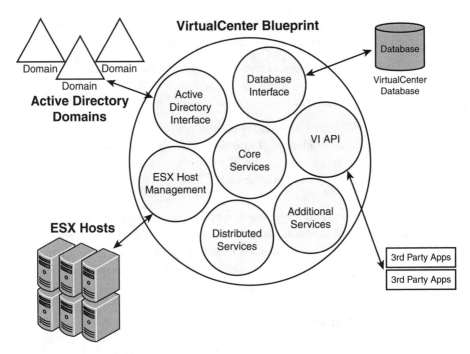

FIGURE 5.1 **vCenter blueprint.**

The following different architectural pieces make up the blueprint:

▸ **Core Services:** The main module of vCenter, the basic heart of the application that gives way to VM provisioning, Task Scheduler, events logging, and so on.

▸ **Distributed Services:** The module that gives way to features like vMotion, HA, and DRS. This is the place where the features that require a separate license stem from.

▸ **Additional Services:** The place where independent modules stem from, technologies such as VMware Converter Enterprise and Update Manager.

▸ **Database Interface:** The link that is established with a database server that provides VC with a centralized repository for all its data.

▸ **ESX/ESXi Host Management:** The interface that allows VC to plug into ESX/ESXi hosts and manage them.

▸ **Active Directory Interface:** The link that is established with an Active Directory domain to extend user and group support to vCenter.

▶ **vSphere Application Programming Interface (API) and vSphere Software Development Kit (SDK) :** The programming code that provide a framework for developers of custom applications.

vCenter communicates and issues commands to ESX Servers it manages using the vpxa daemon. However, if you are using the vSphere Client to connect directly to the ESX/ESXi host and issue commands to manage it that way, the vmware-hostd daemon, also known simply as hostd, is used.

vCenter Preinstallation

As with any application with a critical role in the enterprise, proper planning, sizing, and preinstallation steps and tasks exist that you should be familiar with to successfully complete vCenter installation. Before you can size hardware and software, you need to know the minimum requirements, and that is what we cover in the following sections.

vCenter Hardware Requirements

The minimum hardware requirements for a vCenter Server vary depending on the roles the server will play. The more roles you add to a server, the more hardware you will most likely throw at it for it to perform its functions in an optimal manner. Therefore, if you decide that the server hardware will run the vCenter Server and also the vCenter database, the hardware requirements are one thing, and if the server hardware will support only the vCenter Server, the hardware is in a different configuration. The following minimum requirements are for a server that runs vCenter Server only:

▶ **CPU:** Two 64-bit processors or one 64-bit processor with dual cores. Minimum clock speed of 2GHz or more.

▶ **Memory:** 3GB or more.

▶ **Storage:** A minimum of 1GB is needed. However, 2GB is recommended, and if the vCenter database is on the same server, you will need to allocate space accordingly.

▶ **Networking:** A network interface card (NIC) that supports 10/100MB, with 1GB being the best practice recommendation.

vCenter Software Requirements

Now that we have covered the minimum hardware requirements, let's shift our attention to the software requirements needed to host vCenter Server 4.1.

Keep in mind that vCenter 4.1 is a 64-bit application and therefore is supported on 64-bit operating systems. The following operating systems are supported, however:

- Windows XP Professional 64-bit
- Windows Server 2003 64-bit
- Windows Server 2008 64-bit (Standard, Enterprise, Datacenter)
- Windows Server 2008 R2

> **Caution**
>
> VMware vCenter 4.1 is a 64-bit only application. As you prepare for the VCP exam, keep in mind that vCenter 4.0 supported a 32-bit operating system. Be careful not to fall for a question on the exam.

vCenter Database Design

The server is only as good as the data repository that supports it, so no matter how great vCenter is, it is only as good as the database that supports it. For this reason, designing a good database backend is imperative for performance, scalability, and stability.

When you are planning for a vCenter database, best practice calls for hosting the database on a separate dedicated server. In other words, it is not recommended to have the database and vCenter on the same server. That being said, the following databases are supported by vCenter Server:

- Microsoft SQL Server 2005 Express
- Microsoft SQL Server 2005
- Microsoft SQL Server 2008
- IBM DB2 9.5
- Oracle 10g and 11g

> **Caution**
>
> When you use Microsoft SQL Server 2005 Express, the database size limit is 4GB. If the VC database reaches this size limit, performance degradation occurs. Best practice calls for using this type of database only for test or demonstration purposes, but not for production.

ExamAlert

VMware supports the Microsoft SQL Express database for up to five ESX/ESXi hosts with a maximum of 50 virtual machines on each.

Prior to installing vCenter Server, you need to complete the following preparatory steps if you choose to use Microsoft SQL Server as your database software of choice:

► You need to create a database on the database server and a database user with either the sysadmin server role or the db_owner fixed database role assigned to it.

► You should create a system DSN, otherwise known as an ODBC connection, on the vCenter Server that points to the database server. This process ensures that when the installation wizard needs to connect to the database, it knows how to communicate with it.

► You need to configure your DSN connection to use SQL server authentication.

Note

The only time you should use Windows authentication is when your vCenter Server and your SQL Server are on the same server host.

ExamAlert

SQL authentication is supported on both local and remote instances of a SQL database server.

Database Sizing

After installing vCenter Server, you are provided with a small bunch of useful tools; among them is a calculator that allows you to design your database size based on a number of different parameters. For instance, you tell the calculator how many ESX/ESXi hosts you have and how many virtual machines you have, and it estimates the database size you need. Figure 5.2 illustrates what this calculator looks like.

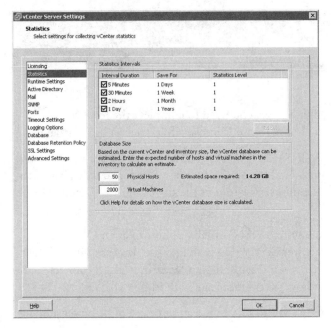

FIGURE 5.2 **vCenter database sizing.**

To access this sizing tool, follow these steps:

1. Log in to vCenter using the vSphere client.

2. Select Administration.

3. Choose vCenter Server Settings.

4. Choose Statistics from the left pane.

On the right pane of the Statistics window, you enter your values, and the calculator crunches your numbers for you.

vCenter Installation

vCenter Server can be installed on a physical server or on a VM. The advantages of hosting it on a VM are endless, including its capability to participate in HA and DRS, making the server even more reliable and stable. Some administrators might hesitate to put vCenter on a VM and allow it to participate in HA or DRS because they fear that they don't want to put the server that published these technologies in a position where it is also taking advantage of its technologies due to fear of complications. VMware does recommend and support this type of configuration for vCenter. With the many deployments that we have made, we think this solution is a good one.

When you are ready to perform the installation, you should become familiar with the components of vCenter and the order in which they should be installed so as to avoid any complications. For that matter, this order is recommended:

1. **Database Server:** This step includes creating the database on the database server, assigning it the proper permissions, and creating the associated ODBC connection on the vCenter Server.

2. **License Server:** The use of a license server is imperative for backward compatibility. If you are in a mixed environment with ESX/ESXi hosts pre-version 4, the presence of a license server is needed to enable enterprise-level features and provide centralized license management.

3. **vCenter Server:** This is the actual application server software to be installed.

4. **vSphere Client:** This is the application that you use to log in to vCenter from a GUI and manipulate it.

During the installation of vCenter, you have the opportunity to modify the communications ports that vCenter will use. You have a chance to modify the following. In most cases, the default values work just fine.

▶ **HTTP Web Service:** Configured by default on port 80 and used for client connections to VC via a web browser.

▶ **HTTPS Web Service:** Configured by default on port 443 and used for client connections to VC via a secure web browser.

▶ **Heartbeat (UDP):** Configured by default on UDP 902 and used by VC to maintain ESX/ESXi host connectivity. In other words, as long as VC is receiving packets from the ESX/ESXi hosts on these ports, the ESX/ESXi host is online and communicating, and if VC stops receiving a heartbeat, it assumes the ESX/ESXi host is down.

▶ **Web Server Port:** Configured by default on port 8086 and used by the Apache web server.

vCenter Services

If you installed vCenter on a server that is part of an Active Directory domain, you can add users and groups from that domain and any trusted domain directly into VC. Furthermore, once part of a domain, the Domain Admins group is automatically added and granted full control over hosts and VMs. So, if this is not something you want, you should plan accordingly. After the installation of VC, a number of Windows services are added, as follows:

▶ **VMware Capacity Planner Service:** This service controls the Guided Consolidation feature of VC.

▶ **VMware Converter Enterprise Service:** This service controls VMware Converter, which allows you to migrate physical machines to virtual machines or virtual machines to virtual machines.

▶ **VMware vCenter Management Web Services:** This service controls your ability to access vCenter management services from a web interface.

▶ **VMware License Server:** This service controls whether the license server is online or offline. This will only be installed if the license server is installed.

▶ **VMware Mount Service for vCenter Service:** This service is used during the creation or cloning of VMs.

▶ **VMware Update Manager Service:** As the name implies, this service controls the Update Manager.

▶ **VMware vCenter Server Service:** The most important service and heart of VC, this service is what makes vCenter Server run. If this service is not running, VC will not run, and as a result, all its service offerings will not run either.

▶ **VMware vCenter Orchestrator Configuration:** Orchestrator is a workflow engine that allows the administrator to automate tasks.

▶ **VMware VCMSDS:** This is the service that allows vCenter to leverage LDAP directory services.

▶ **VMware Tools Service:** The VMware Tools service will only appear if vCenter is installed on a virtual machine, and only after the tools have been installed.

> **Note**
>
> Some of the services listed assume that the license server and vCenter Server are installed on the same server per best practices. Some of these services may not be present in your deployment based on the method by which you installed the different components in your environment.

vCenter Licensing

As with any enterprise class technology, vCenter requires licensing so that you can enable or disable certain features based on the types of licenses you have purchased. Licensing is a great source of income for VMware, but it can be costly for you if you are not sure what types of licenses you need for your environment and how many licenses you need.

vCenter also comes in different editions, as follows:

- ▶ **vCenter for Essentials Kits:** This edition is well suited when purchasing any of the vSphere Essentials kits.

- ▶ **vCenter Foundation:** This edition allows you to manage up to three ESX/ESXi hosts.

- ▶ **vCenter Standard:** This is the enterprise-level edition of vCenter and gives you access to all the features and functionality.

While vCenter has three editions to choose from, vSphere has a wide variety of licensing choices. The VCP exam is sure to have a few questions on the differences in licensing. Table 5.2 consolidates the different licensing versions and features.

TABLE 5.2 vSphere Licensing Editions

Licensing	ESXi Stand alone	Essential	Essential Plus	Standard	Advanced	Enterprise	Enterprise Plus
vCenter	X	Essentials	Essentials	Foundation/ Standard	Foundation/ Standard	Foundation/ Standard	Foundation/ Standard
Cores	6	6	6	6	12	6	12
Physical RAM	256GB	256GB	256GB	256GB	256GB	256GB	Unlimited
CPU Support		3 hosts with 2 CPUs each	3 hosts with 2 CPUs each	Per Processor	Per Processor	Per Processor	Per Processor
vSMP	4	4	4	4	4	4	8
Features							
Update Manager		✓	✓	✓	✓	✓	✓
vStorage APIs – Data Protection		✓	✓	✓	✓	✓	✓
Thin Provisioning		✓	✓	✓	✓	✓	✓
Data Recovery		X	✓	✓	✓	✓	✓
HA		X	✓	✓	✓	✓	✓
vMotion		X	✓	✓	✓	✓	✓
Hot Add		X	X	X	✓	✓	✓
vShield Zones		X	X	X	✓	✓	✓
Fault Tolerance		X	X	X	✓	✓	✓
DRS/DPM		X	X	X	X	✓	✓
vStorage APIs – Multipathing		X	X	X	X	✓	✓
vStorage APIs – Array		X	X	X	X	✓	✓
Storage vMotion		X	X	X		✓	✓
Storage I/O Control		X	X	X	X	X	✓
Network I/O Control		X	X	X	X	X	✓
Host Profiles		X	X	X	X	X	✓
vDS		X	X	X	X	X	✓

Upgrading from vCenter Foundation to vCenter Standard is easy; you simply need to acquire a new license and switch the editions. You do not need to reinstall vCenter Server.

How the License Key Functions

The license key is a 25 character alphanumeric key, constructed to enable or disable features of ESX/ESXi Server and vCenter. Currently, the license key is configured in two ways:

▶ Per processor

▶ Per instance

It is important for you to know which parts of the vSphere suite are configured on a per processor basis and which ones are configured on a per instance basis.

Per Processor

vSphere 4 currently licenses its entire feature set per processor with the exception of vCenter, which is licensed on a per instance basis. When you purchase licenses from VMware, they are sold in increments of one, and these licenses, if deployed on the vCenter server (server-based licensing), can be used by any host that is being managed by vCenter server. You can also deploy these license keys directly to the ESX/ESXi hosts, and in the event that you should add these hosts to vCenter at a later time, they will then automatically be managed by vCenter.

To make things simple, when you purchase a server, calculate the number of physical processors in it. Figure how many sockets you have in a server that can host a processor. If you purchased a dual socket processor server, you need two licenses. If you purchased a quad socket processor, you need four licenses.

ExamAlert

Many processors today have cores, so you might see dual socket processors dual cores, dual socket processors quad cores, quad sockets processors quad cores, or any other combination. You should always count only how many sockets you have in your server.

You cannot partially license a host. A quad socket processor server requires four licenses; you cannot use two license keys and just license half of it. This also applies to the features.

Per Instance

Per instance licensing is simple and straightforward and falls within the realm of how licensing works traditionally. You buy the software, and it comes with a license. You can install the software on a server, regardless of the number of processors.

vCenter is licensed on a per instance licensing model.

Per VM

As cloud computing continues to accelerate and become more widely used, the unit of measurement shifts to a per VM basis. A per VM basis licensing model is more flexible and allows you to better control your licensing needs and enforce detailed chargebacks. VMware is moving all products to a per VM licensing model; however, as of this writing only select products can be purchased on a per VM basis per the following guidelines:

> After December 15, 2010, VMware vCenter AppSpeed, CapacityIQ, Chargeback and Site Recovery Manager (SRM) can only be purchased on a Per VM basis.

The vSphere suite of products will continue to use the per processor and per instance model for now. However, continue to check with VMware for more updated information. We don't think the switch will happen to per VM on the vSphere suite until the next major version is released.

Cram Quiz

Answer these questions. The answers follow the last question. If you cannot answer these questions correctly, consider reading the section again.

1. Which of the following is not a vSphere licensing mode?

   ○ **A.** Per VM

   ○ **B.** Per Instance

   ○ **C.** Per Processor

   ○ **D.** Per Core

2. Which of the following is not part of vCenter Architecture?

   ○ **A.** Active Directory Interface

   ○ **B.** Core Services

   ○ **C.** Additional Services

   ○ **D.** Database Interface

   ○ **E.** VMkernel Interface

   ○ **F.** ESX/ESXi Host Management

3. Which two technologies are considered vCenter plug-ins?

   ○ **A.** Guided Consolidation

   ○ **B.** VMware Consolidated Backup

   ○ **C.** Update Manager

   ○ **D.** VMware vCenter Converter

Cram Quiz Answer

1. **D** is correct. vSphere does not have a per core licensing model. The three models supported today are per instance, per processor, and per VM.

2. **E** is correct. VMkernel Interface is not part of the architectural blueprint that makes up vCenter. All the other choices are valid components.

3. **C** and **D** are correct. The two technologies that are vCenter plug-ins are VMware Update Manager and VMware Converter.

Designing a Functional vCenter Inventory

▶ **Datacenters**

▶ **Folders**

▶ **Clusters**

Cram**Saver**

If you can correctly answer these questions before going through this section, save time by skimming the Exam Alerts in this section and then completing the Cram Quiz at the end of the section.

1. Which option is not a vCenter inventory hierarchy?

○ **A.** Hosts and Clusters

○ **B.** Datacenters

○ **C.** Networking

○ **D.** Datastores

2. Which view do you need to be in to organize VMs in folders?

○ **A.** Hosts and Clusters

○ **B.** VMs and templates

○ **C.** Networking

○ **D.** Datastores

○ **E.** All of the above

Answers

1. **B** is correct. Datacenters is not a correct vCenter hierarchy; the other hierarchy that is missing from the list is VMs and Templates.

2. Answer **B** is correct. You can only organize VMs in folders if you are under the VMs and Templates view. If you are under the Hosts and Clusters, you can organize hosts but not VMs. You cannot organize VMs if you are on the Datastores and Networking views.

Depending on the size of your environment and how much you expect it to grow in the future, designing a functional vCenter inventory is critical because doing so makes it much easier for you to apply security and enact role-based access to the different hosts and VMs within this inventory. An organizational hierarchy is important also because it gives you quick access to the systems you are trying to reach, whereas putting all the hosts and all the VMs in one folder makes finding what you are looking for more time consuming and frustrating if you are dealing with several dozen virtual machines. In the following sections, we discuss the different ways you can group and organize resources to gain the maximum flexibility and the easiest management and controlled access possible.

Folders

At the top of the inventory's hierarchy sits the *root folder*, which is, as the name implies, the topmost structure. The *alpha* folder presents itself sometimes as Hosts and Clusters and other times as VMs and Templates, depending on the Inventory view you are in. You can use folders and subfolders to organize VMs and hosts in a way that is functional to your enterprise. A word of caution here: Make sure you do not overuse or overorganize your hierarchy because that, too, can make finding objects difficult for you and for others browsing the inventory.

If you want to break the VMs into folders, you can divide them based on the overall function they serve. Some people might want to break them down based on the function of the server. So, for example, file servers go in one folder, whereas database servers go in another and so on. We have found that dividing the VMs based on what they do in the enterprise may be easier. For example, if you have a Citrix or Terminal Server implementation in your environment and you group all your Citrix or Terminal Server-related VMs in one folder, users can more easily find the server they are looking for. You would use the same approach for Microsoft Exchange, where you group all servers in the same folder.

Datacenters

Before you can add any hosts or VMs to the inventory, you need to create at least one *datacenter*. A datacenter is the logical repository of hosts and VMs. You can create a folder under the root and then add a datacenter, but you cannot create a folder and add hosts and VMs before first adding a datacenter. The best approach to a datacenter setup is to follow what you currently have in your organization. Therefore, if you have two datacenters, create two datacenter objects and group them in folders accordingly and based on geographical location.

Virtual machines in one datacenter cannot be vMotioned to another datacenter. Objects are manipulated in their parent datacenter. However, you can clone a virtual machine from one datacenter to another.

Clusters

Clusters are created by grouping multiple ESX/ESXi hosts. By doing that, you allow these ESX/ESXi hosts to pool resources and distribute load among them in the most efficient way. You also allow these hosts to calculate and take into consideration one or more host failures and the ability to restart VMs on different hosts. When you create a cluster, you can enable it to be a High Availability cluster only, a Distributed Resource Scheduler cluster only, or both at the same time, which is what best practice calls for. Keep in mind that when you are creating a cluster, the maximum number of hosts that it can support is 32. Figure 5.3 illustrates a cluster that is both VMware HA and VMware DRS enabled.

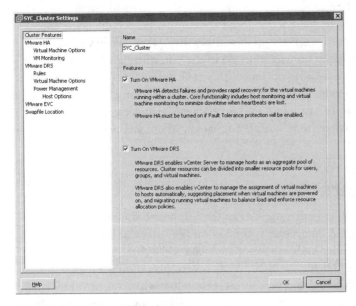

FIGURE 5.3   **HA and DRS cluster.**

Cram Quiz

Answer these questions. The answers follow the last question. If you cannot answer these questions correctly, consider reading the section again.

1. True or false: VMs in one datacenter can easily be vMotioned to another datacenter.

   ○ **A.** True

   ○ **B.** False

2. True or false: Clusters are a way of allocating more hardware resources to VMs.

   ○ **A.** True

   ○ **B.** False

Cram Quiz Answers

1. **B**, False, is correct. VMs in one datacenter cannot be vMotioned to another datacenter. This is by design.

2. **A**, True, is correct. Clusters are a way of combining ESX/ESXi hosts and leveraging their physical resources to yield them back to VMs.

Administration with vCenter

▶ **vSphere Client Tabs**

▶ **Lockdown Mode**

▶ **vCenter Maximums**

▶ **VMware vCenter High Availability**

▶ **VMware vCenter Clustering**

▶ **VMware vCenter Heartbeat**

Cram**Saver**

If you can correctly answer these questions before going through this section, save time by skimming the Exam Alerts in this section and then completing the Cram Quiz at the end of the section.

1. What is the maximum number of registered virtual machines that can be managed by a single vCenter Server?

   ○ **A.** 1000

   ○ **B.** 2000

   ○ **C.** 10000

   ○ **D.** 15000

2. Which file is responsible for holding the system logs?

   ○ **A.** vpxd-logs

   ○ **B.** vpxd-events

   ○ **C.** vpxd-alerts

   ○ **D.** vpxd-index

3. True or false: vCenter can be protected by VMware Fault Tolerance.

   ○ **A.** True

   ○ **B.** False

Answers

1. **D** is correct. The VMware Configuration Maximum states that the maximum number of registered virtual machines to be managed by a single VC Server is 15000.

2. **D** is correct. The file responsible for holding the system logs is vpxd-index.

3. **B** is correct. VMware FT cannot be used to provide fault tolerance for vCenter as the minimum vCenter hardware requirements conflict with what FT can support.

When you access vCenter via the vSphere Client, you are presented with numerous tabs from which you can administer, manage, and support your infrastructure. The following sections focus on these tabs and tools in vCenter and how you can use them in an efficient way.

Linked Mode

Linked mode vCenter allows you to group multiple vCenter servers and manage all their resources by logging in to any of the vCenter servers participating in linked mode. This process is ideal in enterprise deployments especially when the configuration maximums of a single vCenter have been reached and the need for scalability remains. Using linked mode vCenter you can scale the number of registered VMs, running VMs, managed hosts, and more.

vSphere Client Tabs

The following subsections cover the following vSphere Client tabs:

- Inventory
- Scheduled Tasks
- Events
- Administration
- Maps
- Consolidation

Inventory Tab

The Inventory tab enables you to switch the view of the hierarchy between

- Hosts and Clusters
- VMs and Templates
- Networking
- Datastores

As their names imply, a view of Hosts and Clusters primarily focuses on displaying the hosts and the different cluster configurations. You can, however, still drill down on every host or in every cluster and find the VM or template you are looking for. On the other hand, a view of VMs and Templates displays all the VMs and templates available. Similarly, a view of Networking or Datastores primarily displays the different network configurations and the available datastores. Figure 5.4 shows where you can change the views.

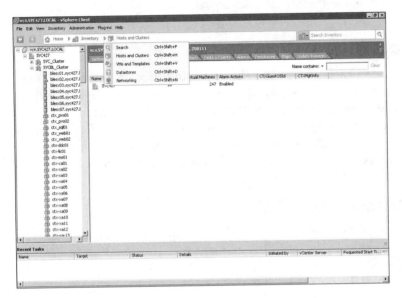

FIGURE 5.4 **Inventory views.**

Scheduled Tasks Tab

Scheduled tasks are helpful in automating certain tasks to be performed at a given time. Without scheduled tasks, get ready to be up bright and early at 3:00 a.m. to power down a host or run an update or perform any other task that would be required after hours or when load is at a minimum. Scheduled tasks allow you to perform these tasks in an automated manner. Figure 5.5 shows the Scheduled Tasks tab and some available scheduled tasks.

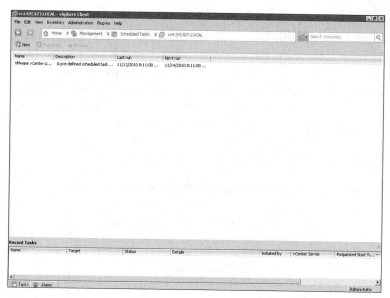

FIGURE 5.5   **Scheduled tasks.**

Events Tab

The Events tab is an imperative first step in any troubleshooting undertaking that you will engage in. This panel displays the different events that have occurred. This may include errors that have been registered, alarms that have been triggered, or tasks that have been completed. From this panel, you also have access to search with query keywords and display relevant results. If looking at all the events in one panel is too cumbersome and you want a more focused list, you can select any object in the inventory and browse its Tasks & Events window, which displays information on this object only.

Administration Tab

The Administration tab offers several tabs that allow you to manipulate different functions in the infrastructure. These tabs are

- ▶ **Roles:** This tab is discussed in greater detail with security and access control topics in Chapter 7, "vSphere Security and Web Access." On this tab, you can define or view a defined role based on access to vCenter.

- ▶ **Sessions:** This tab shows you who is currently logged in to vCenter and how long that user has been logged in. It also enables you to send messages to these sessions in case you need to make an announcement.

- ▶ **Licenses:** This tab allows you to view licenses within the environment.

▶ **System Logs:** Like events, system logs are imperative when you are troubleshooting, and this tab gives you a list of system-related logs that you can browse through. You may also search system logs by keyword. Because there may be more than one version of the vpxd-index file, which is the file that holds the system logs, make sure you are using the latest one. The most recent one is usually incremented by a number, and the higher the number, the more recent the file. So, for example, you may have vpxd-2.log and vpxd-3.log, the latter being the more recent one. Figure 5.6 illustrates this tab in greater detail.

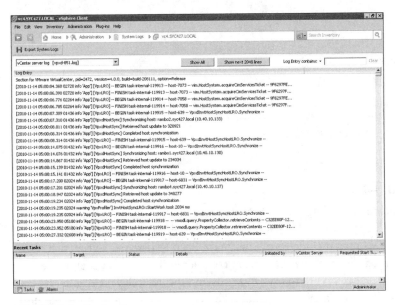

FIGURE 5.6 **System logs.**

Maps Tab

Maps are a fantastic way of graphically understanding the topology and what is connected to what. They can be used in many different ways. Say you want to find out which hosts are connected to which datastores or which VMs are on which hosts. Maps can be useful in making sure the vMotion requirements are met by inspecting the ESX/ESXi hosts in question and making sure they see the correct networking and storage. The more seasoned you become with ESX, the more you will appreciate the power that maps offer you, especially in larger, more complicated environments. Figure 5.7 shows the Maps tab; it shows, on the right, the different criteria that can be selected that would update maps to reflect your selection.

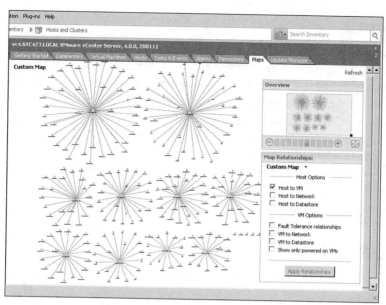

FIGURE 5.7   **Maps tab.**

Consolidation Tab

Guided Consolidation is covered in greater detail in Chapter 6, "Virtual
Machine Operations." On this tab, you plan and execute a Guided
Consolidation. The tools under this tab allow you to discover, analyze, and
consolidate physical servers into virtual machines on ESX/ESXi hosts.

Lockdown Mode

Lockdown mode allows you to control direct vSphere Client access to an ESXi
host. In other words, you shouldn't directly log in to hosts that are being managed by vCenter because this may cause issues. To prevent administrators from
logging in to a host directly, you can modify the Security Profile by selecting
an ESXi host, choosing Configuration > Security Profile > Edit, and checking
the Enable Lockdown Mode box. This prevents direct root access to this ESXi
host, but a configured user with admin rights can still access.

> **ExamAlert**
>
> As of this writing, the Lockdown mode is available and shows up only on ESXi
> hosts.

Plug-ins

Plug-ins are applications that can be enabled from within vCenter. Plug-ins extend the capabilities of vCenter by giving it more features. Plug-ins are written to connect through the framework that vCenter provides. There are several plug-ins for vCenter; most notable are VMware Update Manager, Guided Consolidation, and VMware Converter. This is not to say that VMware could not release a plug-in tomorrow that would take advantage of the VC framework; that's the beauty and power of VC. Plug-ins are also installed and upgraded separately, which makes installing them independent from the VC installation. When a plug-in is enabled, the vSphere Client GUI is modified, and new features appear accordingly to help manage the new plug-ins.

Client Settings

Because the vSphere Client is the arm by which you manipulate vCenter, knowing how to tweak some of its settings is an important step. You can modify the Timeout settings of the vSphere Client so it is more tolerant to slow WAN connections or even limit the number of vSphere Clients that can concurrently connect to VC. You can access these settings from the File menu: Select Edit and then Client Settings.

vCenter Maximums

When you are planning, designing, and building any environment, it is critical that you know your limits so that you can plan accordingly and be able to scale properly. Table 5.3 provides some configuration maximums for vCenter.

TABLE 5.3   **vCenter Limits**

Description	Limit
Powered on VMs per vCenter	10000
Registered VMs per vCenter	15000
ESX/ESXi hosts per vCenter	1000
ESX/ESXi hosts per Datacenter	400
Linked mode vCenter Servers	10
ESX/ESXi in Linked mode vCenter Servers	3000
Powered on VMs in Linked mode vCenter Servers	30000
Registered VMs in Linked mode vCenter Servers	50000
Concurrent vSphere Client Connections	100
ESX/ESXi per cluster (HA and DRS)	32

Cram Quiz

Answer these questions. The answers follow the last question. If you cannot answer these questions correctly, consider reading the section again.

1. How many ESX/ESXi hosts can you have per cluster?

   ○ **A.** 16

   ○ **B.** 24

   ○ **C.** 32

   ○ **D.** 36

2. What is the maximum number of powered on virtual machines that can be managed by a single vCenter Server?

   ○ **A.** 1000

   ○ **B.** 2000

   ○ **C.** 10000

   ○ **D.** 15000

3. What is the maximum number of ESX/ESXi hosts that can be managed by linked vCenter Servers?

   ○ **A.** 1000

   ○ **B.** 2000

   ○ **C.** 3000

   ○ **D.** 4000

Cram Quiz Answers

1. **C** is correct. The maximum number of ESX/ESXi hosts that is supported per cluster is 32.

2. **C** is correct. The VMware Configuration Maximum states that the maximum number of powered on virtual machines to be managed by a single VC Server is 10000.

3. **C** is correct. The VMware Configuration Maximum states that the maximum number of ESX/ESXi hosts to be managed by linked vCenter Servers is 3000.

vCenter Server Backup and High Availability

The first thing you should know before we get into the discussion of how to back up and recover vCenter is that if the vCenter Server goes offline, your environment will not stop working. As a matter of fact, everything will continue to function normally. You will be limited only to what new tasks you can perform, and when the vCenter Server is back online, it will resume its responsibilities.

Now let's talk about what you can do to back up vCenter Server or to provide some redundancy and High Availability. First, you can put your vCenter Server on a VM and make it part of a cluster. That way, it is taking advantage of both HA and DRS. This takes care of ensuring the server stays up but does not protect you in case of operating system corruption or crashes. To protect against that, you can always have a copy of the vCenter virtual machine stored somewhere safe that you can recover from in case of emergency.

vCenter Heartbeat

The vCenter Heartbeat allows you to have two vCenter servers that are a replica of one another. The primary vCenter server is constantly sending an "I'm alive" message to the secondary. In the event that the primary should fail, the secondary assumes its identity, network configuration, and duties. For more information on how to install and configure vCenter Heartbeat, check out the vCenter Heartbeat Quick Start Guide at http://www.vmware.com/pdf/heartbeat_63_quick_start.pdf.

Clustering vCenter

If the idea of having vCenter on a VM does not appeal to you, you can have a cold standby server that is the exact replica of the vCenter Server in production. In the event that the production server goes offline, you can recover in a relatively short period. You can also mix and match. Therefore, instead of having a physical server in standby, doing nothing and collecting dust, you can P2V (Physical to Virtual conversion) your vCenter to a VM and turn it off. Then you can use it in the event your physical server should go offline. Being able to do this would not hold you up until you recover your physical server.

Another approach would also be to use Microsoft clustering (MSCS) of the vCenter Server, either between two physical servers or two virtual servers, or a mix of physical and virtual. Clustering can also be extended to the database because both Microsoft SQL and Oracle offer clustering.

ExamAlert

VMware Fault Tolerance cannot be used with vCenter Server. FT can only protect VMs with one vCPU, whereas the minimum hardware requirement for a vCenter server is two CPUs.

The options and configurations you can use to protect against a vCenter failure are numerous. The choice you make depends on what you see as the most efficient solution for your environment. Remember to keep it simple. As long as you have a good backup of your database and a good strategy on how to handle outages in VC, you should be good to go.

Cram Quiz

Answer these questions. The answers follow the last question. If you cannot answer
these questions correctly, consider reading the section again.

1. True or false: vCenter as a VM can participate in High Availability and Distributed
   Resource Scheduler.

   ○ **A.** True

   ○ **B.** False

2. True or false: Microsoft clustering cannot be used to provide protection for
   vCenter Server.

   ○ **A.** True

   ○ **B.** False

Cram Quiz Answers

1. **A**, True, is correct. If you virtualize vCenter, it can participate in VMware HA and
   DRS.

2. **B**, False, is correct. Microsoft clustering can be used to protect a vCenter server,
   whether it is physical, virtual, or a mixture of both.

CHAPTER 6

Virtual Machine Operations

This chapter covers the following VCP exam topics:

▶ Cold Migrations

▶ Snapshots

▶ Guided Consolidation

▶ Virtual Appliances

▶ vApps

▶ Templates

▶ Open Virtualization Format (OVF)

▶ VMware Tools

▶ Virtual Disk

▶ VMware Converter

▶ Capacity Planner

▶ Virtual Hardware

▶ Virtual Machine Files

▶ Virtual Machine Maximums

(For more information on the VCP exam topics, see "About the VCP Exam" in the introduction.)

In this chapter, we start tackling some of the daily operations that an administrator faces when working with a VMware vSphere environment, such as the creation and administration of virtual machines—one of the fundamental reasons we use a virtual infrastructure in the first place. As far as the VCP exam goes, you can rest assured that the topic of virtual machine operations dominates because it is one of the most basic functions an administrator is expected to perform and understand thoroughly.

Virtual Machine Defined

▶ **Virtual Hardware**

▶ **Virtual Machine Files**

▶ **Virtual Machine Maximums**

Cram**Saver**

If you can correctly answer these questions before going through this section, save time by skimming the Exam Alerts in this section and then completing the Cram Quiz at the end of the section.

1. How many available PCI devices can you add to a virtual machine?

    ○ **A.** 4

    ○ **B.** 5

    ○ **C.** 6

    ○ **D.** 8

2. A VM is made up of a collection of files. What is the purpose of the .vmsd file?

    ○ **A.** It is the VM's swap file.

    ○ **B.** It contains the BIOS of the VM.

    ○ **C.** It contains information about any available snapshots for this VM.

    ○ **D.** It contains information about the available log files in the VM.

Answers

1. **B** is correct. You can add a maximum of six PCI devices to a virtual machine; however, because one PCI device is always allocated for the video adapter, you have only five available PCI devices you can add.

2. **C** is correct. The file with the .vmsd extension contains information about the VM's available snapshots. The VM's swap file is contained in a file with a .vswp extension whereas the bios is in a .nvram and the log has a .log extension. Therefore: Answers A, B and D are incorrect.

A virtual machine (VM) serves the same purpose and behaves in the same manner as a physical machine except, instead of being a collection of hardware devices, it is a collection of software or virtual devices. A virtual machine is made up of the same components found in a physical machine, and similar to the way a physical machine's components establish a baseline upon which you can install a guest operating system, a virtual machine's virtual components establish a similar framework upon which you can install a guest operating system. In this sense, a virtual machine is made up of a bunch of files that carry its configuration and specify its name, how many CPUs are assigned to it, how much memory is allocated, and so on.

> **Tip**
>
> When you are naming a virtual machine, best practices call for not using special characters in its display name because the Service Console might have issues with that.

Virtual Hardware

The power of a virtual machine is that it provides a uniform platform upon which an operating system can be installed. It does this by allocating a standardized motherboard for all supported guest operating systems to use. This motherboard is based on an Intel 440BX with an NS338 SIO chipset. This standardization is what makes the VM so portable and so compatible with a wide collection of supported operating systems.

When you are installing an operating system, it does not matter whether you are installing it on *physical* or *virtual hardware*. As a matter of fact, the guest OS does not even know the difference between physical and virtual; the only thing that matters is that it sees the necessary components it needs to complete the installation.

A virtual machine can have several different virtual hardware components added to it:

- ▶ **6 virtual PCI devices:** Although six virtual PCI devices are supported, one is automatically allocated to the virtual video adapter, thereby leaving you with five available PCI devices that you can allocate to Ethernet and SCSI adapters.

- ▶ **4 SCSI adapters with 15 devices otherwise known as hard drives:** You can allocate a maximum of four SCSI adapters. Given that these are PCI devices and that you have only five *available* PCI slots in every VM, you have to plan accordingly.

- ▶ **4 IDE devices per VM:** You can have up to four CD-ROM/DVD-ROM drives.

- ▶ **10 virtual NICs:** You can have a maximum of 10 network interface cards in every VM.

> ▶ **2 floppy drives:** You can have up to a maximum of two floppy drives.

> ▶ **Up to 8 vCPUs:** To take advantage of the ability to add up to eight vCPUs per VM, you need to use the Enterprise Plus license.

> ▶ **255GB RAM:** Up to 255GB of RAM can be physically allocated to a VM's use.

> ▶ **4 serial ports:** Up to four serial ports can be allocated to a VM's use.

> ▶ **3 parallel ports:** Up to three parallel ports can be allocated to a VM's use.

ExamAlert

At this time, ESX/ESXi 4.1 VMs have limited support for USB and no support for audio adapters.

Figure 6.1 illustrates these different virtual hardware components.

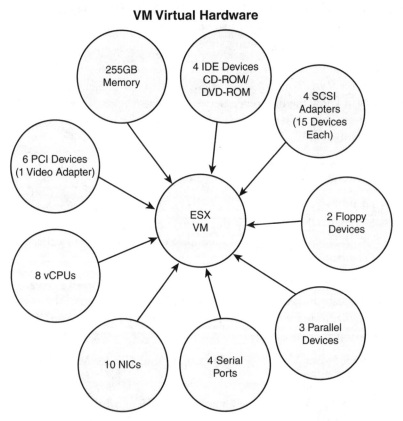

FIGURE 6.1 **VM virtual hardware.**

The bare minimum components required for every virtual machine are as follows:

- vCPU
- Memory
- Boot mechanism (CD-ROM, floppy, or virtual disk)

All other components are considered optional.

Virtual Machine Files

Every virtual machine is made up of files that together make up its environment. You should become intimately familiar with these files because they are at the core of your proper understanding of how a virtual machine is constructed. These files are as follows:

- **name_of_VM.vmx:** This file contains the configuration of the VM—the way it is built and constructed. This file is literally the blueprint of the VM that defines how many vCPUs are assigned, how much memory is allocated, and so on.

- **name_of_VM.vmdk:** This file contains all the relevant information about the VM's virtual hard disk.

- **name_of_VM-flat.vmdk:** This file makes up the hard drive and contains all the data.

- **vmware.log:** This file contains the VM's log files.

- **.nvram:** This file contains the BIOS of the VM.

- **vmware-#.log:** This file contains old VM logs, and the # enumerates starting with 1.

- **name_of_VM.vswp:** This is the VM's swap file.

- **name_of_VM.vmsd:** This file contains information about any available snapshots for this VM.

The VM may have additional files if snapshots exist or if raw disk mappings are in place. Raw disk mappings can be in the form of a SAN LUN that is directly attached to the VM. Another point to note here is that when you have only one hard drive configured for a VM, the files that make up the hard drive appear as VM.vmdk and vm-flat.vmdk, but when you add a second hard drive, the second hard drive's files appear as vm_1.vmdk and vm_1-flat.vmdk. Adding a third hard drive enumerates accordingly, but it is important to note that the enumeration process starts at 1.

Virtual Machine Maximums

The VCP exam will surely quiz you on configuration maximums for virtual machines. For this reason, we provide you with Table 6.1, which supplies the configuration maximums for virtual machines with ESX 4.1.

TABLE 6.1 **Virtual Machine Configuration Maximums**

Component	Maximum
vCPUs	8
Memory	255GB
SCSI disk size	2TB – 512 bytes
Devices per VM (Windows and Linux)	60
NICs	10
IDE devices	4
Floppy devices	2
CD-ROM/DVD-ROM devices	4
SCSI controllers	4
Devices per SCSI controller	15
Parallel ports	3
Serial ports	4
VM swap size	255GB
PCI devices	6
VMDirectPath PCI/PCIe	2
VMDirectPath SCSI targets	60
Remote console connections	40

Cram Quiz

Answer these questions. The answers follow the last question. If you cannot answer these questions correctly, consider reading the section again.

1. What is the maximum amount of physical memory that you can allocate to a virtual machine?

   ○ **A.** 16GB

   ○ **B.** 32GB

   ○ **C.** 64GB

   ○ **D.** 128GB

   ○ **E.** 255GB

2. What is the maximum disk size you can allocate to a virtual machine?

   ○ **A.** 1TB

   ○ **B.** 2TB-512bytes

   ○ **C.** 4TB

   ○ **D.** 8TB

Cram Quiz Answers

1. **E** is correct. ESX 4 introduced increased memory support for VMs, raising it to 255GB of memory per VM.

2. **B** is correct. The maximum disk size you can allocate to a virtual machine is 2TB-512bytes.

Creating a Virtual Machine

▶ **VMware Tools**

▶ **Virtual Disk**

Cram**Saver**

If you can correctly answer these questions before going through this section, save time by skimming the Exam Alerts in this section and then completing the Cram Quiz at the end of the section.

1. Which three SCSI adapters are available with vSphere 4.1?

   ○ **A.** BusLogic SAS

   ○ **B.** BusLogic Parallel

   ○ **C.** LSI Logic SAS

   ○ **D.** VMI Logic

   ○ **E.** VMware Paravirtual

   ○ **F.** VMDirectPath

2. True or false: When using a VM, you can attach a LUN directly into the VM without going through VMFS.

   ○ **A.** True

   ○ **B.** False

Answers

1. **B, C,** and **E** are correct. The three available SCSI adapters are BusLogic Parallel, LSI Logic SAS, and VMware Paravirtual. BusLogic SAS and VMI Logic do not exist, while VMDirectPath is not a SCSI adapter.

2. **A**, True, is correct. You can attach a LUN directly into a VM. This is called Raw Device Mapping (RDM). When using this method, you choose to bypass VMFS altogether and give the VM native access to the LUN.

The process of creating a virtual machine is one that you should be comfortable with as you are preparing to take the VCP exam. Therefore, we do not go into detailed steps as to how to go about creating the VM because this straightforward wizard-driven process allows you to configure all the components we have discussed up to this point in the chapter. These components include vCPU, memory, virtual disk, and so on. We do, however, want to highlight the importance of the configuration of the virtual disk during the creation of the virtual machine. We do that in the next section, but first let's quickly tackle a few issues pertaining to how to launch console access to the VM to manipulate it.

The vSphere client is the tool used to initially launch the VM's console to install a guest operating system on it. After a guest operating system is installed, though, the VM console is not typically used, but rather tools like RDP, SSH, or VNC are used. That being said, the console can be used to access the VM's BIOS or to control power cycling the VM or editing some of its settings.

> **Tip**
>
> When you are using the vSphere client to launch the console, if a Windows operating system is installed, you can use the key combination Ctrl+Alt+Ins to initiate a Ctrl+Alt+Del command to access the Graphical Identification and Authentication (GINA) and log in. You can also do this by clicking VM on the File menu of the console and selecting Send Ctrl+Alt+Del.

Installing a Guest Operating System

The easiest way to install a guest operating system inside a VM is to mount an ISO file as a CD-ROM and install it that way. The other options that you have are to mount either the ESX CD-ROM or the client from where you are connecting, meaning the machine you are using to access the VM Console, which can be your local desktop or laptop. You can use the CD-ROM devices to install the guest operating system. Figure 6.2 illustrates these options.

However, the most efficient way is to store the ISO image files in a shared location, whether on a VMFS datastore or an NFS datastore that is accessible by all ESX servers. This makes deployment easier and more reliable. ESX 4 currently supports the following guest operating systems:

- Windows NT 4.0 all the way to Windows Server 2008 R2

- Red Hat Enterprise Linux 2.1, 3, 4, and 5

- Red Hat Linux 7 to 9

- Ubuntu 5.04, 5.10, 6.06, 6.1, all the way to 10.04

- NetWare 4.2, 5.1, 6.0, and 6.5

- Solaris 10 x86

- SLES 7 to 10

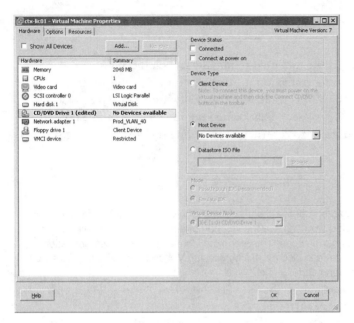

FIGURE 6.2   **Virtual machine settings.**

For a full list of supported operating systems, consult The VMware document, "Guest Operating System Installation Guide" at www.vmware.com/pdf/GuestOS_guide.pdf.

Virtual Disk

A few clicks into the VM creation wizard, and you are presented with a screen that prompts you to select the storage adapter type, as shown in Figure 6.3. Your options are either BusLogic Parallel, LSI Logic Parallel, LSI Logic SAS, and VMware Paravirtual. The setup wizard selects the ideal adapter based on the operating system you are about to install; however, this step allows you to customize this selection if the need arises. Keep in mind that if you choose Typical at the beginning of the virtual machine creation wizard, you are not shown this step. To be prompted with this step, you must select Custom at the beginning of the virtual machine creation wizard.

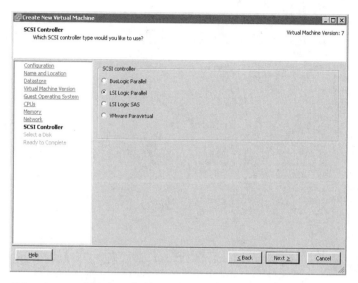

FIGURE 6.3   **SCSI adapter type.**

Next, you are prompted to select a disk, and, as you can see in Figure 6.4, your options are as follows:

▶ **Create a New Virtual Disk:** As the name implies, this option creates a new virtual disk.

▶ **Use an Existing Virtual Disk:** With this option selected, you can browse for an existing virtual disk and associate it with the virtual machine you are creating.

▶ **Raw Device Mappings:** This option is the one you would use if you were attaching a SAN LUN directly to this virtual machine.

▶ **Do Not Create Disk:** This option does not create a virtual disk and therefore renders this VM as a shell only. The VM cannot be powered on unless you specify some kind of a booting mechanism, such as booting from a CD-ROM, an ISO image, or even a floppy.

ExamAlert

You can create a VM without a virtual disk, but it needs some kind of booting mechanism that directs it to the virtual disk.

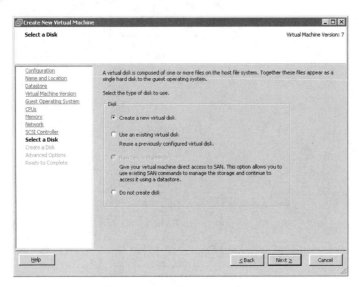

FIGURE 6.4   **Provision virtual disk.**

If you choose to create a new virtual disk, your next screen in the setup wizard looks like Figure 6.5. Here, you can enter the desired size of the virtual hard disk. Keep in mind while you're doing this that the maximum size of disk you can use is 2TB-512bytes. But more important in this screen is the method of storing the virtual disk. Your options are Store with the Virtual Machine and Specify a Datastore. This choice is important because it allows you to separate multiple hard disks associated with a single VM to different locations. The importance of this lies in performance, so for instance, in one scenario you may opt to separate the operating system files from the data files.

You also have the option of using thin provisioning by selecting the Allocate and Commit Space on Demand (Thin Provisioning) check box. If you select the Support Clustering Features Such As Fault Tolerance check box, you are committing the entire space. In other words, you are zeroing out the disk and using thick provisioned disks. This type of disk is mandatory if you intend on using clustering and is known as Eagerzeroedthick.

The final step in the virtual disk configuration is illustrated in Figure 6.6. Here, you can configure the virtual disk on a specific SCSI node. This step also gives you the option to tweak the disk mode. By default, the disk mode allows you to use snapshots. If you opt to use independent disks, by checking Independent, you sacrifice the use of snapshots because they are not supported. An independent disk has two modes, as follows:

▶ **Persistent:** This option means that the changes made to the disk are immediately committed to the disk and are final; you cannot undo them.

▶ **Nonpersistent:** This mode means that when the VM is powered off or recycled, all the changes since the last power on are discarded and you revert to the original state of the disk.

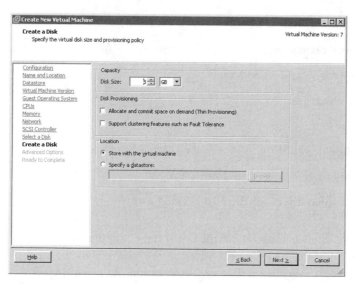

FIGURE 6.5 **Disk capacity and storage location.**

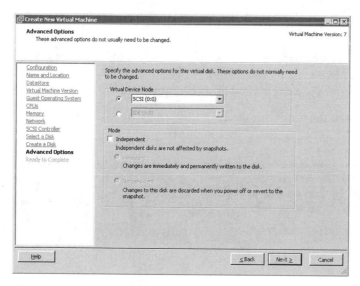

FIGURE 6.6 **Independent disk modes.**

Understanding VMware Tools

VMware Tools is a software package that is installed after the guest operating system is up and running. It provides performance and other enhancements to the VM's operability:

▶ A better virtual NIC adapter driver

▶ An enhanced SCSI adapter driver

▶ Better memory management

▶ OS quiescing for snapshots and VCB

▶ Time synchronization

▶ VM heartbeat

▶ A better mouse driver

▶ The capability to gracefully shut down a VM

▶ An enhanced video driver for the virtual video card

When the VMware Tools package is installed, you can configure the tools further by double-clicking the VMware Tools icon in the taskbar. One of the more important tasks to consider is time synchronization. By default, when the VMware Tools are installed, time synchronization is disabled between the VMs and the ESX/ESXi host. This feature is disabled by default because Windows-based VMs sync time with the domain controller that has the FSMO role of PDC emulator.

When you choose to sync with the PDC emulator it is possible that the time of the Windows VM will run too fast if the VM gets only a few CPU cycles. Syncing time with the VMware Tools will prevent this.

VMs will always sync the time with the ESX host when the VM is powered on, regardless of the setting in the VMware Tools.

> **ExamAlert**
>
> Time synchronization is an important design consideration. For more information on this topic, refer to the VMware white paper "TimeKeeping in Virtual Machines" at www.vmware.com/pdf/vmware_timekeeping.pdf.

Cram Quiz

Answer these questions. The answers follow the last question. If you cannot answer these questions correctly, consider reading the section again.

1. VMware Tools provides which of the following enhancements? (Choose all that apply.)

   ○ **A.** Time Synchronization

   ○ **B.** CPU Management

   ○ **C.** Disk Management

   ○ **D.** Fault Tolerance

   ○ **E.** High Availability

2. True or false: You can use thin provisioned vDisks with clustering technologies such as fault tolerance.

   ○ **A.** True

   ○ **B.** False

Cram Quiz Answers

1. **A** is correct. Out of the current list, VMware Tools provides time synchronization.

2. **B**, False, is correct. When using any kind of clustering technologies, only Eagerzeroedthick disk is supported; therefore, the full size of the disk is allocated and committed.

Understanding and Working with Templates

▶ **Templates**

▶ **Open Virtualization Format (OVF)**

Cram**Saver**

If you can correctly answer these questions before going through this section, save time by skimming the Exam Alerts in this section and then completing the Cram Quiz at the end of the section.

1. Which two methods can be used to create a template?

   ○ **A.** Clone to Template

   ○ **B.** Convert to Template

   ○ **C.** Make Template

   ○ **D.** Snapshot to Template

2. True or false: Templates can only be stored in thick formats (Eagerzeroed and Eagerzeroedthick) and cannot be thin provisioned.

   ○ **A.** True

   ○ **B.** False

Answers

1. **A** and **B** are correct. The two methods to create a template are Clone to Template and Convert to Template.

2. **B**, False, is correct. Templates can be thin provisioned and do not necessarily have to be a thick format when stored.

Everything in a virtual infrastructure is derived one way or another from your day-to-day functions. Consider the concept of *templates*, for example. Templates in a virtual infrastructure are the equivalent of images in a physical environment. So, before the concept of virtualization became popular, what administrators and engineers did—and still do—is provision servers from images. Images are created by configuring a system either by creating just an operating system image or by creating an operating system and application's image. When the time comes for a new server to be deployed, you do so from these images, thus saving time and effort.

Templates are the same: They are a quick and easy way to provision VMs on the fly. The advantage of templates over traditional images is not just in the significant speed by which you can provision VMs, but also in your ability to update the template.

Templates in a vSphere environment allow for the quick provisioning of similarly configured virtual machines. Templates are objects that cannot be powered on.

Creating Templates

There are a couple of different ways to create a template, depending on the situation you are in and what you are trying to accomplish. To create a template, you first have to create a virtual machine, configure this virtual machine to your liking in terms of operating system tweaks, and install the necessary drivers and applications. When you are ready to create a template, simply right-click this VM and scroll down to Templates. You are presented with the following two options:

- ▶ **Clone to Template:** With this option, you are cloning the current VM to a template. You use this option if you want to continue to use the existing VM because by turning it into a template. You cannot power it on anymore.

- ▶ **Convert to Template:** With this option, you convert the VM into a template that is powered off. You typically use this option if the sole purpose of creating the VM is to make it into a template.

> **ExamAlert**
>
> When you are cloning to template, you should turn off the source VM that you are about to clone.

Now that you have created a template, you should also be familiar with how to update this template. As you are likely aware, master images constantly need updating, whether for security patches, new application versions, or anything else. To accomplish this, you simply find the template you want to update, right-click it, and select Convert to Virtual Machine. At this point, that template is converted back to a VM. You can power it on, update accordingly, and then when you are ready, convert it back to a template.

Templates Storage

Storage seems to dominate almost every aspect of a virtual infrastructure, and the reason is simple: You are doing everything in files, and files need to be stored somewhere. Understanding the different options available makes finding things and sharing things easier, but can also help save on space if you tweak certain settings at your disposal. During the process of creating a template, you are offered two methods by which to store it. As shown in Figure 6.7, the choices are as follows:

▶ **Same Format as Source:** As the name implies, this choice uses the same format as the source disk being converted to template.

▶ **Thin Provisioned Format:** Supported on VMFS-3 and above, this storage type logically allocates the full size of the disk but only commits on demand as needed.

▶ **Thick Format:** This storage type uses the Eargerzeroedthick approach and allocates and commits the full size to disk.

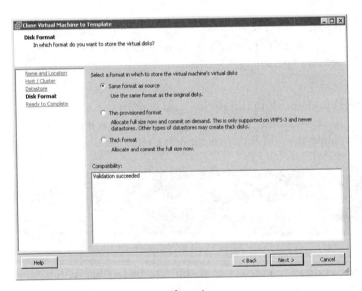

FIGURE 6.7 **Template storage format.**

Guest OS Customization

When you are deploying from a template or master image, one of the challenges is making sure the newly deployed VM has its own unique identity and is not an exact replica of the template or any other VM on the network because that would cause numerous issues. Two completely identical VMs cannot and should not exist. For that matter, many tools exist from OS vendors to address these issues. VMware ESX leverages these tools and streamlines the customization process.

Windows-Based OS Guest Customization

Windows-based operating systems use what is known as the Sysprep files, which are a bunch of small applications and tools that Microsoft makes available to customize its operating systems. For vCenter to take advantage of this feature, these files need to be copied to the vCenter server in the following location:

- **Pre-Windows Server 2008:** C:\Documents and Settings\All Users\ Application Data\VMware\VMware VirtualCenter\Sysprep\<OS>

- **Windows Server 2008:** %ALLUSERSPROFILE%\VMware\VMware VirtualCenter\sysprep which translates to C:\ProgramData\VMware\ VMware VirtualCenter\sysprep by default

Linux-Based OS Guest Customization

Linux-based operating systems do not need any special attention. All the files and tools needed for configuration are installed as part of the vCenter install because they are open source and can be included in the VC distribution without any licensing requirements. Guest OS customization for Linux allows you to customize the following parameters:

- Computer name

- Domain name

- DHCP or static IP settings

- DNS

Deploying Virtual Machines

Deploying a virtual machine is a straightforward task; you can deploy it in two ways:

- **Deploy from Template:** Simply identify the template you want to use, right-click it, and choose Deploy from Template. This option preserves the template in its existing state and creates a duplicate as a virtual machine. It's as simple as that.

▶ **Clone:** Simply identify a virtual machine, right-click it, and select Clone. This option creates an exact replica of the virtual machine that is currently running. We strongly recommend you use guest operating system customization to avoid issues on your network and in your domain, such as SID conflicts, same IP conflict, and so on. You can also use Clone to clone an existing template. Say you want to keep a certain template but create an additional one with extra features. You can clone the template by creating a baseline image you can work from and then modify the new template.

It is important to know that you can clone or deploy virtual machines across datacenters.

Cram Quiz

Answer these questions. The answers follow the last question. If you cannot answer these questions correctly, consider reading the section again.

1. What must be installed on vCenter for Guest OS customization to work for Windows-based systems?

   - ○ **A.** Sysprep files
   - ○ **B.** RIPREP
   - ○ **C.** SID Changer
   - ○ **D.** Nothing; all files are copied during VC install

2. vCenter is installed on a Windows Server 2008 machine. Where should the Sysprep files be located?

   - ○ **A.** %ALLUSERSPROFILE%\VMware\VMware VirtualCenter\sysprep
   - ○ **B.** %ALLUSERS%\VMware\VMware vCenter\sysprep
   - ○ **C.** C:\ProgramFiles\VMware\VMware vCenter\sysprep
   - ○ **D.** C:\ProgramData\VMware\VMware VirtualCenter\sysprep

Cram Quiz Answers

1. **A** is correct. The Sysprep files need to be copied to the vCenter for every Windows operating system that uses Guest OS customization.

2. **A** and **D** are correct. On Windows Server 2008, the default location for the Sysprep files is %ALLUSERSPROFILE%\VMware\VMware VirtualCenter\sysprep which translates to C:\ProgramData\VMware\VMware VirtualCenter\sysprep. Therefore, answers B and C are incorrect paths to the Sysprep files.

Managing Virtual Machines, Virtual Appliances, and vApps

▶ **Cold Migrations**

▶ **Snapshots**

▶ **Virtual Appliances**

▶ **vApps**

Cram**Saver**

If you can correctly answer these questions before going through this section, save time by skimming the Exam Alerts in this section and then completing the Cram Quiz at the end of the section.

1. What is the default format of a virtual appliance?

   ○ **A.** OVB

   ○ **B.** OVE

   ○ **C.** OVF

   ○ **D.** OVC

2. What is the maximum number of snapshots that a VM can have?

   ○ **A.** 10

   ○ **B.** 15

   ○ **C.** 20

   ○ **D.** None of the above

Answers

1. **C** is correct. The correct format of a virtual appliance is OVF, which stands for Open Virtualization Format.

2. **D** is correct. The maximum number of snapshots per VM is 496. Therefore, all the other answers are incorrect.

At the heart of the Virtual Infrastructure (VI) environment is the management of virtual machines because they enable you to perform your daily tasks. The following sections are dedicated to some important techniques you need to be familiar with to make it easier for you to manage your environment.

Cold Migration

A *cold migration* is used to move a virtual machine from one ESX/ESXi host to another while the machine is powered off. Cold migrations are useful because they allow you to move VMs between ESX/ESXi hosts that may have different CPU families that would otherwise prevent vMotion from working properly. Cold migrations are also useful to move VMs to local disks that may or may not be visible to all ESX/ESXi hosts.

What Are Snapshots?

Snapshots are a moment-in-time capture of a virtual machine's state; this includes its settings, memory, and disk states. This feature is useful especially in development or testing when you need to repeatedly go back to a point in time and try different fixes to a potential problem. This feature is also useful in educational areas where you are trying to demonstrate something but need to repeatedly revert to a VM's state after the demonstration is over.

A virtual machine can have multiple snapshots that are all managed by the Snapshot Manager, which you can access by right-clicking a VM and selecting Snapshots and then Snapshot Manager.

Virtual machine snapshots consist of the following files:

- ▶ **name_of_VM-00000#-delta.vmdk:** This is the differences file that basically registers the changes that have happened on this VM. The # is a sequential number that is enumerated starting at 1.

- ▶ **name_of_VM-00000#.vmdk:** This file contains the snapshot description.

- ▶ **name_of_VM-Snapshot#.vmsn:** This file holds the state of the memory and is typically the size of the maximum memory allocated for this VM.

ExamAlert

Snapshots are a key topic and are most certainly going to show up on the VCP-410 exam. The maximum number of snapshots per VM is 496.

By default, a VM can have a maximum of 496 snapshots, and while there is no documented way of controlling this value, you can edit a VM's .vmx file and type the following line: snapshot.maxSnapshots="n" where *n* is the maximum number of snapshots allowed for this VM.

Deploying Virtual Appliances

Virtual appliances have grown in popularity, and many vendors offer them as a means of easing a system deployment. The concept here is that vendors can preconfigure a VM, load it with all the necessary software and drivers, and make it available or download into your vSphere infrastructure. This saves significantly on installation and setup times of a vendor's software.

VMware has created a Marketplace, an online area where vendors can make their appliances available for download. To access the Marketplace and browse the available templates, all you have to do while you are logged in to vCenter is to click File > Browse VA Marketplace. Alternatively, you can go to www.vmware.com/appliances.

Deploy an OVF Template

Virtual appliances have a standard format known as OVF, which stands for Open Virtualization Format. This format was created to make it easier to move appliances across different platforms. Importing an appliance into your virtual infrastructure is easy. While logged in to vCenter, click on File, Deploy OVF and then follow the wizard.

Similarly, if you want to create your own appliance as an OVF format, you can export any VM as an appliance by clicking on the File > Export > Export OVF Template option from the File menu and following the onscreen instructions.

What Is VMware vApp?

A vApp is a container similar to a resource pool and can contain one or more VMs or other vApps. The idea behind a vApp is that you can group VMs that are interdependent in one way or another. For example, if you have a web application that requires an IIS server frontend and a SQL Server backend and possibly a file server as well, you can group them together and manage them as a single entity. When you group VMs inside a vApp you are then able to control the sequence by which they are powered on or off.

A vApp shares some similar functionality with VMs in general. For example, vApps can be powered on and off and can be cloned. You can view vApps either from the Hosts and Clusters view or the VM and Templates view.

When configuring a vApp, you can also define how IP addresses are allocated to the different applications within the vApp. You can choose from three options:

- *Fixed* simply implies that an IP address will be manually assigned.

- *Transient* implies that IP addresses will be assigned from the vCenter managed IP range. These IP assignments will be lost on power off.

- *DHCP* of course means that an IP address will be assigned from a Dynamic Host Configuration Protocol service running on the network somewhere.

Similar to a resource pool, you can also configure the vApp's resource allocation, configuring options such as CPU and memory shares.

Cram Quiz

Answer these questions. The answers follow the last question. If you cannot answer
these questions correctly, consider reading the section again.

1. True or false: You control the maximum number of snapshots per VM.

   ○ **A.** True

   ○ **B.** False

2. True or false: You can only have a maximum of 5 Snapshots per VM.

   ○ **A.** True

   ○ **B.** False

Cram Quiz Answers

1. **A**, True, is correct. While the method of controlling a VM's maximum allowed
   snapshots is not documented, you can modify a VM's .vmx file and add the line
   snapshots.maxSnapshots-"n" entry, where n is the maximum number of snapshots allowed for this VM.

2. **B**, False, is correct. There is no maximum on the number of snapshots you can
   take.

Advanced VM Operations

▶ **VMware Converter**

▶ **Guided Consolidation**

▶ **Capacity Planning**

CramSaver

If you can correctly answer these questions before going through this section, save time by skimming the Exam Alerts in this section and then completing the Cram Quiz at the end of the section.

1. Which two services from the following list are required for proper Guided Consolidation operation?

   ○ **A.** vCenter Collector Service

   ○ **B.** VMware Guided Consolidation Service

   ○ **C.** VMware ESX/ESXi host vCenter Server Service

   ○ **D.** VMware Converter Service

2. Which cloning modes are valid cloning modes? (Choose two.)

   ○ **A.** LUN-based

   ○ **B.** Volume-based

   ○ **C.** Disk-based

   ○ **D.** Partition-based

Answers

1. **A** and **D** are correct. VMware Guided Consolidation requires the vCenter Collector Service and the VMware Converter Service to be running for the entire process to work. The vCenter Collector Service discovers analysis and recommends systems for virtualization, while the Converter turns them into virtual machines.

2. **B** and **C** are correct. The two valid cloning modes are Volume-based and Disk-based. Partition-based and LUN-based do not exist.

There are advanced VM operations that you can take advantage of that cam make your administrative life a bit easier. In this section, we cover VMware vCenter Converter and VMware vCenter Guided Consolidation.

Using VMware vCenter Converter

VMware vCenter Converter is an add-on product that is used to extend vCenter capabilities. Its primary function is to convert physical or virtual machines into ESX-compatible virtual machines. vCenter Converter can be used to accomplish the following tasks:

- ▶ **P2V and V2V:** vCenter Converter can convert a physical machine to a virtual machine (P2V) and also can convert other VMware VMs, such as Workstation, Fusion, ACE, and Player to ESX VMs (V2V).

- ▶ **Convert third-party VMs to ESX VMs**

- ▶ **Restore VCB images to ESX VMs**

- ▶ **Export ESX VMs to other formats**

- ▶ **Customize vCenter VMs**

When using vCenter Converter against a Windows operating system, you are able to customize and resize the volume being restored and also change its identity, whereas if you are using a non-Windows operating system, you are bound by the original settings and cannot modify them.

vCenter Converter Components

As with any other product, vCenter Converter has a prerequisite set of components that need to interact together to make the process work. These components are as follows:

- ▶ **Server:** This component initiates import and export of VMs through the vSphere client or via CLI.

- ▶ **CLI:** The command-line interface component actually carries out the commands issued by the server component. Whether the server commands were issued from the vSphere client or CLI, the CLI component is the one responsible for carrying them out.

- ▶ **Agent:** This component is tasked with preparing a physical machine for conversion.

- ▶ **Client Plug-in:** This component modifies the vSphere Client GUI and enables the vCenter Converter features.

vCenter Converter Installation

VMware vCenter Converter is a Windows-based application that is typically installed on the same server as vCenter because it requires intimate connection with this server in any case. However, you can install vCenter Converter on a standalone physical or virtual server, provided that a connection exists to vCenter. vCenter Converter has the following requirements:

- ▶ Windows 2000 Server SP4

- ▶ Windows XP Professional SP3 (32- and 64- bit)

- ▶ Windows Server 2003 (32- and 64-bit)

- ▶ Windows Vista (32- and 64-bit)

- ▶ Windows Server 2008 (32- and 64-bit)

- ▶ Windows Server 2008 R2

After it is installed, VMware vCenter Converter needs to be enabled from within the vSphere Client. To do so, do the following:

1. Click Plugins from the File menu.

2. Click Manage Plugins.

3. Select Available Plugins.

4. Select Install.

> **ExamAlert**
>
> After installing any plug-ins, always make sure you enable them from the Plugins > Manage Plugins > Installed menu.

Cloning

Cloning is the process of copying or converting a physical or virtual disk to a new virtual disk. Cloning makes an exact replica of the source disk. VMware vCenter Converter is capable of the following cloning methods:

- ▶ **Hot cloning:** The process of cloning a machine while it is online without taking it offline or affecting its productivity.

- ▶ **Cold cloning:** The process of cloning a machine while it is not online.

- ▶ **System reconfiguration:** The process of rehabilitating an imported virtual machine so that it functions properly in an ESX environment.

▶ **Remote cloning:** The process of cloning a machine using the agent over the network. This means you do not need to physically be there or manipulate it in any way; everything is done remotely.

▶ **Local cloning:** The process of cloning with the vCenter Converter software being present on the local machine, such as on a CD-ROM.

Cloning Modes

When cloning, you are offered two methods by which you can clone:

▶ **Volume-based cloning:** You clone only the volumes available on the source machine. This method is useful because it allows you to resize the volumes being cloned. For example, if you want to resize a volume to a smaller size, you can do that, at which point the conversion takes place at a file level rather than at a block level, had you not modified the size downward. It is done at a file level to ensure no data loss occurs. Block level does not understand what exists and simply clones block by block whether or not data exists on these blocks. This mode is supported by hot and cold cloning.

▶ **Disk-based cloning:** This method takes the exact copy of the entire disk and creates a replica. It replicates everything, even free space. If you are cloning a 6GB hard drive, you end up with a 6GB hard drive. This mode is supported only with cold cloning.

Using vCenter Guided Consolidation

vCenter Guided Consolidation is a feature of vCenter aimed particularly at new users who are just starting out in virtualization and server consolidation as a whole. This intelligent concept is a scaled-down version of a more robust product offering from VMware known as Capacity Planner. Guided Consolidation is ideally used in small- to medium-sized organizations with about 100 physical servers. Guided Consolidation can discover and analyze only Windows-based operating systems. As mentioned earlier, the aim of this product is to quickly introduce new users to the benefits and power of virtualization.

Guided Consolidation analyzes systems based on their performance metrics and determines whether they are good candidates for virtualization. The machines that Guided Consolidation can discover and analyze in the enterprise are not limited to physical machines; they can be virtual machines as well, running a different platform than ESX. As long as they are Windows boxes, they can be discovered and analyzed. The final step in the Guided

Consolidation process is to recommend and implement a plan that will convert physical or non-ESX virtual machines to ESX virtual machines and place them on the most suited ESX/ESXi host. This process is done while these machines are live and therefore not jeopardizing any uptime for these systems.

Guided Consolidation depends on the following two services to function properly:

- **VMware vCenter Collector Service:** Also known as the Data Collector service, this service is installed on the vCenter Server and is responsible for discovering the systems by using either LAN Manager or Active Directory. When the systems are discovered, this service is responsible for querying them for performance metrics to make recommendations on whether they are virtualization candidates.

- **VMware Converter Service:** This service is responsible for converting physical and virtual machines to ESX virtual machines. We covered the Converter in detail earlier in this chapter. Think of it as the implementation arm of Guided Consolidation: The Converter does the actual dirty work and implements the Guided Consolidation recommendations on potential virtualization systems.

Configuring Guided Consolidation is easy. From the Home screen of your vCenter Server, in the Solutions and Applications section, click on Guided Consolidation. Once you are in the Guided Consolidation window, you can click on the Configuration tab, which allows you to configure all the Guided Consolidation options including Active Directory. You can select which Active Directory domain(s) you want Guided Consolidation to be able to crawl when searching for target devices.

Discovery and Analysis

The Discovery and Analysis task is the first step in the Guided Consolidation process. To start this process, log in to vCenter using the vSphere client and from the Home screen select Guided Consolidation. Then click on the Analysis tab. This brings you to a window that prompts you to start the analysis. After you click Start Analysis, a wizard starts and guides you through the Discovery and Analysis process.

For this process to work properly, you need a user account with the following privileges:

- Member of local administrators group on vCenter server.

- User must have the Log on as Service user right.

▸ User must have Read access to Active Directory to be able to query it.

▸ User with Administrator rights on target machines to be queried. You can enter different credentials for this step of the process.

> **Tip**
>
> Typically, you would create a single user account for the purpose of doing all these tasks. We described the simplest approach to doing this.

Performing the Consolidation

When the Discovery and Analysis is complete, you are shown a list of servers that can be consolidated; you can then select these servers and click on Plan Consolidation. This starts the process and walks you through the consolidation process, which uses vCenter Converter to convert the servers to ESX VMs and gives you the option of placing them on specific ESX/ESXi hosts if you choose to do so.

Cram Quiz

Answer these questions. The answers follow the last question. If you cannot answer these questions correctly, consider reading the section again.

1. True or false: VMware vCenter Converter requires that you install a client on every machine that needs to be converted into a VM.

   O **A.** True

   O **B.** False

2. True or false: VMware Guided Consolidation queries only Windows-based machines.

   O **A.** True

   O **B.** False

Cram Quiz Answers

1. **B**, False, is correct. VMware vCenter Converter does not require you to manually install a client on machines you want to convert to VMs.

2. **A**, True, is correct. VMware Guided Consolidation queries and analyzes only Windows-based machines. This product is intended for new users as a way to introduce them to virtualization. For a more robust analysis, you should use VMware Capacity Planner.

CHAPTER 7

vSphere Security and Web Access

This chapter covers the following VCP exam topics:

- ▶ Roles
- ▶ Privileges
- ▶ Permissions
- ▶ vpxuser
- ▶ Web Access
- ▶ Virtual Machine Shortcut
- ▶ WebAccess Tasks
- ▶ WebAccess Requirements

  (For more information on the VCP exam topics, see "About the VCP Exam" in the introduction.)

With great power comes great responsibility. Your responsibility is to make sure that the virtual infrastructure you have deployed is secure and that role-based access has been implemented so that the right users have the necessary security permissions to perform their daily tasks. This chapter is dedicated to security in vSphere.

vSphere Security Model

▶ **Roles**

▶ **Permissions**

▶ **Privileges**

▶ **vpxuser**

CramSaver

If you can correctly answer these questions before going through this section, save time by skimming the Exam Alerts in this section and then completing the Cram Quiz at the end of the section.

1. What is a collection of privileges called in the security model of a vSphere?

   ○ **A.** Role

   ○ **B.** Right

   ○ **C.** Access

   ○ **D.** Permission

2. Choose two roles that are default vCenter roles.

   ○ **A.** Night-shift Operator

   ○ **B.** VCB User

   ○ **C.** Backup Administrator

   ○ **D.** Virtual Machine User

Answers

1. **A** is correct. A collection of privileges is known as a role in a vSphere.

2. **B** and **D** are correct. From the list provided, the two roles that are available by default on a vCenter server are VMware Consolidated Backup (VCB) User and Virtual Machine User.

The vSphere security model consists of both vCenter security and ESX Server security. The security model revolves around users and groups that are assigned *roles*. These roles constitute a collection of rights or *privileges* to perform certain tasks.

Users, Roles, Privileges, and Permissions

The cornerstones of the vSphere (VI) security model are the users, groups, roles, privileges, and permissions that you can assign at different levels and to different objects within your infrastructure. Properly configuring and assigning these rights and permissions enables you to enforce accountability. Taking a closer look at each of these cornerstones helps you better design your security solution:

- ▶ **User and group:** An account that is allowed to log in to the VMware infrastructure. A group is a collection of accounts with rights to log in and perform other tasks within the vSphere.

- ▶ **Role:** A collection of privileges that a user or group is allowed to perform.

- ▶ **Privilege:** An allowed action or function within a role. In other words, a privilege allows a user or group to perform a certain task.

- ▶ **Permission:** A right assigned to an object in the inventory and grants a user or group the right to interact with that object according to selected roles and privileges.

> **Note**
>
> You can choose from more than 100 preconfigured privileges.

Working with Roles

Familiarizing yourself with roles is an imperative task of building your access control into the Virtual Infrastructure. To help you get started, Table 7.1 shows a set of default roles available to you.

TABLE 7.1   **Default Roles**

Default ESX Roles	Default vCenter Roles	Custom Roles
No Access	No Access	User-created roles
Read-Only	Read-Only	
Administrator	Administrator	
	Virtual Machine Administrator	
	Datacenter Administrator	
	Virtual Machine Power User	
	Virtual Machine User	
	Resource Pool Administrator	
	VCB User	

The easiest way to get to the Roles panel is to log in to ESX Server or
vCenter using your vSphere client. Click the Administration tab and then the
Roles tab, as shown in Figure 7.1.

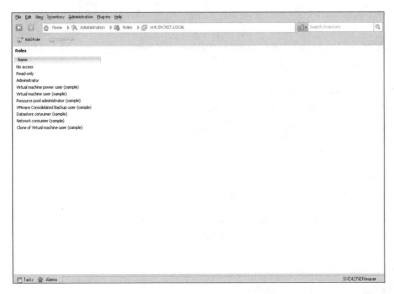

FIGURE 7.1 **Roles panel.**

On the Roles panel, you can right-click any role and edit it. However, we recommend that you maintain the integrity of the existing roles and create your own
custom roles if the need arises. To do so, you can right-click anywhere in the
Roles panel and click Add to start the new role creation, as shown in Figure 7.2.

Note

Custom roles cannot be shared between ESX Server and vCenter.

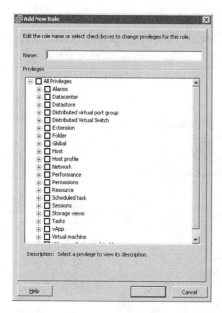

FIGURE 7.2 **Add new role.**

Assigning Permissions

After you have crafted the appropriate roles for your environment, it is time to apply them to the right inventory object to allow your users and groups access only to the part of the inventory tree that you want them to have access to. To apply permissions, find the object in the tree on which you want to implement security, right-click it, and select Add Permission. This brings you to a screen similar to the one shown in Figure 7.3 that allows you to choose a user or group and assign the corresponding role that you want the user or group to have for this inventory object.

When assigning permissions, you may choose to have these permissions propagate from the object where the permission originated and downward to all the child objects. To do this, simply place a check mark in the check box next to Propagate to Child Objects, as shown in Figure 7.3.

If a conflict arises when assigning permissions, the most restrictive of the permissions takes precedence. For instance, if a user is part of a group in the Administrator role but the user is explicitly assigned a Read-Only role on a particular object, the most restrictive of the permissions takes precedence, thereby allowing the user only Read-Only permissions to the object. Keep in mind though that if permissions do not propagate down to any child objects, the user has Read-Only permission over the object but has full permissions over the child objects. The reason behind this is Propagate permissions is not enabled, which means you are slapping explicit permissions on this object only, but not its child object. The child objects in this case inherit the permissions given to the user's group.

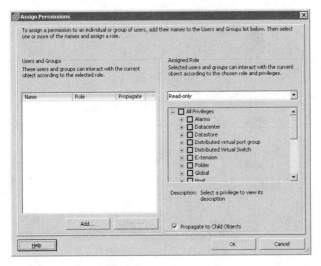

FIGURE 7.3   **Assign permissions.**

ExamAlert

Knowing how permissions are applied and the precedence of permissions are topics that are sure to come up on the exam.

When explicitly assigned, permissions take precedence, and the most restrictive permissions are enforced.

vCenter Security

vCenter is a Windows-based application to be installed on a Windows-based operating system. It has two types of directory repositories to select from:

▶ **Local:** If vCenter is installed on a Windows server that is part of a workgroup, the users and groups that are local members of this server can be configured to have access in vCenter.

> ▶ **Domain:** If vCenter is part of an Active Directory domain, in addition to the ability to configure local users and groups, you can also configure users and groups from Active Directory.

By default, the local Administrators group is assigned the Administrator role at the top of the inventory list in vCenter. If the VC server is member of a domain, the Domain Admins group is also added by default.

ESX Server Security

The ESX Server security revolves around the Service Console, and because the Service Console operating system is based on Red Hat Linux, the users and groups that you find in the ESX Server are Linux users and groups. These users and groups can be configured to grant direct access to an ESX host.

Note

ESX Server users and groups do not sync and cannot be used to assign roles and privileges in vCenter.

Tip

Do not configure permissions using ESX users and groups. The permissions you assign on a per ESX Server level do not propagate to other ESX hosts; therefore, using a common users and groups directory makes it easier to manage permissions.

By default, the following users are assigned the Administrator role in ESX Server:

> ▶ *root* is the equivalent of the administrator in the Windows world and is the highest user account that is created by default.

> ▶ *vpxuser* is added to the Administrators group in ESX after the ESX Server is joined to vCenter. vCenter uses this user to authenticate itself to the ESX host to send preapproved commands.

While the vpxuser is used to authenticate vCenter to ESX Server and pass preapproved commands, the root account actually executes these commands. So in this case, the vpxuser acts merely as a secure bridge between vCenter and the ESX host, while the root user account is tasked with executing vCenter tasks.

Cram Quiz

Answer these questions. The answers follow the last question. If you cannot answer these questions correctly, consider reading the section again.

1. True or false: ESX Server and vCenter Server users and groups can be synchronized.

   ○ **A.** True

   ○ **B.** False

2. Which two user accounts are assigned to the ESX Server Administrator role by default?

   ○ **A.** adm

   ○ **B.** vpxuser

   ○ **C.** vpx

   ○ **D.** root

3. Choose the roles that are not default ESX Server roles.

   ○ **A.** Read-Only

   ○ **B.** No Access

   ○ **C.** Datacenter Administrator

   ○ **D.** Resource Pool Administrator

4. True or false: When using Web Access, you can access VMs only by accessing the vCenter Server WebAccess.

   ○ **A.** True

   ○ **B.** False

Cram Quiz Answers

1. **B**, False, is correct. ESX Server and vCenter Server users and groups cannot be synchronized.

2. **B** and **D** are correct. The two user accounts that are assigned the administrator role by default on the ESX Server are root and vpxuser.

3. **C** and **D** are correct. The two roles that are not default ESX Server roles are Datacenter Administrator and Resource Pool Administrator.

4. **B**, False, is correct. You can access the Web Access console by either pointing to the ESX Server or vCenter Server IP address or FQDN. When pointing to the ESX host, you see only the VMs on that host, whereas when pointing the web access to the VC server, you see all the VMs.

Web Access

- ▶ Web Access
- ▶ Virtual Machine Shortcut
- ▶ WebAccess Tasks
- ▶ WebAccess Requirements

Cram**Saver**

If you can correctly answer these questions before going through this section, save time by skimming the Exam Alerts in this section and then completing the Cram Quiz at the end of the section.

1. Which version of Internet Explorer is the minimum that can be used with Web Access?

- ○ **A.** 4.0
- ○ **B.** 5.0
- ○ **C.** 6.0
- ○ **D.** 7.0

2. True or false: Web Access can be used to create virtual machines.

- ○ **A.** True
- ○ **B.** False

Answers

1. **C** is correct. Internet Explorer version 6.0 is the minimum that can be used to access Web Access.

2. **B**, False, is correct. Web Access cannot be used to create virtual machines. Web Access can be used only to manage VMs. To create virtual machines, you need to use the vSphere client.

Web Access is designed to allow you to manage virtual machines from anywhere without requiring special software to be installed on the host from which you are trying to connect. Web Access is not as robust or feature friendly as the vSphere client. It allows for limited functionality, but can be useful when you need to perform certain tasks from a machine that does not have the vSphere client installed or if you need to pass an administrative tool with limited features to a group like the helpdesk, for example.

To access Web Access, you need to point your Internet browser to either the IP address or fully qualified domain name (FQDN) of your ESX host or your vCenter Server. If you point to your ESX host, you are able to manage virtual machines that are on this host only. If you log in to vCenter Web Access, you are able to manage all your VMs.

After logging in to Web Access, you can select any VM in the list and you are able to perform the following tasks, shown in Figure 7.4:

- ▸ Enumerate VMs

- ▸ Launch console access to a VM

- ▸ Manipulate all VM power functions

- ▸ View a VM's status

- ▸ Edit VM configuration

- ▸ Monitor Datacenters, ESX hosts, and VMs

- ▸ Create and manage VM snapshots

- ▸ Generate VM Remote Console URL

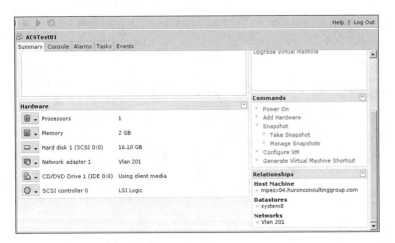

FIGURE 7.4   **Virtual machine Web Access view.**

ExamAlert

The exam will surely challenge your knowledge of the difference between Web Access and the full vSphere client. Know the limitations of the Web Access compared to the full vSphereclient.

> **Caution**
>
> You cannot create VMs from Web Access; this function requires the vSphere client to be completed.

> **Note**
>
> To launch a VM's console from Web Access, you need to have installed the VMware vSphere plug-in in your browser.

Web Access Minimum Requirements

The minimum system requirements to successfully connect and log in to Web Access are as follows:

On a Windows machine:

- ▶ Internet Explorer 6.0 or higher
- ▶ Firefox 2.0 or higher

On a Linux machine:

- ▶ Firefox 2.0 or higher

Remote Console URL

One of the cool things you can do with Web Access is generate a regular web URL to a particular virtual machine. This URL gives you or any user you send it to direct access to this virtual machine. This capability is useful when you want to provide someone access to a virtual machine directly; you can just as easily paste the URL link into an email and send it to that person.

To generate a URL for a VM, you can simply click the Generate Virtual Machine Shortcut link shown in Figure 7.4.

This brings you to a screen similar to the one shown in Figure 7.5 that allows you to configure different settings to control which user interface features the user has access to.

FIGURE 7.5   **Generate Virtual Machine Shortcut window.**

Cram Quiz

Answer these questions. The answers follow the last question. If you cannot answer these questions correctly, consider reading the section again.

1. Approximately how many privileges are there by default in vSphere?

   ○ **A.** 50+

   ○ **B.** 75+

   ○ **C.** 85+

   ○ **D.** 100+

2. Which version of Mozilla Firefox is the minimum that can be used with Web Access?

   ○ **A.** 1.0.4

   ○ **B.** 1.0.5

   ○ **C.** 2.0.0

   ○ **D.** 2.1.0

Cram Quiz Answers

1. **D** is correct. There are approximately 100 privileges by default.

2. **C** is correct. The minimum version of Mozilla Firefox that is supported with Web Access is 2.0.

CHAPTER 8

Managing vSphere Resources

This chapter covers the following VCP exam topics:

▶ Resource Pools

▶ Clusters

▶ Shares

▶ Limit

▶ Reservation

▶ Expandable Reservation

▶ vMotion

▶ Storage vMotion

▶ Eagerzeroed

▶ Distributed Resource Scheduler (DRS) Cluster

▶ VMware EVC

▶ Affinity Rules

(For more information on the VCP exam topics, see "About the VCP Exam" in the introduction.)

Understanding resource management is the single most important component of designing and maintaining your virtual infrastructure. To properly identify how many virtual machines (VMs) you can load on your ESX/ESXi hosts, you must understand how resource management works. Furthermore, to plan for scalability and high availability, you must thoroughly understand resource management. This chapter covers resource management in a VMware Infrastructure 3 environment.

VM CPU and Memory Management

▶ **Limit**

▶ **Reservation**

▶ **Shares**

▶ **Resource Pools**

▶ **Clusters**

▶ **Expandable Reservation**

CramSaver

If you can correctly answer these questions before going through this section, save time by skimming the Exam Alerts in this section and then completing the Cram Quiz at the end of the section.

1. Which items are not settings that would affect a virtual machine's resource allocation? (Select all that apply.)

   ○ **A.** Cycles

   ○ **B.** Expandable

   ○ **C.** Reservations

   ○ **D.** Shares

2. When do CPU Shares kick in?

   ○ **A.** They are on at all times to balance and regulate.

   ○ **B.** When there is a shortage of resources.

   ○ **C.** When you enable DRS.

   ○ **D.** When you enable High Availability.

Answers

1. **A** and **B** are correct. Cycles and Expandable are not settings that you can use to control a virtual machine's resource allocation. Cycles is not valid, and Expandable is available only on resource pools. The three settings that affect a VM's resource allocation in terms of CPU and Memory are Shares, Reservations, and Limits; therefore, answers C and D are incorrect.

2. **B** is correct. CPU Shares only kick in when there is a shortage of resources. Shares enforce quality of service for VMs from a vCPU perspective. Answers A, C, and D are incorrect.

Understanding how virtual machines address their resources, particularly their CPU and memory resources, is extremely important. As Figure 8.1 illustrates, the three settings that control the VM's CPU and Memory resource management are as follows:

▶ *Limit* defines the maximum that a VM can consume in CPU (measured in megahertz, or MHz) and memory (measured in megabytes, or MB).

▶ *Reservation* is the minimum that a VM needs in terms of CPU and memory resources to be able to function properly.

▶ *Shares* identify the frequency and priority a VM has in terms of accessing time slices on the physical CPU and memory. All VMs are assigned shares. The more shares a VM is assigned, the more priority it has over physical resources.

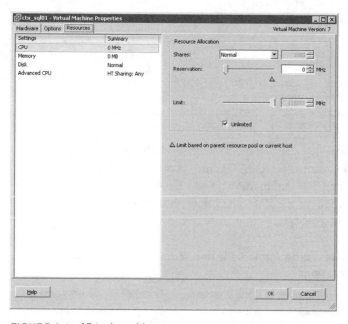

FIGURE 8.1 **Virtual machine resource management.**

A virtual machine's vCPUs are always scheduled at the same time. When you're assigning shares, keep in mind the number of vCPUs configured for any given VM. A reservation of 1,000 MHz might be adequate for a VM that has only one vCPU, but a VM of two vCPUs will have to divide these 1,000 MHz into 500 MHz per vCPU, and that might or might not be adequate depending on what this VM's function will be. Similarly, reservation of 1,000 MHz for a VM that has four vCPUs renders each vCPU with 250 MHz, which further diminishes the functionality of the VM.

Exam Alert

Shares are ignored when there is no resource contention. For example, two VMs with varying CPU share reservations get equal access to the host's CPU when there is no shortage of resources. Therefore, shares only kick in when there is a shortage of resources.

The Available Memory setting, which is a fourth setting option enabled only for the memory configuration of a VM, is the initial memory that you configure for a VM during its creation. You can always modify this option, after the VM is created. With this in mind, if the Available Memory and Reservation values differ, the VMkernel compensates for this discrepancy by creating a swap file for the difference between the two values. An example of this would be if the Available Memory setting is configured for 2GB and the reservation is set to 1GB; then the VMkernel creates a swap file to compensate for the difference.

Note

A virtual machine does not power on if its CPU and memory reservation is not met by the ESX/ESXi host it is running on.

When assigning shares to a virtual machine, you have four options: High, Normal, Low, and Custom. Table 8.1 outlines how these settings translate in number of shares for CPU and memory. The values in Table 8.1 are currently valid for resource pools; as for VMs, the values should read High=2000, Normal=1000, and Low=500.

TABLE 8.1 **CPU/Resource Pools CPU and Memory Share Value Calculations**

Share Setting	Number of CPU Shares	Number of Memory Shares
High	2000 * # of vCPUs	20 * Available memory
Normal	1000 * # of vCPUs	10 * Available memory
Low	500 * # of vCPUs	5 * Available memory
Custom	Manually specified	Manually specified

Using Resource Pools to Govern CPU/Memory Resources

A *resource pool* enables you to group virtual machines and apply the same resource policy on them. Resource pools can be created for a single ESX/ESXi host or to a *Distributed Resource Scheduler (DRS)* cluster to govern the CPU and memory resources. Grouping virtual machines also makes it easier to implement security and delegate administration to other users and groups. You should also know that you can create child resource pools and further compartmentalize VMs.

> **ExamAlert**
>
> Every ESX/ESXi host, by default, is a resource pool known as the Root Resource Pool. The Root Resource Pool exists prior to your creating any resource pools under this host.

Resource pools have the same settings as virtual machines; therefore, you can control a resource pool's CPU and memory shares, limits, and reservations. As Figure 8.2 illustrates, a resource pool has an additional *expandable reservation* option, which allows a child resource pool to tap into the parent resource pool and harness whatever resources are available to satisfy its own shortage. An expandable resource is used only when the resource pool cannot secure enough resources to satisfy its policy.

> **Tip**
>
> Use expandable reservation wisely because it can consume all the parent's resources.

You can view a resource pool's data using either of the following methods:

▶ Highlight the resource pool in the inventory and then select the Summary tab.

▶ Choose the Resource Allocation tab while the resource pool is selected in the inventory.

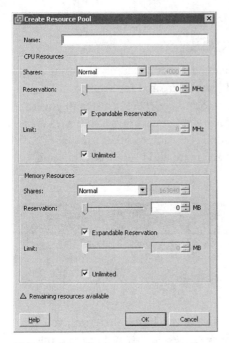

FIGURE 8.2 Resource pool properties.

Cram Quiz

Answer these questions. The answers follow the last question. If you cannot answer these questions correctly, consider reading the section again.

1. Which setting controls the maximum CPU time measured in MHz that a virtual machine is allowed to use?

   ○ **A.** Limit

   ○ **B.** Reservation

   ○ **C.** Shares

   ○ **D.** Affinity

2. True or false: If a virtual machine's available memory and its reservation memory setting differ, the VMkernel generates a VM-specific swap file for the difference between the two settings.

   ○ **A.** True

   ○ **B.** False

3. What is the name given to the topmost resource pool?

   ○ **A.** Resource Pool

   ○ **B.** Default Resource Pool

   ○ **C.** Root Resource Pool

   ○ **D.** Master Resource Pool

4. True or false: Resource pools can be used with a standalone ESX/ESXi host or a DRS cluster.

   ○ **A.** True

   ○ **B.** False

Cram Quiz Answers

1. **A** is correct. Limit is the setting that controls the maximum a CPU can use measured in MHz; therefore, answers B, C, and D are incorrect.

2. **A**, True, is correct. When the Available Memory and the Memory Reservation settings differ, the VMkernel generates a swap file for the difference.

3. **C** is correct. The Root Resource Pool is the name given to the topmost resource pool; therefore, answers A, B, and D are incorrect.

4. **A**, True, is correct. Resource Pools can be created for a single ESX/ESXi host or for a DRS cluster.

vMotion and Storage vMotion

▶ **vMotion**

▶ **Storage vMotion**

▶ **Eagerzeroed**

CramSaver

If you can correctly answer these questions before going through this section, save time by skimming the Exam Alerts in this section and then completing the Cram Quiz at the end of the section.

1. Which of the following is not a requirement of the source and destination host for vMotion to work properly?

   ○ **A.** Gigabit Ethernet

   ○ **B.** Virtual switches that are configured and labeled identically

   ○ **C.** Access to the same shared storage

   ○ **D.** Access to each host's Service Console

2. Which of the following circumstances will prevent the vMotion process from being successfully completed? (Choose two.)

   ○ **A.** CPUs with different multimedia instruments

   ○ **B.** CPUs with different numbers of cores

   ○ **C.** CPU of different manufacturers

   ○ **D.** If Hyperthreading is enabled on one of the hosts

Answers

1. **D** is correct. Access to each host's service console is not a requirement for the successful vMotion process; therefore, answers A, B, and C are incorrect.

2. **A** and **C** are correct. The vMotion process will not successfully complete if you are trying to vMotion across CPUs from Intel and AMD for example. The process will also fail if the multimedia instruments on the CPUs differ.

vMotion is probably the most popular and most sought after feature in the VMware infrastructure suite. The vMotion feature allows a running virtual machine to be migrated without interruption from one host to another, provided that some prerequisites are met on the originating and destination hosts.

Storage vMotion, on the other hand, allows you to migrate a VM's data files from one storage location to another without interruption. The vMotion suite collectively allows you to control a VM's host placement and its data file placement at any time for performance or organization purposes without downtime.

vMotion

vMotion is an enterprise-level feature and thereby requires vCenter before it can be enabled. vMotion, as you see later in the section "Distributed Resource Scheduler," is used in conjunction with DRS to make sure VMs are always spread out on the most appropriate host, thereby balancing the resource availability of these hosts.

vMotion Host Prerequisites

With vMotion, for the VM to successfully port from one host to another, the following requirements must be satisfied on the source and destination hosts:

- ▶ Access to all datastores on which the VM is configured

- ▶ Virtual switches that are labeled the same, so that when the VM is ported from one host to another, its configuration is the same and finds the same resources

- ▶ Access to the same physical networks for the VM to continue to function after being ported from one host to another

- ▶ Compatible CPUs

- ▶ Gigabit network connection

When you initiate a vMotion from one host to another, the wizard that starts the process warns you if there are errors that prevent the migration from completing successfully. The vMotion wizard also provides warnings that you take into account and possibly address after the migration is completed. Warnings do not prevent the vMotion process from completing successfully, whereas errors do. Table 8.2 outlines the different scenarios that might generate an error or a warning.

TABLE 8.2 **vMotion Errors and Warnings**

vMotion Errors	vMotion Warnings
A VM is connected to an internal vSwitch on the source host.	A VM is configured for an internal vSwitch but is not connected to it.
A VM has a removable disk such as a CD/DVD-ROM or floppy connected to it.	A VM is configured for a removable CD/DVD-ROM or floppy but is not connected to it.
A VM has CPU affinity assigned.	A VM has a snapshot. A heartbeat cannot be detected from the VM to be migrated.

Tip

If your ISO or FLP image files are mounted in a shared network location where all the ESX/ESXi hosts involved have access, you receive a warning only during vMotion. That's whether the virtual CD or floppy drive is connected.

Enabling vMotion

To enable vMotion, you need to create a VMkernel port group with vMotion enabled on all ESX/ESXi hosts that will participate in the vMotion process, as shown in Figure 8.3. The virtual switch where this port group is created should bear the same label on all ESX/ESXi hosts. Typically, vMotion is configured on a dedicated virtual switch on all ESX/ESXi hosts.

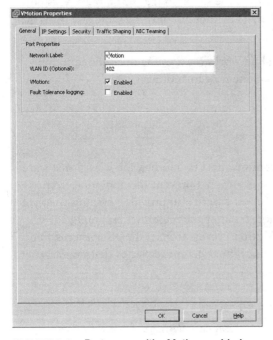

FIGURE 8.3 **Port group with vMotion enabled.**

vMotion also requires that the physical NIC that you choose to service the virtual switch where vMotion is enabled should be a Gigabit or higher.

vMotion CPU Requirements

One of the main obstacles to a successful vMotion migration is the CPU; vMotion requires a strict CPU approach, so keep the following guidelines in mind:

- ▶ vMotion does not work across CPU vendors, so if you have an ESX/ESXi host that is running an AMD processor and one that is running an Intel processor, vMotion errors out and does not work.

- ▶ vMotion does not work across CPU families, so you are not able to migrate between a Pentium III and a Pentium 4, for example.

- ▶ Hyperthreading, the number of CPU cores, and the CPU cache sizes are not relevant to vMotion.

- ▶ vMotion does not work across CPUs with different multimedia instructions—for example, a CPU with *Streaming SIMD Extensions 2* (SSE2) and a CPU with *Streaming SIMD Extensions 3* (SSE3).

- ▶ NX/XD hides or exposes advanced features in the CPU of an ESX Server. In most cases, this hidden feature is controlled by VMware for stability reasons (see Figure 8.4). In the event that the guest operating system requires it, however, the vSphere client exposes this feature in the properties of a VM. If it is enabled, the CPU characteristics of the host and destination must match; if disabled, an occurring mismatch is ignored and vMotion proceeds.

CPU vendors Intel and AMD now offer a technology known as *virtualization assist* that aids virtualization. Intel has its VT technology, and AMD has its AMD-V technology, both of which are enabled in the BIOS of a computer.

> **Note**
>
> Virtualization assist needs to be enabled before you can migrate 64-bit VMs from one host to another.

In the presence of these technologies, you can enable the VMs whose operating system supports the virtualization assist technology to improve their performance. To do this, you can right-click the VM in question and click Edit Settings. Click the Options tab, find the Paravirtualization section, and enable it. Figure 8.5 illustrates this process clearly.

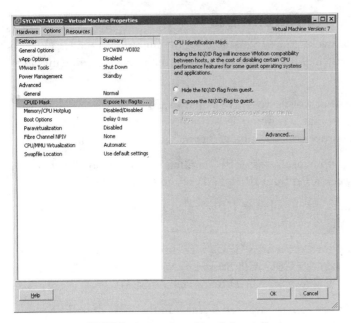

FIGURE 8.4   **NX/XD feature exposed in vSphere client.**

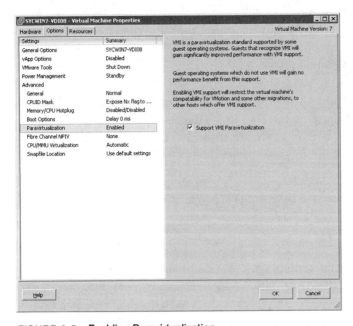

FIGURE 8.5   **Enabling Paravirtualization.**

The vMotion Stages

Because the virtual machine to be vMotioned resides on a datastore that is visible and accessible to both the source and the destination ESX/ESXi host, the only thing that vMotion needs to do is to copy the VM's memory from one host to another. Because the VM's memory resides on the physical memory of the source host, that memory is what needs to be copied. That being said, the two ways to initiate a vMotion are as follows:

▶ Select one or more VMs and then right-click and choose Migrate.

▶ Simply choose the Change host option.

When the vMotion process begins, the four stages that it goes through are as follows:

1. Once vMotion is initiated, a memory bitmap is created to track the changes, and the process of copying the physical RAM from one host to another begins.

2. Quiesce the VM and copy the contents of the memory bitmap. Quiesce can be defined in simpler terms as a cut-over. This is the only time at which the VM is unavailable. This is a short period of time that for the most part is transparent to the user.

ExamAlert

The Quiesce period is the only time during which the VM is not available, but the outage time is short, typically between 1/2 to 1 1/2 seconds. This time period is so transparent that you may lose a single ping in some cases.

3. The virtual machine on the destination host starts and moves all connectivity to it from the source host to the destination host.

4. The VM is removed from the source host.

During your monitoring of the vMotion process, you might notice that it pauses at 10% completion as part of the identification process.

Note

The speed at which vMotion completes its process depends on bandwidth availability and congestion on the vMotion network, as well as the size of the RAM dedicated to the VM being moved.

Storage vMotion

Storage vMotion is the process of migrating all the VM's files from one storage to another while the VM is powered on and without any interruption. Traditional vMotion moves the logical representation of a VM from one ESX/ESXi host to another while it is powered on while keeping the files that constitute this VM in the same storage space. Storage vMotion complements this by allowing you to move the VM files as well thereby contributing to a complete VM migration from one location to another without an interruption in service.

Storage vMotion was introduced in Virtual Infrastructure 3.5 but only at the command-line level; with vSphere 4, you can now do Storage vMotion from a GUI. To initiate a Storage vMotion from the GUI you follow the same steps as you would for a normal vMotion, which is to right-click a VM and select Migrate. The difference is the screen shown in Figure 8.6 has been completely changed with the following options:

- **Change Host:** This is obviously the traditional vMotion option, which moves the VM while it is powered on or off from one ESX/ESXi host to another.

- **Change Datastore:** This is the option to do a Storage vMotion thereby moving all the VM's files from one storage to another while the VM is powered on or off.

- **Change Both Host and Datastore:** As the name implies you can move both the VM and its corresponding files from one host to another with one catch, the VM has to be powered off.

> **Note**
>
> While the option to simultaneously move host and datastore cannot be done while the VM is powered on there is no reason why you cannot run these tasks consecutively thereby achieving the goal of migrating the VM and its files while it is powered on.

The next screen shown in Figure 8.7 prompts you to select the destination datastore where you want to move the files to. It is important to note that with vSphere 4 all protocols are now supported, which means, iSCSI, Fiber Channel, Fiber Channel over Ethernet (FCoE), NFS, and RDMs.

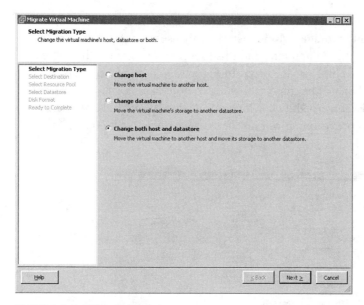

FIGURE 8.6 **Migrate Wizard.**

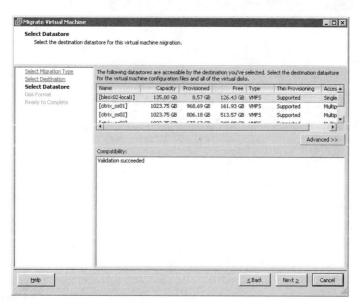

FIGURE 8.7 **Datastore destination.**

This brings us to the last step in the Storage vMotion wizard, which is the disk format. While Storage vMotion is primarily used to move VM files from one storage to another you might find this tool useful to change the disk format from Thin to Thick or vice versa. In Figure 8.8, note two options for disk type: Thin and Thick. The important thing to note here is that the reference to Thick is the Eagerzeroedthick, which means that the VMDK will be zeroed, thus thin provisioning will not be possible once this is converted to this type of Thick.

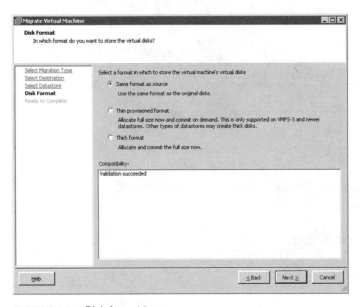

FIGURE 8.8 **Disk format type.**

Cram Quiz

Answer these questions. The answers follow the last question. If you cannot answer these questions correctly, consider reading the section again.

1. Storage vMotion and vMotion can be run simultaneously while_____.

   ○ **A.** The VM is powered on.

   ○ **B.** The VM is powered off.

   ○ **C.** The VM is powered on or off.

   ○ **D.** They cannot be run simultaneously under any circumstance.

2. Which virtual disk type writes zeros across all the capacity of the virtual disk?

   ○ **A.** Eagerzeroed

   ○ **B.** Eagerzeroedthick

   ○ **C.** Zeroedthick

   ○ **D.** Thick

Cram Quiz Answers

1. **B** is correct. You cannot run Storage vMotion and vMotion simultaneously while the VM is powered on. You can run them while the VM is powered off, or you can schedule them to run consecutively.

2. **B** is correct. Eagerzeroedthick is the virtual disk type that writes zeroes across the entire capacity of the disk and commits it all, thereby thin provisioning would not be possible. All other types are incorrect.

Distributed Resource Scheduler

▶ **Distributed Resource Scheduler (DRS) Cluster**

▶ **Affinity Rules**

▶ **VMware EVC**

Cram**Saver**

If you can correctly answer these questions before going through this section, save time by skimming the Exam Alerts in this section and then completing the Cram Quiz at the end of the section.

1. What color is assigned to a DRS cluster that is overcommitted?

   ○ **A.** Red

   ○ **B.** Orange

   ○ **C.** Blue

   ○ **D.** Yellow

2. How do you configure two VMs so that they are never present on the same host at the same time?

   ○ **A.** Affinity

   ○ **B.** Policy

   ○ **C.** Permissions

   ○ **D.** Anti-Affinity

Answers

1. **D** is correct. A DRS cluster that is overcommitted is assigned the color yellow; therefore, answers A, B, and C are incorrect.

2. **D** is correct. Configuring an Anti-Affinity rule would be the correct course of action and the correct answer to the question. Affinity rules force VMs to stay together on the same host. Choices B and C are incorrect.

VMware DRS is an enterprise-level feature that uses vMotion to load balance the CPU and memory resources of all ESX/ESXi hosts within a given DRS cluster. DRS is also used to enforce resource policies and respect placement constraints.

DRS functions efficiently using *clusters*. A cluster is the implicit collection of CPU and memory resources across ESX/ESXi hosts that are members of this cluster to allow for the creation of VMware DRS clusters and VMware High

Availability (HA) clusters. A cluster is an object that appears in the vCenter inventory and, like all other objects, can be assigned permissions. It can have a maximum of 32 nodes, or 320 VMs per host, or 3000 VMs per cluster, whichever maximum is reached first.

In other words, you can have 32 hosts in the cluster, but you are then limited to only 93 VMs per host, or you can have 300 VMs on 10 hosts, or 20 hosts with 150 VMs, and so on.

After you add ESX/ESXi hosts as nodes in a DRS cluster, DRS then monitors these ESX/ESXi hosts. If DRS detects high CPU utilization or high memory utilization on a particular host, it uses vMotion to migrate some VMs off the host with resource constraints to a host that is not experiencing resource constraints. DRS constantly plays this role to ensure that all ESX/ESXi hosts never have resource constraints.

DRS Automation Process

The DRS automation process involves *initial placement* of the virtual machines when they are first powered on and later on dynamically load balancing VMs on the best-suited host that will render the best performance. As shown in Figure 8.9, the automation process options are as follows:

- ▶ **Manual:** If you select this option, vCenter suggests which VM needs to be initially placed on which host at power on and later suggests which VM should be migrated to a different host; however, vCenter does not perform either task automatically.

- ▶ **Partially Automated:** If you select this option, VMs are automatically placed at power on; however, for future load balancing, vCenter only suggests the migration but does not perform it.

> **Note**
>
> The advantage of using Manual or Partially Automated is that you get greater control of which VMs are moved where and when. The disadvantage, of course, is you have to manually intervene for this task to be completed. Typically, Manual or Partially Automated is used on sensitive VMs that you want to constantly monitor.

- ▶ **Fully Automated:** If you select this option, vCenter suggests and performs the initial placement of VMs at power on and automatically migrates them to maintain the most adequate load balancing.

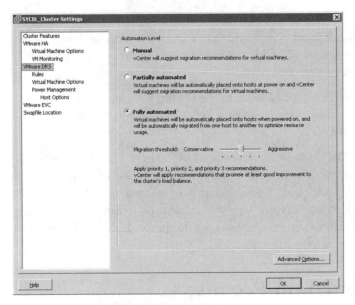

FIGURE 8.9   **DRS cluster automation.**

When set to Manual or Partially Automated, DRS recommends VMs that
need to be migrated to improve performance and maintain proper load balancing in the cluster. To view these recommendations, you can select the DRS
cluster in the vCenter inventory and click the DRS Recommendations tab, as
shown in Figure 8.10.

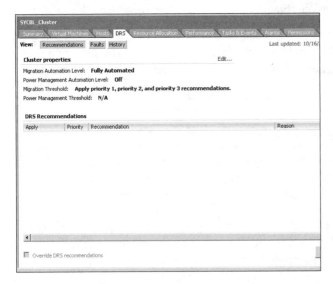

FIGURE 8.10   **DRS recommendations.**

If you choose a fully automated load-balancing schedule, you can also control the frequency at which migrations occur. DRS analyzes the VMs and rates them on a five-star basis, with five stars meaning the VM must move from one host to another and one star meaning the VM does not necessarily need to move or, if moved, the change is not significant. Your options are as follows:

▶ **Most Conservative:** This option means DRS migrates VMs very infrequently and only when it must (that is, when VMs have five stars).

▶ **Moderately Conservative:** This option means that DRS migrates VMs with four stars or more. This option promises significant improvement.

▶ **Default:** This option moves VMs with three stars or more and promises good improvement.

▶ **Moderately Aggressive:** This option moves VMs with two stars or more and promises moderate improvement.

▶ **Aggressive:** This option migrates VMs with one star or more and promises slight improvement.

DRS automation levels can also be managed on the virtual machine level, where you manually assign the automation level for each VM in the cluster. To configure the automation level based on the VM, right-click the cluster where the VM is a member and go to Edit Settings. On the left pane, select Virtual Machine Options. You then are presented with a list of VMs that are members of this cluster on the right. You can change the automation level manually. Figure 8.11 shows an example.

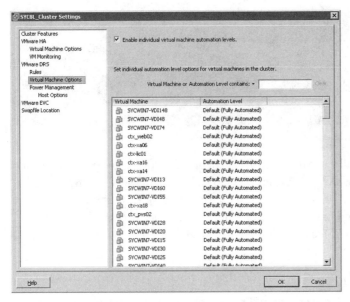

FIGURE 8.11   **VM level automation.**

DRS Cluster Validity

Monitoring a DRS cluster to ensure that there are no errors is critical. A resource pool can be in one of three states: valid, overcommitted, or invalid. A DRS cluster is considered to be valid, functioning, and healthy when the resource availability satisfies all the reservations and supports all running VMs. In the event that a DRS cluster is not considered valid, resource pools notify you that there is a problem by changing the color of the resource pool in the vSphere client as follows:

▶ *Yellow* means that the resource pool is *overcommitted* in terms of resources.

▶ *Red* means that the resource pool has violated the DRS cluster rules or high-availability rules and is thereby considered *invalid*.

DRS Rules

DRS enables you to set rules that govern whether VMs can exist on the same ESX/ESXi host at the same time or if they should always be separated and never exist on the same host at the same time. This capability can be useful if you are trying to avoid a single point of failure for a particular VM and want to make sure that the DRS algorithm never places VMs assigned in the rules on the same host. That being said, you can choose to have the VMs on the same host at all times, so if one VM is migrated, the other follows as well. These rules are known as VM-VM Affinity rules and have two options:

- **Affinity:** This rule implies that VMs should be on the same ESX/ESXi host at all times.

- **Anti-Affinity:** This rule implies that VMs cannot exist on the same ESX/ESXi host at the same time.

The release of vSphere 4.1 introduced a new Affinity rule known as *VM-Host Affinity Rules*. These rules determine whether groups of VMs can or cannot exist on groups of ESX/ESXi hosts. With these rules, you can build groups of specific VMs and groups of specific ESX/ESXi hosts and then implement Affinity or Anti-Affinity rules. VM-Host affinity rules have the following options:

- **Must run on hosts in group:** This rule implies it is a requirement that the VM group be on the same ESX/ESXi host group at all times.

- **Should run on hosts in group:** This rule implies it is preferred that the VM group be on the same ESX/ESXi host group at all times.

- **Must not run on hosts in group:** This rule implies it is a requirement that the VM group NOT be on the same ESX/ESXi host group at all times.

- **Should not run on hosts in group:** This rule implies it is preferred that the VM group NOT be on the same ESX/ESXi host group at all times.

> **ExamAlert**
>
> Affinity rules changed with the release of vSphere 4.1; they now fall under two categories, VM-VM Affinity rules, which are the traditional affinity rules known as Affinity and Anti-Affinity, and the new VM-Host Affinity rules. The VCP exam may test your knowledge on this topic.

You can access these rules by right-clicking your cluster and pointing to Edit Settings. You then see the Rules section on the left. Select it and click Add. Figure 8.12 shows an example of how you can set a rule to never allow two VMs to be on the same host at the same time.

FIGURE 8.12   **DRS rules.**

VMware EVC

As we have been discussing in this chapter, vMotion has certain CPU requirements that need to be met before a successful live migration of VMs can take place between hosts. Considering OEM server manufacturers constantly upgrade the CPUs that ship with their server models, it can become challenging when you purchase servers at different intervals. At some point, you are bound to have hardware of different CPU families.

VMware Enhanced vMotion Compatibility is similar in function to the NX/XD feature, except it is configured on a cluster basis and affects the hosts in the cluster while the NX/XD feature is implemented on a VM level. When creating an EVC cluster, you are instructing vSphere to find the lowest common denominator between all the hosts' CPUs thereby allowing the highest level of vMotion compatibility.

As you can see in Figure 8.13, creating a VMware EVC cluster is easy. Choose Edit Settings on your existing DRS cluster and select VMware EVC from the left pane. You can then configure the options appropriately.

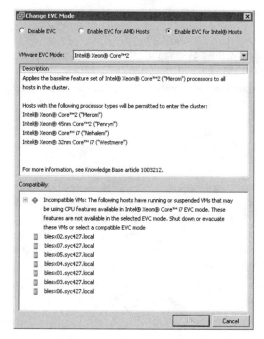

FIGURE 8.13 **VMware EVC enabled cluster.**

Cram Quiz

Answer these questions. The answers follow the last question. If you cannot answer these questions correctly, consider reading the section again.

1. Which setting is an invalid level when Fully Automated DRS cluster load balancing is selected?

   ○ **A.** Conservative

   ○ **B.** Aggressive

   ○ **C.** Default

   ○ **D.** Low

2. Which of the following is not a DRS cluster automation level? (Select all that apply.)

   ○ **A.** Manual

   ○ **B.** Semi Manual

   ○ **C.** Fully Automated

   ○ **D.** Semi Automated

3. How many cluster nodes are supported for each DRS cluster?

   ○ **A.** 16

   ○ **B.** 24

   ○ **C.** 32

   ○ **D.** 36

Cram Quiz Answers

1. **D** is correct. Low is not a valid frequency level when Fully Automated is selected; therefore, answers A, B, and C are incorrect.

2. **B** and **D** are correct. Semi Manual and Semi Automated are invalid and do not exist. The three levels of automation are Manual, Partially Automated, and Fully Automated; therefore, answers A and C are incorrect.

3. **C** is correct. VMware DRS clusters support up to 32 ESX/ESXi hosts or nodes per cluster; therefore, answers A, B, and D are incorrect.

CHAPTER 9

Monitoring vSphere Resources

This chapter covers the following VCP exam topics:

- ▶ Hyper-Threading
- ▶ Hardware Execution Context (HEC)
- ▶ Transparent Memory Page Sharing
- ▶ Balloon-Driver
- ▶ Hypervisor Swap
- ▶ Memory Compression
- ▶ Alarms
- ▶ Virtual CPU
- ▶ Virtual Memory
- ▶ CPU
- ▶ Memory
- ▶ Disk

    (For more information on the VCP exam topics, see "About the VCP Exam" in the introduction.)

This chapter focuses primarily on how to monitor your VMware Infrastructure. You learn about optimizing and monitoring resources used by virtual machines (VMs) and hosts, including virtual CPUs and virtual memory. The chapter concludes with a discussion of alarms.

Resource Optimization Concepts

▶ **Virtual CPU**

▶ **Virtual Memory**

▶ **Balloon-Driver**

▶ **Hyper-Threading**

▶ **Hardware Execution Context (HEC)**

▶ **Transparent Memory Page Sharing**

▶ **Hypervisor Swap**

▶ **Memory Compression**

Cram**Saver**

If you can correctly answer these questions before going through this section, save time by skimming the Exam Alerts in this section and then completing the Cram Quiz at the end of the section.

1. True or false: Transparent memory page sharing is enabled by default and cannot be turned off.

   ○ **A.** True

   ○ **B.** False

2. Which virtual memory technology is used to consume the memory of a virtual machine and release it to the VMkernel for allocation to other VMs? (Select all that apply.)

   ○ **A.** Balloon-driver

   ○ **B.** VMkernel swap

   ○ **C.** Transparent memory page sharing

   ○ **D.** Vmmemctl

3. True or false: The Service Console is constantly scheduled on different HECs.

   ○ **A.** True

   ○ **B.** False

The two most important resources for virtual machines are virtual CPU and virtual memory. Knowing and understanding the different concepts and techniques used to manipulate these two resources are absolutely critical and are fundamental in your understanding of how the VMware hypervisor works. This section focuses on the different mechanisms used by ESX for virtual CPU and virtual memory optimization.

Virtual CPU

You can configure a virtual machine with up to eight virtual CPUs (vCPUs). For a vCPU to get physical CPU time, the vCPU needs to be scheduled on a *Hardware Execution Context (HEC)*. An HEC is a thread that is scheduled on a physical processor. The number of HECs available for scheduling depends on the number of physical cores available in the system. vCPUs must be scheduled at the same time or not at all, so, for example, a two-vCPU virtual machine must be scheduled on two HECs at the same time or not all. The same applies to a four-vCPU virtual machine; it either gets scheduled on four HECs at the same time or not at all.

Note

To configure a VM with eight vCPUs, you must have the vSphere 4 Enterprise Plus Edition.

ExamAlert

If any physical CPU in an ESX/ESXi host fails, the entire host will crash, and there will be no redundancy capabilities.

To determine the number of HECs available, you have to look at the physical processor configuration of your system. Today, processors with multiple cores are available; a socket is a complete processor that is either packaged with other cores in the same socket or available alone. If you have a single socket , dual core system without hyper-threading, for example, you then have two HECs. If you have a single socket, quad core, you then have four HECs and so on. The following sections describe hyper-threading and vCPU load balancing.

Hyper-Threading

Hyper-threading is an Intel Corporation technology that allows you to schedule multiple threads on the same processor at the same time. Hyper-threading does not increase CPU capacity, however. Hyper-threading is enabled in the BIOS of the system, and when enabled, it increases the number of available HECs on which vCPUs can be scheduled. Even with the capability to schedule multiple threads on the same physical CPU at the same time, if contention occurs, one thread would have to wait while the other finishes execution. For this reason, when VMs have high vCPU utilization, the VMkernel ignores the second thread if it exists. That is, hyper-threading does not increase a VM's vCPU capabilities if the VM is CPU intensive.

vCPU Load Balancing

The VMkernel is responsible for dynamically scheduling vCPUs and the Service Console (SC). VMkernel schedules and reschedules vCPUs on different HECs every 20 milliseconds, with the exception of the Service Console, which is always scheduled on the first HEC or physical CPU 0 and is never changed.

The VMkernel's sole purpose in this constant migration of the vCPUs from one HEC to another is to maintain the most adequate load. The VMkernel determines where it schedules the different vCPUs and on which HECs.

> **ExamAlert**
>
> The VCP exam will challenge your knowledge of on which physical CPU the SC is always scheduled.

Virtual Memory

The VMkernel uses the following techniques to control and allocate virtual memory when memory is scarce:

- ▸ Transparent memory page sharing

- ▸ Balloon-driver or vmmemctl

- ▸ Hypervisor swap

> **ExamAlert**
>
> The VCP exam may use the term *balloon-driver* at times and at other times may use the official name of the technology, which is *vmmemctl*, so be prepared.

The following sections dig into each one of these concepts. You find out how they work and how they yield and release memory to satisfy an ESX/ESXi host in times of memory need.

Transparent Memory Page Sharing

Transparent memory page sharing detects when VMs are accessing the same memory pages, and instead of allocating different copies of the same memory space for each VM, it maps all the VMs that are accessing the same memory space to a single copy. The technique of transparent memory page sharing holds true as long as the VMs are just reading the same memory space—so in other words, as long as they are in Read-Only mode.

As soon as a VM needs to write to memory, the VMkernel creates a copy of this memory space specifically for this VM, which can then write to it. Transparent memory page sharing is enabled by default unless specifically disabled.

Consider an example of how this mechanism works. Say you have 10 VMs that are all running Windows Server 2003. Because they all run the same operating system, they are all accessing the same file and thus require the same memory pages. So these 10 VMs can access the same memory pages in Read-Only mode. As soon as any one of these VMs needs to write to memory, a private copy is then created for it.

Balloon-Driver (vmmemctl)

A *balloon-driver* (also referred to as *vmmemctl*) is a guest operating system device driver that is installed as part of the VMware Tools installation. Its function is simple: When an ESX system comes under physical memory strain, the VMkernel randomly selects a VM and inflates the device driver inside the guest operating system. This inflation forces the guest OS to swap rarely used pages to disk and release these pages to the vmmemctl driver. It then releases this acquired memory to the ESX system to ease its memory requirements. When the need for this memory ceases to exist, the device driver is deflated or stopped, and the memory is returned to the guest operating system.

This mechanism comes into play only when an ESX system is hungry for memory resources. It is also worth noting that VMs are completely unaware of this concept. To a VM, a device driver simply started inside the guest operating system and consumes all this memory.

You can configure the balloon-driver to consume up to 75% of the memory of the virtual machine. This is an advanced VMkernel setting named `Mem.CtlMaxPercent` and can be set between 0% and 75%. It is set to 65% by default. As you can see in Figure 9.1, to modify this setting, you need to go to the Configuration tab on your ESX/ESXi host, select Advanced Settings on the left pane, and click on Mem.

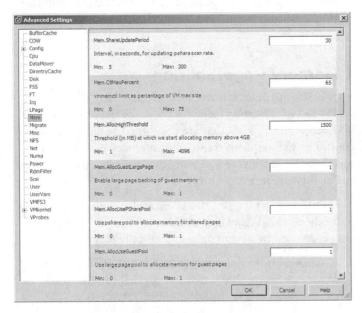

FIGURE 9.1   **Mem.CtlMaxPercent setting.**

Memory Compression

vSphere 4.1 introduced a fourth technique for memory management called Memory Compression. This technique is very cool and precedes Hypervisor Swapping. Since access to compressed memory is much faster than access to memory swapped to disk, this technique makes perfect sense as a step before swapping to disk. vSphere of course attempts to first use Transparent Memory Page Sharing (TPS). If that does not resolve the memory contention it reverts to Ballooning, and if that fails as well it initiates Memory Compression.

Memory Compression intercepts 4k memory pages that are destined to be swapped and compresses them by 50% or more, resulting in a 2k (or less) page, which is then stored in the VM's memory.

By default, the compression cache size is up to 10% of the VM's memory; however, you can change that setting from the Advanced Settings dialog box of an ESX/ESXi host, select Mem from the left pane and browse to Mem.MemZipMaxPct. You can also disable Memory Compression altogether from the same dialog box.

> **Note**
>
> If Memory Compression is not able to compress 4k memory pages by 50% or more, the 4k file is then swapped to disk.

Hypervisor Swap

Every virtual machine needs a swap file that is created when the VM is powered on and is deleted when the VM powers off. The swap file size is the difference between the VM's memory limit and its reservation. Unless otherwise specified, the swap file is located with the VM's boot disk.

When the hypervisor requires memory, the VM's memory pages are copied into the swap file to allow the VM to continue to function and then relinquish this memory to the hypervisor. This measure is a last resort in case the balloon-driver cannot allocate enough memory to satisfy the hypervisor's needs. As with any other system, when heavy paging occurs, the VM's performance suffers.

Because ballooning can consume only up to 75% of a VM's memory and because ballooning is set to 65% by default, the 10% difference would have to be allocated by the VMkernel swap. For example, in the event that an ESX/ESXi host becomes starved for memory resources and a VM's balloon-driver is inflated for 65% of its memory but the VMkernel has requested 75%, the remaining 10% is allocated by swap. You should note that swapping is less desirable than ballooning and causes a VM's performance to suffer, whereas ballooning has less of a performance strain on the VM. It is important to note that when the hypervisor swaps memory to disk, a significant performance penalty is noticeable.

> **Exam Alert**
>
> Although we don't expect the VCP exam to play the name game, note that VMware now references the VMkernel as the hypervisor. Thus it is important to pay attention and know that they are one and the same.

> **Note**
>
> If the hypervisor requests it, a VM's entire memory is written to the page file and released to the hypervisor. This happens only in times of extreme memory strain on the ESX/ESXi host.

Cram Quiz

Answer these questions. The answers follow the last question. If you cannot answer these questions correctly, consider reading the section again.

1. True or false: A virtual machine's swap file is deleted once the VM is powered off.

   ○ **A.** True

   ○ **B.** False

2. True or false: The balloon-driver, if inflated, is configured by default at 75% of the VM's memory.

   ○ **A.** True

   ○ **B.** False

3. What is the interval at which the VMkernel dynamically and constantly changes the vCPU's HECs?

   ○ **A.** 20 seconds

   ○ **B.** 20 milliseconds

   ○ **C.** 25 seconds

   ○ **D.** 25 milliseconds

4. How many physical CPUs are needed to support a virtual machine that is configured with four vCPUs? (Select all that apply.)

   ○ **A.** Single socket, quad core

   ○ **B.** Quad socket processor

   ○ **C.** Dual socket, single core

   ○ **D.** Single socket, dual core

5. On which physical processor does the Service Console always run?

   ○ **A.** CPU0

   ○ **B.** CPU1

   ○ **C.** CPU2

   ○ **D.** Distributes the load on multiple CPUs for redundancy

6. Which technology allows for the scheduling of multiple threads on the same CPU?

   ○ **A.** CPU affinity

   ○ **B.** CPU threading

   ○ **C.** Memmaker

   ○ **D.** None of the above

Cram Quiz Answers

1. **A**, True, is correct. A virtual machine's swap file is deleted when the VM is powered off and is re-created when the VM is powered on.

2. **B**, False, is correct. The balloon-driver is configured by default at 65% of the VM's memory and can be set to 75% as a maximum.

3. **B** is correct. The VMkernel dynamically and constantly changes the vCPU's HECs every 20 milliseconds; therefore, answers A, C, and D are incorrect.

4. **A** and **B** are correct. A virtual machine with four vCPUs requires four physical CPUs to be scheduled on; therefore, answers C and D are incorrect.

5. **A** is correct. The Service Console is always scheduled on physical CPU0 and never changes; therefore, answers B, C, and D are incorrect.

6. **D** is correct. The technology that allows for the scheduling of multiple threads on the same CPU is known as hyper-threading; therefore, answers A, B, and C are incorrect.

Monitoring Virtual Machines and Hosts

▶ **CPU**

▶ **Memory**

▶ **Disk**

▶ **Alarms**

Cram**Saver**

If you can correctly answer this question before going through this section, save time by skimming the Exam Alert in this section and then completing the Cram Quiz at the end of the section.

1. What is the key indicator that a virtual machine's vCPU is losing competition time for physical CPU scheduling?

   ○ **A.** CPU ready time

   ○ **B.** CPU time

   ○ **C.** Context switches

   ○ **D.** % CPU Scheduler

Answers

1. **A** is correct. The key indicator that a virtual machine is losing compete time for a physical CPU time slice is the CPU ready time; therefore, answers B, C, and D are incorrect.

Monitoring the resource usage of a virtual machine or a host is a critical first step in a troubleshooting process or if you are planning an expansion and need to know where your performance metrics stand as far as resources. The vSphere client offers you the Performance tab for both virtual machines and hosts; this tab allows you to view real-time or historical graphs for the following resources:

▶ CPU

▶ Memory

▶ Disk

▶ Network

Tip

To compare multiple VMs, you can tear off the performance charts of those VMs and arrange them side by side to make comparing them easier.

In the sections to follow, we cover those resources in greater detail and examine how you can gather the necessary performance metrics needed. Performance metrics are great to have for troubleshooting purposes, of course, but they are also useful in justifying additional hardware purchases or hardware upgrades.

CPU

The most important indicator that a VM is not getting enough time on the physical CPU is the CPU ready metric, which indicates that a vCPU is requesting a time slice on the physical CPU but cannot get scheduled fast enough. The vCPU is thereby queued, which results in poor performance. Figure 9.2 shows a vCPU's ready graph that is available only in real-time.

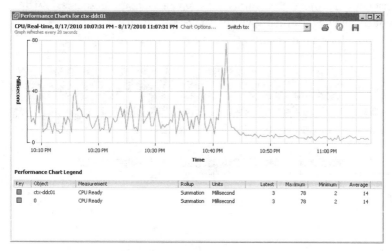

FIGURE 9.2   **CPU ready graph.**

The following conditions can affect the CPU ready time:

▶ **Overall CPU utilization:** This can affect CPU ready time because when the overall CPU utilization is high, other VMs are also competing for this resource, which drives up this counter.

▶ **Number of resource consumers:** When an ESX/ESXi host is running several VMs, it is more than likely that the VMkernel will start to queue the VMs' access times to the physical CPU as a result of the numerous simultaneous requests.

▶ **Load correlation:** This means that if a task being executed on the physical CPU initiates multiple other tasks or threads when it is completed, ready time is affected.

▶ **Number of vCPUs in a VM:** When multiple vCPUs are present in the VMs, they are scheduled at the same time on the physical CPUs or not at all. A four-vCPU VM requires four physical CPUs to be available for the schedule to be successful. In high ready times, this is challenging because all the CPUs must be free of contention to be scheduled.

Memory

You can monitor memory usage in the same manner as you would CPU usage. However, when a virtual machine is running out of memory, check the performance graph and monitor the amount of ballooning, which may be consuming memory. In this event, you can VMotion the VM to another host that is not experiencing memory constraints, or you can increase its shares, which would give it priority over other VMs. Figure 9.3 shows a VM's memory graph with the ballooning metric.

> ### Exam**Alert**
>
> vMotioning a VM does not reduce the amount of ballooned memory. Only power off does.

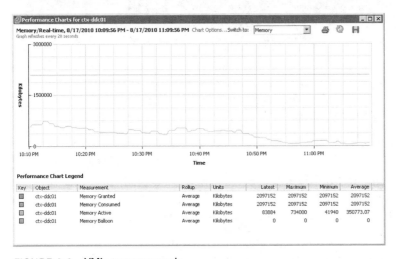

FIGURE 9.3   **VM's memory graph.**

Disk

Disk contention is a performance metric that many people often dismiss as a nonissue. Disk contention, however, can significantly degrade virtual machine performance. You can monitor disk saturation using the performance graph inside the VI client or using third-party tools. In the event that disk saturation is detected, you should move the VM's files to another storage device that is not having disk contention, change the path that leads to the storage device if that path is saturated, and then ensure that you are using a RAID level that is adequate for the application you have deployed.

> **Note**
>
> Keep in mind that the installation of the VMware Tools improves disk access, so make sure they are installed.

Network

Network bandwidth-intensive applications often require you to migrate the VMs to other physical NICs that are less utilized to maximize performance. You may also consider traffic shaping as another technique by which you can control network bandwidth. The use of the performance graphs or other third-party tools can help you detect high utilization of network bandwidth.

Monitoring with Alarms

Alarms are thresholds that you configure on either a host or a virtual machine. The alarm sends you a notification when a certain threshold has been reached. Alarms allow you to quickly respond to a potential problem and address it before it causes major problems.

When an alarm threshold is reached, the VI client displays a message. Because you typically are not monitoring or logged in all the time, you can configure options to notify you of this alarm. Figure 9.4 shows the Actions tab in Alarm Settings and the different methods by which you can configure the alarm to notify you. You can also configure it to perform a certain task when an alarm threshold is reached, such as run a script, send an email, or even use the Short Message Service (SMS).

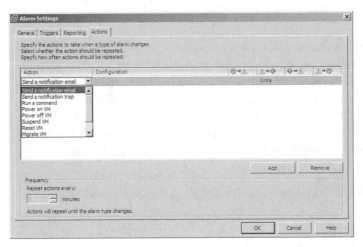

FIGURE 9.4   Alarm Actions tab.

After you have configured your alarms with the proper actions to perform, you should make sure that vCenter delivers these messages to you. If you chose to be notified by email when a certain threshold is reached, for example, you need to configure VC with the proper SMTP settings to route this email to you successfully. The same goes for SNMP traps. From within VC, click on Administration > vCenter Server Settings. As you can see in Figure 9.5, you can then click on the Mail to configure email delivery or SNMP to configure its settings

ExamAlert

If the SMTP server is reporting the alarm, you may never be notified because the server that is charged with delivering the notification is suffering from a warning. Situations like these are what necessitates that you have alternate means of notification delivery, such as a monitoring server, for example.

FIGURE 9.5   vCenter Management server configuration.

Cram Quiz

Answer this question. The answer follows. If you cannot answer this question correctly, consider reading the section again.

1. How can you reduce the amount of ballooning that occurs inside a VM?

   ○ **A.** vMotion to a different host

   ○ **B.** Reboot/Power Off

   ○ **C.** Restart VMware Tools Service

   ○ **D.** End Balloon-Driver Process

Cram Quiz Answer

1. **B** is correct. To reduce or eliminate a VM's ballooning, it would require the reboot or power off tasks. All other answers are incorrect.

CHAPTER 10

Backup and High Availability

What good is an environment without a good backup strategy? This chapter explores the different options by which you can back up your VMware Infrastructure. The chapter also explores VMware High Availability (HA) and the ability to sustain host failures and ensure that your critical virtual machines (VMs) can be restarted on other hosts that are online.

Backup Scenarios

▶ **Host Backup**

▶ **VMware Consolidated Backup (VCB)**

▶ **Data Recovery**

Cram Saver

If you can correctly answer this question before going through this section, save time by skimming the Exam Alerts in this section and then completing the Cram Quiz at the end of the section.

1. What are the two types of virtual machine backups? (Select all that apply.)

   ○ **A.** Differential

   ○ **B.** File-level

   ○ **C.** Shadow-copy

   ○ **D.** Image-level

Answers

1. **B** and **D** are correct. The two types of VM level backups are file-level and image-level backups; therefore, answers A and C are incorrect.

You should think of and treat backup strategies for VMs and their ESX/ESXi host the same way you would approach physical machines. The same best practices and methodologies apply. The only different scenario covered is VMware Consolidated Backup (VCB).

Virtual Machine Backup Options

As far as virtual machines are concerned, you can back them up using any of the following methods:

▶ Installing a backup agent inside the guest operating system. This is the same as when you install a backup agent inside a physical machine's guest operating system. You can then do file-level backups as frequently as your data changes or as frequently as your environment requires.

▶ Backing up the virtual machine files. Because a virtual machine is encapsulated inside regular files, you can back up or archive these files. When using this method, you can power off the VM and back up the files. Alternatively, if you need the VM to continue to be online, you can take a snapshot of it and back up the VMDK files.

When considering backup of virtual machine data, make sure that you have your application files stored on separate drives. This makes the process of backing up the data easier. This also concentrates the backup process on the data rather than the operating system files, which should be backed up infrequently because they do not change and you don't want to have to back them up repeatedly. The system drive should be backed up in the event that you want to restore the entire virtual machine to the state it was in when you made the backup. The point to keep in mind here is that you are backing up the system drive for the Registry and the application-specific files that are installed with the virtual machine.

Host Backup Options

The ESX/ESXi host is primarily the Service Console. Because the Service Console is used for command-line advanced options, its files rarely change and most of the configurations you make in your VMware Infrastructure are stored in the vCenter database. That being said, backing up the Service Console is not really worth the time and effort involved. You can easily reinstall ESX and make the changes rather than deal with executing a backup and restore operation of the Service Console.

However, if you want to back up your Service Console, you can do so using one of the following two methods:

▶ Install a backup agent inside the Service Console and back up the files accordingly. This would be the same traditional agent backup approach that you would take with any physical machine running any guest operating system.

▶ Use third-party software to create a complete image of the ESX server and then use this same third-party software to restore the entire image and return the state of the ESX/ESXi host to the point when you took the image originally.

ExamAlert

Pay attention to the host backup section because you are sure to get a question on this topic on the VCP exam.

VMware Consolidated Backup

VMware Consolidated Backup (VCB) is an alternative method of backing up and restoring virtual machines at the file level or image level. VCB runs on a

Windows server and makes a snapshot of the VM, and for file-level backups, it mounts the VMDK as a disk on the Windows backup server. Once the VMDK is mounted, you can see the contents of the VMDK appear under a specified directory on the VCB server. Now your file-level backup agent can access these files and write them to tape or any other backup destination.

When you want to make a full image backup, VCB also makes a snapshot but then copies the full VMDK as a file to a special backup LUN, which should be at least the size of the VMDK. After copying the VMDK to the LUN, the snapshot of the VM is released and your file-level backup agent can pick up the VMDK from the backup LUN.

To be able to do this, the VCB server has to have a direct connection to the LUNs on which the VMs reside. Keep in mind that VCB is not a backup product itself, but just a tool to help your traditional backup product access your VMs.

Consequently, you have taken the network out of the equation all the way to the backup server. Now, obviously, depending on what type of backup system you are using and how the backup server is connected to your backup robot, the network can remain out of the equation or can be used to move the files from the backup server to the backup tape library.

By using VCB, you have the following advantages:

- ▶ Because you are dealing with snapshot-level backups, there is no need for a backup window because no downtime is required to back up the VM. The VM is backed up while it is powered on.

- ▶ Backup load is moved away from the ESX/ESXi host because you are taking a snapshot and moving this snapshot to another location to be backed up directly by the VCB proxy server. By doing so, you offload all the processing requirements needed from the ESX/ESXi host to the backup server.

- ▶ The backup agent is optional. When using VCB, you take advantage of the VMware Tools that are installed inside the VM that allow for VCB to take place, thereby giving you the option to use the backup agent only if you want to restore directly to this virtual machine. Instead of restoring directly to a VM, you may opt to install a backup agent on a select few VMs and then restore any files to these VMs. At that point, you can copy the restored files to their final destination. This would save money and management of backup agents on multiple virtual machines.

When running VCB, you have full support for file-level backup of Microsoft Windows guest operating systems and image-level backups of any guest operating system.

Data Recovery

Data Recovery is a new backup and recovery tool for VMs feature that is introduced with vSphere 4, aimed at small to medium-sized companies. Data Recovery is a Linux-based appliance that can be imported into vCenter and controlled through a vSphere Client plug-in.

The Data Recovery appliance is an agentless backup to disk type solution. Your destination backup location can be to VMware VMFS Datastores on local disk, iSCSI, FC, or it can be on an NFS Datastore. You can even back up using Data Recovery to Windows Common Internet File System (CIFS) shares.

Tip

Destination Virtual Disks or RDMs would have to manually be added to the Data Recovery Appliance.

A single Data Recovery Appliance can support the following:

▶ Up to 100 VMs.

▶ Up to 100 backup jobs.

▶ Each backup job can have a maximum of one destination.

▶ Each VM configured in a backup job is backed up once every 24 hours.

Note

The configuration of the backup jobs is saved on the Data Recovery appliance. However, after the completion of a successful backup, a copy of the configuration is stored on the destination location as well. This allows for easier restore to a new appliance should the need arise.

How to Configure the Data Recovery Appliance

Setting up the Data Recovery Appliance is straightforward. After obtaining all the files necessary, follow these steps:

1. Deploy the Data Recovery OVF template to vCenter by going to File > Deploy OVF Template and following the wizard.

2. Configure the networking stack to allow for connectivity through the appliance's console.

3. Configure the appropriate time zone settings through the appliance's console.

4. Add destination storage to the appliance. To accomplish this, you would add a virtual disk to this appliance the same way you would any other VM by going to Edit Settings.

5. Install the Data Recovery plug-in for the vSphere Client.

Once you have installed and configured the appliance, you can access it via your vSphere client from the Home screen in the Solutions and Applications.

> **ExamAlert**
>
> The ESX/ESXi host that the appliance will be deployed on and the host that carries the VMs that will be backed up both need to be licensed for Data Recovery.

> **Tip**
>
> After you configure the networking settings of the appliance, you can access its web interface from a supported browser by pointing to its IP address. From there, you can configure many of the settings you can configure via console, such as the time zone.

Backup Process

Backing up VMs using the Data Recovery Appliance is easy and wizard-driven. Once you initiate the wizard, it leads you step by step to a successful backup job creation. The backup job wizard is capable of enumerating all objects in the vCenter inventory, which means you can back up any VM regardless of its logical grouping or location.

When you run the backup wizard, you are warned if

▶ You have selected more than 100 VMs for backup.

▶ If a selected VM is on a nonlicensed host.

To start the backup job wizard, point to the Data Recovery Appliance in vCenter and select the Backup tab. You can then either select New at the top right-hand corner or right-click anywhere and click New.

The backup wizard prompts you to

▶ Select the VM to back up or select certain components of a VM to back up, such as vdisks.

▶ Select the destination target from your available options.

▶ The Backup Window is next; specify the times that backup is allowed to run.

▶ Retention Policy settings are up next, as shown in Figure 10.1. This screen allows you to configure how long you retain data on the destination and how many backups to retain.

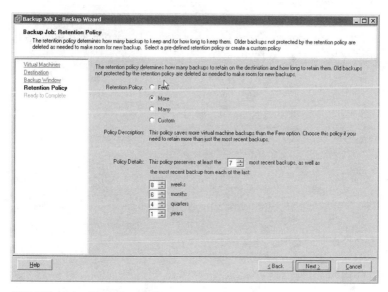

FIGURE 10.1 **Retention Policy.**

Restore VMs and Files

The restore process using the Data Recovery Appliance is just as easy as the backup process and is completely wizard driven. You can

- ► Restore a single file back to a VM (Windows and Linux support only).

- ► Restore a VM to a different host, datastore, or resource pool.

- ► Restore a VM due to deletion or corruption.

- ► Restore a VM to an earlier point in time.

- ► Restore a VM's virtual disks.

To initiate the restore wizard, find the Data Recovery Appliance in your vCenter inventory and click on the Restore tab. You can then click on the Restore link in the top right-hand corner. This initiates the restore wizard, which prompts you to select what to restore. Based on the guidelines we discussed earlier, you can select anything from a full VM restore all the way to a specific vdisk restore.

Now to restore a file back into a VM, additional software needs to be downloaded from the VMware website. You need to download the restore client for Windows or Linux. This restore client is then installed in the VM allowing you to mount a restore point from the Data Recovery Appliance and select the appropriate file for restore directly to the VM.

Cram Quiz

Answer these questions. The answers follow the last question. If you cannot answer these questions correctly, consider reading the section again.

1. True or false: It is a recommended and crucial task that you back up the Service Console to preserve the ESX/ESXi host configuration.

   ○ **A.** True

   ○ **B.** False

2. True or false: VMware Consolidated Backup supports file-level backup for all guest operating systems.

   ○ **A.** True

   ○ **B.** False

Cram Quiz Answers

1. **B**, False, is correct. Although backing up the Service Console is an option, it is really not required because most of the ESX/ESXi host configuration is stored in the vCenter database. The Service Console files rarely change, and those that do don't merit a backup. It is thereby easier to reinstall ESX than it is worth backing up the SC.

2. **B**, False, is correct. VMware Consolidated Backup supports only file-level backups on Windows-based systems and image-level backups for all guest operating systems.

High Availability

▶ **High Availability (HA)**

▶ **Admission Control**

▶ **Cluster-in-a-Box**

▶ **Cluster-Across-Boxes**

▶ **Physical-to-Virtual Cluster**

▶ **Host Isolation**

▶ **MSCS Clustering**

▶ **Fault Tolerance**

Cram**Saver**

If you can correctly answer this question before going through this section, save time by skimming the Exam Alerts in this section and then completing the Cram Quiz at the end of the section.

1. What are the two VMware HA clusterwide settings that you can configure? (Select all that apply.)

   ○ **A.** Host Failures

   ○ **B.** DRS

   ○ **C.** Admission Control

   ○ **D.** Fault Tolerance

2. Which outgoing TCP and UDP ports are used for heartbeats and state synchronization? (Choose all that apply.)

   ○ **A.** TCP 2150–2250

   ○ **B.** UDP 2150–2250

   ○ **C.** TCP 2050–2250

   ○ **D.** UDP 2050–2250

Answers

1. **A** and **C** are correct. The two settings that you can configure clusterwide for VMware HA are Host Failures and Admission Control; therefore, answers B and D are incorrect.

2. **C** and **D** are correct. The outgoing TCP and UDP ports are 2050 through 2250; therefore, answers A and B are incorrect.

VMware *High Availability (HA)* deals primarily with ESX/ESXi host failure and what happens to the virtual machines that are running on this host. HA can also monitor and restart a VM by checking whether the VMware Tools are still running. When an ESX/ESXi host fails for any reason, all the running VMs also fail. VMware HA ensures that the VMs from the failed host are capable of being restarted on other ESX/ESXi hosts.

Many people mistakenly confuse VMware HA with fault tolerance. VMware HA is not fault tolerant in that if a host fails, the VMs on it also fail. HA deals only with restarting those VMs on other ESX/ESXi hosts with enough resources. Fault tolerance, on the other hand, provides uninterruptible access to resources in the event of a host failure.

> ### Exam**Alert**
>
> The VCP exam is sure to challenge your knowledge on the difference between HA and fault tolerance. Make sure you have a clear understanding of the difference.

VMware HA maintains a communication channel with all the other ESX/ESXi hosts that are members of the same cluster by using a heartbeat that it sends out every 1 second in vSphere 4.0 or every 10 seconds in vSphere 4.1 by default. When an ESX server misses a heartbeat, the other hosts wait 15 seconds for the other host to respond again. After 15 seconds, the cluster initiates the restart of the VMs on the failing ESX/ESXi host on the remaining ESX/ESXi hosts in the cluster. VMware HA also constantly monitors the ESX/ESXi hosts that are members of the cluster and ensures that resources are always available to satisfy requirements in the event of a host failure.

> ### Tip
>
> VMware HA is a reactive system, which means it kicks in to react to a problem; in this case, the problem is a failed host. A reactive system would be perfect if combined with a proactive system, and this is exactly what you get if you enabled VMware HA and VMware DRS on the same cluster. DRS is a proactive system that is constantly busy trying to load-balance resources on ESX/ESXi hosts.

Virtual Machine Failure Monitoring

Virtual Machine Failure Monitoring is technology that is disabled by default. Its function is to monitor virtual machines, which it queries every 20 seconds via a heartbeat. It does this by using the VMware Tools that are installed inside the VM. When a VM misses a heartbeat, VMware HA deems this VM as failed and attempts to reset it. Think of Virtual Machine Failure Monitoring as sort of High Availability for VMs.

> **Note**
>
> Virtual Machine Failure Monitoring can detect whether a virtual machine was manually powered off, suspended, or migrated, and thereby does not attempt to restart it.

HA Configuration Prerequisites

HA requires the following configuration prerequisites before it can function properly:

- ▶ **vCenter:** Because VMware HA is an enterprise-class feature, it requires vCenter before it can be enabled.

- ▶ **DNS resolution:** All ESX/ESXi hosts that are members of the HA cluster must be able to resolve one another using DNS.

- ▶ **Access to shared storage:** All hosts in the HA cluster must have access and visibility to the same shared storage; otherwise, they would have no access to the VMs.

- ▶ **Access to same network:** All ESX/ESXi hosts must have the same networks configured on all hosts so that when a VM is restarted on any host, it again has access to the correct network.

Service Console Redundancy

Recommended practice dictates that the Service Console have redundancy. VMware HA complains and issues a warning if it detects that the Service Console is configured on a vSwitch with only one vmnic. As Figure 10.2 shows, you can configure Service Console redundancy in one of two ways:

- ▶ Create two Service Console port groups, each on a different vSwitch.

- ▶ Assign two physical network interface cards (NICs) in the form of a NIC team to the Service Console vSwitch.

Service Console NIC Team Redundancy

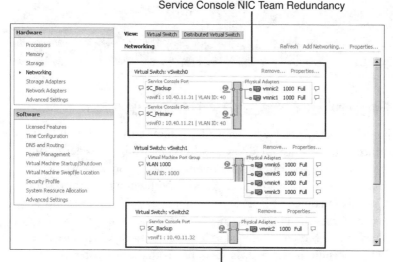

Service Console second separate vSwitch Redundancy

FIGURE 10.2   **Service Console redundancy.**

In both cases, you need to configure the entire IP stack with IP address, subnet, and gateway. The Service Console vSwitches are used for heartbeats and state synchronization and use the following ports:

- ▶ Incoming TCP port 8042

- ▶ Incoming UDP port 8045

- ▶ Outgoing TCP port 2050

- ▶ Outgoing UDP port 2250

- ▶ Incoming TCP port 8042–8045

- ▶ Incoming UDP port 8042–8045

- ▶ Outgoing TCP port 2050–2250

- ▶ Outgoing UDP port 2050–2250

Failure to configure SC redundancy results in a warning message when you enable HA. So, to avoid seeing this error message and to adhere to best practice, configure the SC to be redundant.

ExamAlert

Service Console redundancy is an important topic and will more than likely be one of the questions on the exam.

Host Failover Capacity Planning

When configuring HA, you have to manually configure the maximum host failure tolerance. This is a task that you should thoughtfully consider during the hardware sizing and planning phase of your deployment. This would assume that you have built your ESX/ESXi hosts with enough resources to run more VMs than planned to be able to accommodate HA. For example, in Figure 10.3, notice that the HA cluster has four ESX hosts and that all four of these hosts have enough capacity to run at least three more VMs. Because they are all already running three VMs, that means that this cluster can afford the loss of two ESX/ESXi hosts because the remaining two ESX/ESXi hosts can power on the six failed VMs with no problem if failure occurs.

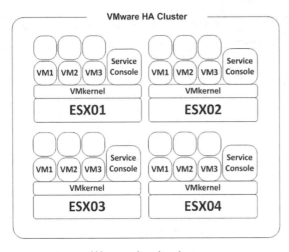

FIGURE 10.3   HA capacity planning.

During the configuration phase of the HA cluster, you are presented with a screen similar to that shown in Figure 10.4 that prompts you to define two clusterwide configurations as follows:

▸ **Host Monitoring Status:**

▸ **Enable Host Monitoring:** This setting enables you to control whether the HA cluster should monitor the hosts for a heartbeat.

This is the cluster's way of determining whether a host is still active. In some cases, when you are running maintenance tasks on ESX/ESXi hosts, it might be desirable to disable this option to avoid isolating a host.

▶ **Admission Control:**

   ▶ **Enable: Do not power on VMs that violate availability constraints:** Selecting this option indicates that if no resources are available to satisfy a VM, it should not be powered on.

   ▶ **Disable: Power on VMs that violate availability constraints:** Selecting this option indicates that you should power on a VM even if you have to overcommit resources.

▶ **Admission Control Policy:**

   ▶ **Host failures cluster tolerates:** This setting enables you to configure how many host failures you want to tolerate. The allowed settings are 1 through 4.

   ▶ **Percentage of cluster resources reserved as failover spare capacity:** Selecting this option indicates that you are reserving a percentage of the total cluster resources in spare for failover. In a four-host cluster, a 25% reservation indicates that you are setting aside a full host for failover. If you want to set aside fewer, you can choose 10% of the cluster resources instead.

   ▶ **Specify a failover host:** Selecting this option indicates that you are selecting a particular host as the failover host in the cluster. This might be the case if you have a spare host or have a particular host that has significantly more compute and memory resources available.

ExamAlert

The VCP exam may present you with a scenario and ask you to identify or configure capacity for HA. Make sure you are comfortable with capacity planning.

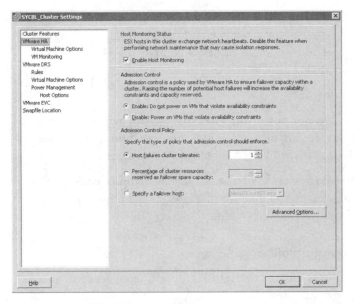

FIGURE 10.4   **HA clusterwide policies.**

Host Isolation

A network phenomenon known as a *split-brain* occurs when the ESX/ESXi host has stopped receiving a heartbeat from the rest of the cluster. The heartbeat is queried for every 1 second in vSphere 4.0 or 10 seconds in vSphere 4.1. If a response is not received, the cluster thinks the ESX/ESXi host has failed. When this occurs, the ESX/ESXi host has lost its network connectivity on its management interface. The host might still be up and running and the VMs might not even be affected considering they might be using a different network interface that has not been affected. However, vSphere needs to take action when this happens because it believes a host has failed. For that matter, the host isolation response was created. Host isolation response is HA's way of dealing with an ESX/ESXi host that has lost its network connection.

You can control what happens to VMs in the event of a host isolation. To get to the VM Isolation Response screen, right-click the cluster in question and click on Edit Settings. You can then click Virtual Machine Options under the VMware HA banner in the left pane. You can control options clusterwide by setting the host isolation response option accordingly. This is applied to all the VMs on the affected host. That being said, you can always override the cluster settings by defining a different response at the VM level.

As shown in Figure 10.5, your Isolation Response options are as follows:

▶ **Leave Powered On:** As the label implies, this setting means that in the event of host isolation, the VM remains powered on.

▶ **Power Off:** This setting defines that in the event of an isolation, the VM is powered off. This is a hard power off.

▶ **Shut down:** This setting defines that in the event of an isolation, the VM is shut down gracefully using VMware Tools. If this task is not successfully completed within five minutes, a power off is immediately executed. If VMware Tools is not installed, a power off is executed instead.

▶ **Use Cluster Setting:** This setting forwards the task to the clusterwide setting defined in the window shown previously in Figure 10.5.

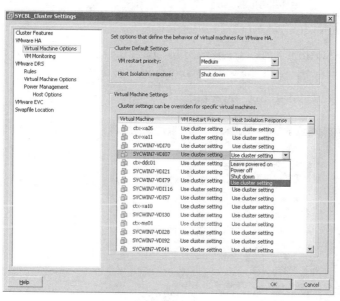

FIGURE 10.5 **VM-specific isolation policy.**

In the event of an isolation, this does not necessarily mean that the host is down. Because the VMs might be configured with different physical NICs and connected to different networks, they might continue to function properly; you therefore have to consider this when setting the priority for isolation. When a host is isolated, this simply means that its Service Console cannot communicate with the rest of the ESX/ESXi hosts in the cluster.

Virtual Machine Recovery Priority

Should your HA cluster not be able to accommodate all the VMs in the event of a failure, you have the ability to prioritize on VMs. The priorities dictate which VMs are restarted first and which VMs are not that important in the event of an emergency. These options are configured on the same screen as the Isolation Response covered in the preceding section. You can configure cluster-wide settings that will be applied to all VMs on the affected host, or you can override the cluster settings by configuring an override at the VM level.

As you can see in Figure 10.6, you can set a VM's restart priority to one of the following:

- **High:** VMs with a high priority are restarted first.
- **Medium:** This is the default setting.
- **Low:** VMs with a low priority are restarted last.
- **Use Cluster Setting:** VMs are restarted based on the setting defined at the cluster level defined in the window shown in Figure 10.6.
- **Disabled:** The VM does not power on.

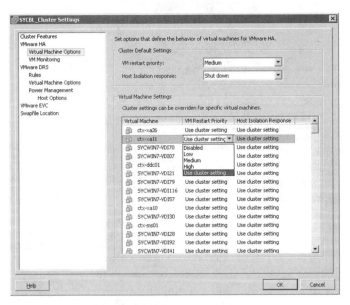

FIGURE 10.6   **VM restart priority.**

The priority should be set based on the importance of the VMs. In other words, you might want to restart domain controllers and not restart print servers. The higher priority virtual machines are restarted first. VMs that can tolerate remaining powered off in the event of an emergency should be configured to remain powered off to conserve resources.

MSCS Clustering

The main purpose of a cluster is to ensure that critical systems remain online at any cost and at all times. Similar to physical machines that can be clustered, virtual machines can also be clustered with ESX using three different scenarios:

▶ **Cluster-in-a-box:** In this scenario, all the VMs that are part of the cluster reside on the same ESX/ESXi host. As you might have guessed, this immediately creates a single point of failure: the ESX/ESXi host. As far as shared storage is concerned, you can use virtual disks as shared storage in this scenario, or you can use Raw Device Mapping (RDM) in virtual compatibility mode.

▶ **Cluster-across-boxes:** In this scenario, the cluster nodes (VMs that are members of the cluster) reside on multiple ESX/ESXi hosts, whereby each of the nodes that make up the cluster can access the same storage so that if one VM fails, the other can continue to function and access the same data. This scenario creates an ideal cluster environment by eliminating a single point of failure. Shared storage is a prerequisite in this and must reside on Fiber Channel SAN, You also must use an RDM in Physical or Virtual Compatibility Mode as virtual disks are not a supported configuration for shared storage. Whereby each of the nodes that make up the cluster can access the same storage so that if one VM fails, the other can continue to function and access the same data.

▶ **Physical-to-virtual cluster:** In this scenario, one member of the cluster is a virtual machine, whereas the other member is a physical machine. Shared storage is a prerequisite in this scenario and must be configured as an RDM in Physical Compatibility Mode.

> **Tip**
>
> When configuring a cluster-across-boxes, it is highly recommended that you create an anti-affinity rule that always separates the VMs that are part of the cluster so that DRS never vMotions them to the same ESX/ESXi host, thereby creating a single point of failure scenario.

Whenever you are designing a clustering solution you need to address the issue of shared storage, which would allow multiple hosts or VMs access to the same data. vSphere offers several methods by which you can provision shared storage as follows:

▸ **Virtual disks:** You can use a virtual disk as a shared storage area only if you are doing clustering in a box—in other words, only if both VMs reside on the same ESX/ESXi host.

▸ **RDM in Physical Compatibility Mode:** This mode enables you to attach a physical LUN directly into a VM or physical machine. This mode prevents you from using functionality such as snapshots and is ideally used when one member of the cluster is a physical machine while the other is a VM.

▸ **RDM in Virtual Compatibility Mode:** This mode enables you to attach a physical LUN directly into a VM or physical machine. This mode gives you all the benefits of virtual disks running on VMFS including snapshots and advanced file locking. The disk is accessed via the hypervisor and is ideal when configuring a cluster-across-boxes scenario where you need to give both VMs access to shared storage.

At the time of this writing, the only VMware-supported clustering service is Microsoft Clustering Services (MSCS). You can consult the VMware white paper "Setup for Failover Clustering and Microsoft Cluster Service" on the topic located at http://www.vmware.com/pdf/vsphere4/r40/vsp_40_mscs.pdf.

ExamAlert

Because there are probably many third-party software vendors that advertise support for clustering inside ESX VMs, it is likely that the VCP exam will challenge your knowledge on the official VMware stand on supported clustering services with VMs.

VMware Fault Tolerance

VMware Fault Tolerance (FT) is another form of VM clustering developed by VMware for systems that require extreme uptime. One of the most compelling features of FT is its ease of setup. FT is simply a check box that can be enabled. Compared to traditional clustering that requires specific configurations and in some instances cabling, FT is simple but powerful.

How Does It Work?

When protecting VMs with FT, a secondary VM is created in lockstep of the protected VM, the first VM. FT works by simultaneously writing to the first

VM and the second VM at the same time. Every task is written twice. If you click on the Start menu on the first VM, the Start menu on the second VM will also be clicked. The power of FT is its capability to keep both VMs in sync.

If the protected VM should go down for any reason, the secondary VM immediately takes its place, seizing its identity and its IP address, continuing to service users without an interruption. The newly promoted protected VM then creates a secondary for itself on another host and the cycle restarts.

To clarify, let's see an example. If you wanted to protect an Exchange server, you could enable FT. If for any reason the ESX/ESXi host that is carrying the protected VM fails, the secondary VM kicks in and assumes its duties without an interruption in service.

> **ExamAlert**
>
> If the initially protected VM should recover from its failure, it would not assume its previous role or identity; it would simply show up in the inventory as a VM.

> **Note**
>
> VMware FT protects the VM from failure but not the guest operating system or any application running on it. If the primary VM should blue screen, the secondary will blue screen as well. If the primary has an application error, so will the secondary.

Table 10.1 outlines the different High Availability and clustering technologies that you have access to with vSphere and highlights limitations of each.

TABLE 10.1   **vSphere HA and Clustering Support Matrix**

	HA	FT	MSCS
Availability Type	High Availability	Fault Tolerance	Fault Tolerance
Downtime	Some	None	Some
Supported OS	All supported OS	All supported OS	Only Microsoft supported OS
Supported Hardware	All supported ESX hardware	All supported ESX hardware with CPUs that support FT	Hardware supported by Microsoft
Use Cases	HA for all VMs	FT for critical VMs	FT for critical applications

Fault Tolerance Requirements

Fault Tolerance is no different from any other enterprise feature in that it requires certain prerequisites to be met before the technology can function properly and efficiently. These requirements are outlined in the following list and broken down into the different categories that require specific minimum requirements:

▸ **Host Requirements:**

  ▸ FT-compatible CPU. Check this VMware KB article for more information: http://kb.vmware.com/kb/1008027.

  ▸ Hardware virtualization must be enabled in the bios.

  ▸ Host's CPU clock speeds must be within 400 MHz of each other.

▸ **VM Requirements:**

  ▸ VMs must reside on supported shared storage (FC, iSCSI & NFS).

  ▸ VMs must run a supported OS. Check out the supported guest OS http://kb.vmware.com/kb/1008027.

  ▸ VMs must be stored in either a VMDK or a virtual RDM.

  ▸ VMs cannot have thinly provisioned VMDK and must be using an Eagerzeroedthick virtual disk.

  ▸ VMs cannot have more than 1 vCPU configured.

▸ **Cluster Requirements:**

  ▸ All ESX/ESXi hosts must be same version and same patch level.

  ▸ All ESX/ESXi hosts must have access to the VM datastores and networks.

  ▸ VMware HA must be enabled on the cluster.

  ▸ Each host must have a vMotion and FT Logging NIC configured.

  ▸ Host certificate checking must also be enabled.

Tip

It is highly advisable that in addition to checking processor compatibility with FT, you check your server's make and model compatibility with FT against the VMware Hardware Compatibility List (HCL) here: http://www.vmware.com/resources/compatibility/search.php.

While FT is a great clustering solution, it is important to note that it also has certain limitations. For example, FT VMs cannot be snapshotted, and they cannot be Storage vMotioned. As a matter of fact, these VMs will automatically be flagged DRS-Disabled and will not participate in any dynamic resource load balancing.

How To Enable FT

Enabling FT is not difficult, but it does involve configuring a few different settings. The following settings need to be properly configured for FT to work:

- ▶ **Enable Host Certificate Checking:** To enable this setting, log on to your vCenter server and click on Administration from the File menu and click on vCenter Server Settings. In the left pane, click SSL Settings and check the vCenter Requires Verified Host SSL Certificates box.

- ▶ **Configure Host Networking:** The networking configuration for FT is easy and follows the same steps and procedures as vMotion, except instead of checking the vMotion box, check the Fault Tolerance Logging box as shown in Figure 10.7.

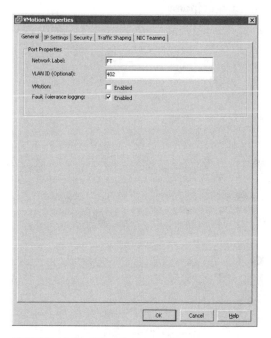

FIGURE 10.7   **FT port group settings.**

▸ **Turning FT On and Off:** Once you have met the preceding requirements, you can now turn FT on and off for VMs. This process is also straightforward: Find the VM you want to protect, right-click it, and select Fault Tolerance > Turn On Fault Tolerance.

Exam**Alert**

FT is an HA technology; therefore, the proper configuration of a VMware HA cluster is an imperative prerequisite for FT.

Note

You cannot turn FT On or Off from the secondary VM. It can only be done on the primary VM.

While FT is a first generation clustering technology, it works impressively well and simplifies overcomplicated traditional methods of building, configuring, and maintaining clusters. FT is an impressive technology for an uptime standpoint and from a seamless failover standpoint.

Cram Quiz

Answer these questions. The answers follow the last question. If you cannot answer these questions correctly, consider reading the section again.

1. When does the phenomenon of split-brain occur?

   ○ **A.** When ESX has lost access to its shared storage

   ○ **B.** When ESX has stopped receiving a heartbeat from its VMs

   ○ **C.** When ESX has stopped receiving a heartbeat from the other nodes in the cluster

   ○ **D.** When ESX cannot resolve DNS

2. Which incoming TCP and UDP ports are used for heartbeats and state synchronization? (Choose all that apply.)

   ○ **A.** TCP 8042–8045

   ○ **B.** UDP 8042–8045

   ○ **C.** TCP 8012–8015

   ○ **D.** UDP 8012–8015

3. How often does an ESX/ESXi host that is part of an HA cluster send out a heartbeat to the rest of the hosts in the same cluster? (Choose all that apply.)

   ○ **A.** 1 second

   ○ **B.** 15,000 milliseconds

   ○ **C.** 5 seconds

   ○ **D.** 20 milliseconds

4. True or false: VMware HA is a fault-tolerance system that allows a VM to have zero downtime in the event that its parent host should fail.

   ○ **A.** True

   ○ **B.** False

5. Which of the following is not a supported VM cluster in ESX?

   ○ **A.** Cluster-in-a-box

   ○ **B.** Cluster-across-boxes

   ○ **C.** ESX-host-cluster

   ○ **D.** Physical-to-virtual cluster

Cram Quiz Answers

1. **C** is correct. This phenomenon occurs when an ESX/ESXi host stops receiving a heartbeat from other members of the HA cluster, and it cannot ping its SC gateway address; therefore, answers A, B, and D are incorrect.

2. **A** and **B** are correct. The incoming TCP and UDP ports are 8042 through 8045; therefore, answers C and D are incorrect.

3. **A** is correct. ESX/ESXi 4.1 hosts that are members of the same HA cluster inform each other that they are still alive via a heartbeat that they broadcast every 1 second; therefore, answers B, C and D are incorrect.

4. **B**, False, is correct. VMware HA is not a fault-tolerance system, and consequently, in the event of a host failure, the VMs running on that host also fail. However, FT can be enabled as part of an HA cluster to extend "never fail" capabilities to VMs in the event that their host should fail. HA natively, however, does not support this feature; it would have to be enabled and configured.

5. **C** is correct. There is no such thing as an ESX-host-cluster other than the vCenter features of DRS and HA; therefore, answers A, B, and D are incorrect.

VCP4 Practice Exam

Hints and Pointers

Other than years of hands-on experience, the best way to prepare for the VMware VCP-410 test is to take practice (or sample) exams. VMware also requires all VCP candidates to take an authorized, instructor-led course leading up to the exam.

It is critical that you learn to approach VMware's certification tests thinking the way VMware wants you to. If you have taken several certification tests from other vendors, you may have a tendency to answer the way other vendors deem correct. That might or might not be correct on a VMware exam. Therefore, take this practice exam and start thinking like a VMware Certified Professional.

This book contains this one printed practice exam in addition to the practice questions provided within each chapter. You can find the answers and explanations to these questions following this practice exam. These practice questions are simply that—practice questions to get you ready for the form, fashion, and types of questions you will encounter on the exam. None are live exam questions.

Electronic VCP4 Practice Exam on CD

A separate practice exam is on the CD that comes with the printed version of this book. It contains 75 new questions. It can grade your performance and allow you to review the questions you missed. You can also customize it to test you on specific exam topics.

After you go through these practice questions a few times, you should have a good idea of what topics you need to brush up on. Other practice tests are also on the market, which may or may not help you. The purpose of the practice questions in this book is to reinforce important, testable concepts, facts, and objectives. The answers and explanations should guide you in filling in voids in your current knowledge base. By all means, supplement your study using the content and Exam Alerts in this book with a thorough review of the VMware Authorized Courseware and the online documents available on the VMware website.

All the questions are single-answer or multiple-answer multiple-choice questions. As you prepare, you should get at least 85% of the answers correct before moving on. Remember, you can, with proper preparation, successfully pass the VCP-410 exam. And this *Exam Cram* will help you.

I encourage you, as you prepare, to check the following websites for updates to the exam and the exam process:

▶ **FAQ:** http://mylearn.vmware.com/portals/certification/faqs.cfm?ui=www#1871

▶ **VCP Certification Page:** http://mylearn1.vmware.com/mgrReg/plan.cfm?plan=12457&ui=www

▶ **VCP Exam Blue Print (Login required):** http://mylearn1.vmware.com/mgrReg/register.cfm?course=70780&user=0&operator=0&pwd=&order=0&mL_method=register&rMethod=register&ui=www_cert&token=none

All the best in your journey to the VCP!

Exam Questions

1. You are considering the vSphere 4 suite as a virtualization solution for your grow-ing enterprise. You are mainly interested in a feature that lets you move a virtual machine from one server to another without having to power it off. Which feature in the vSphere 4 suite interests you?

   ○ **A.** DRS

   ○ **B.** HA

   ○ **C.** vMotion

   ○ **D.** VCB

2. Which of the following vCenter tasks does a virtual machine user have permis-sions to do by default?

   ○ **A.** Create a task

   ○ **B.** Create a virtual machine

   ○ **C.** Add a new disk

   ○ **D.** Remove a disk

3. You want to create an HA cluster using vSphere 4. Which of the following is a requirement to accomplish this?

   ○ **A.** DNS name resolution must be configured for all hosts in an HA cluster.

   ○ **B.** All hosts in an HA cluster must have identical DNS hostnames.

   ○ **C.** All hosts in an HA cluster must have identical IP addresses.

   ○ **D.** All hosts in an HA cluster must be able to resolve hostnames using IP addresses.

4. Which of the following services are provided by the Service Console? (Choose two.)

   ○ **A.** VIC

   ○ **B.** Web Server

   ○ **C.** Firewall

   ○ **D.** CPU Scheduling

5. You want to deploy vCenter in your enterprise. Which is considered a minimum requirement for successfully accomplishing this?

   ○ **A.** 1GB RAM

   ○ **B.** 256MB disk space

   ○ **C.** 10/100 network adapter

   ○ **D.** RHEL 3 Update 6

6. You are configuring your Service Console firewall. Which port controls transmissions from the iSCSI client?

   ○ **A.** 22

   ○ **B.** 902

   ○ **C.** 8000

   ○ **D.** 3260

7. While configuring the Service Console firewall, you notice that port 27000 is open. What does that control?

   ○ **A.** SSH client

   ○ **B.** HTTP transmissions

   ○ **C.** Transmissions from the ESX Server to the License Server

   ○ **D.** Remote Console traffic

8. Which of the following is a limitation of virtual networking on an ESX/ESXi 4.1 host?

   ○ **A.** 512 port groups per standard vSwitch

   ○ **B.** 64 Standard vSwitches

   ○ **C.** 2048 ports per Standard vSwitch

   ○ **D.** 512 ports per Standard vSwitch

9. You are installing ESX 4.1; what is the default size assigned to the /BOOT partition?

   ○ **A.** 5GB

   ○ **B.** 544MB

   ○ **C.** 1100MB

   ○ **D.** 2GB

10. You want to deploy a VMware Consolidated Backup solution on your network. Which of the following are true statements of VCB? (Choose three.)

   ○ **A.** Entire virtual machines can be backed up using VCB.

   ○ **B.** Entire virtual machines can be backed up only using a third-party backup solution.

   ○ **C.** A single VMDK can be backed up using VCB.

   ○ **D.** A single VMDK can be backed up using only a third-party backup solution.

   ○ **E.** Single guest files can be backed up using VCB.

   ○ **F.** Single guest files can be backed up only using a third-party backup solution.

11. Which of the following is considered an ESX/ESXi Server feature in the vSphere 4 suite?

- ○ **A.** vMotion
- ○ **B.** Virtual SMP
- ○ **C.** HA
- ○ **D.** DRS

12. Which of the following are ways of licensing an ESX/ESXi 4 host? (Choose two.)

- ○ **A.** Server based
- ○ **B.** Network based
- ○ **C.** Directory based
- ○ **D.** Host based

13. What are the two ways that a vSphere 4 license key is constructed?

- ○ **A.** Per seat
- ○ **B.** Per server
- ○ **C.** Per processor
- ○ **D.** Per instance

14. Your vSphere 4 enterprise environment is using a centralized License Server for backward compatibility. You have three ESX/ESXi 3.5 hosts. The License Server fails. How long a grace period is available during which all hosts will continue to function without interruption?

- ○ **A.** 10 days
- ○ **B.** 14 days
- ○ **C.** 60 days
- ○ **D.** 90 days

15. You have installed a single instance of vCenter in your enterprise. According to VMware, what is the maximum number of ESX/ESXi 4.1 hosts you can manage with this configuration?

- ○ **A.** 100
- ○ **B.** 200
- ○ **C.** 1000
- ○ **D.** 2000
- ○ **E.** 10,000

16. Your vSphere 4 enterprise environment uses a centralized License Server. You have three ESX/ESXi 3.5 hosts. The License Server fails and you are not able to restore it within the default period allowed. Which features are available after this default period? (Choose two.)

   ○ **A.** vMotion a virtual machine between two hosts

   ○ **B.** Power on a virtual machine

   ○ **C.** Turning on an ESX/ESXi 3.5 host

   ○ **D.** Deleting a virtual machine

17. In vCenter, you are configuring a new virtual machine CPU usage alarm. On the Triggers tab, what are the two possible conditions that this trigger type can have?

   ○ **A.** Is Above

   ○ **B.** Is Below

   ○ **C.** Is Equal To

   ○ **D.** Is Not Equal To

18. In vCenter, you are configuring a new alarm. What variables can you configure on the Triggers tab? (Choose two.)

   ○ **A.** Warning

   ○ **B.** Tolerance

   ○ **C.** Frequency

   ○ **D.** Alert

19. You are configuring an ESX/ESXi 4 host alarm in vCenter. What are two configurable actions that can occur? (Choose two.)

   ○ **A.** Suspend the host

   ○ **B.** Send an email

   ○ **C.** Reset the host

   ○ **D.** Run script

20. You have opted to deploy a virtualization solution in your enterprise using the vSphere 4 suite. Which product do you need to install if you want to connect to a vCenter Server or an ESX/ESXi host from a Windows workstation?

   ○ **A.** HA

   ○ **B.** VCB

   ○ **C.** vMotion

   ○ **D.** vSphere Client

21. Which of the following is not a built-in role found in the Service Console and in vCenter?

- ○ **A.** Read-Write
- ○ **B.** Administrator
- ○ **C.** No Access
- ○ **D.** Read-Only

22. What is the maximum number of ESX/ESXi 4 hosts that can be present in a cluster?

- ○ **A.** 14
- ○ **B.** 24
- ○ **C.** 28
- ○ **D.** 32

23. You want to monitor one of your ESX/ESXi 4 nodes in your vSphere 4 environment. You decide to create an alarm. When you try to configure the alarm, you can select the type of alarm you want to create. Which of the following is an available option on the General tab?

- ○ **A.** Monitor a Cluster
- ○ **B.** Monitor a Server
- ○ **C.** Monitor a Network
- ○ **D.** Monitor a Host

24. Which of the following statements correctly describes a resource pool in a vSphere 4 environment?

- ○ **A.** A container created in Hosts and Clusters view is used to limit the host CPU and memory utilization for a group of virtual machines.
- ○ **B.** A container created in Hosts and Clusters view is used to limit the disk space allocated for a group of virtual machines.
- ○ **C.** A container created in Hosts and Clusters view is used to limit the disk space allocated for a group of hosts.
- ○ **D.** A container created in Hosts and Clusters view is used to allocate throughput for a group of hosts.

25. Which of the following are attributes of a resource pool? (Choose two.)

- ○ **A.** Sessions
- ○ **B.** Throughput
- ○ **C.** Shares
- ○ **D.** Reservations

26. You have added your ESX 4 host to vCenter. What Service Console account is created when you do this, so that VirtualCenter can accomplish tasks on the ESX Server?

- ○ **A.** vpxuser
- ○ **B.** root
- ○ **C.** Administrator
- ○ **D.** VirtualMachineAdministrator

27. You have given Alex sufficient permissions to administer the ESX/ESXi 4 host. You want her to be able to manage all virtual machines on the host except for the Windows Vista machine. You do not want her to have any permission to this VM. What is the easiest way to accomplish this?

- ○ **A.** Delete her account.
- ○ **B.** Rename her account.
- ○ **C.** Configure an IRF.
- ○ **D.** Assign her the No Access Role at the Vista VM.

28. You want to connect to the vCenter Web Access interface. Which of the following can you use to accomplish this?

- ○ **A.** IE 6.0
- ○ **B.** Firefox 1.0.3
- ○ **C.** Netscape Navigator 6.0
- ○ **D.** Opera 8.0

29. Which edition of vSphere 4 gives you access to the vNetwork Distributed Switch feature?

- ○ **A.** Essentials Plus
- ○ **B.** Advanced
- ○ **C.** Standard
- ○ **D.** Enterprise and Enterprise Plus
- ○ **E.** Enterprise Plus

30. Which authentication protocol is used by iSCSI in a vSphere 4 environment?

- ○ **A.** IPSEC
- ○ **B.** PAP
- ○ **C.** CHAP
- ○ **D.** MSCHAPv2

31. Your CIO has informed you that you will be introducing the vSphere 4 product suite into your enterprise. Which product in the vSphere 4 suite provides the virtualization layer on which virtual machines run?

   ○ **A.** DRS
   ○ **B.** ESX/ESXi 4
   ○ **C.** VC
   ○ **D.** SMP

32. Which of the following is a correct representation of an iSCSI Target ID using the following data:

   Date=August 2008

   Domain=pearson.com

   Alternate Name=VM1A

   Host Name=PracticeTest

   ○ **A.** iqn.2008-08.com.pearson:VM1A
   ○ **B.** iqn.pearson.com.VM1A.PracticeTest
   ○ **C.** iscsi. 2008-08.com.pearson:VM1A
   ○ **D.** iscsi.pearson.com.VM1A.PracticeTest

33. You want to create a Windows Server 2003 virtual machine on your ESX/ESXi 4 host. What is the maximum disk size that can be assigned to this VM if you want to use a virtual SCSI disk?

   ○ **A.** 2GB-512bytes
   ○ **B.** 32GB-512bytes
   ○ **C.** 2TB-512bytes
   ○ **D.** 2EB-512bytes

34. You have created a Windows 7 virtual machine. Which file contains virtual hard disk information for this VM?

   ○ **A.** .vmx
   ○ **B.** .vmdk
   ○ **C.** .vswp
   ○ **D.** .vmsd

35. Which of the following vSphere 4 products is licensed using the per processor basis? (Choose all that apply.)

   ○ **A.** ESX/ESXi 4 Host
   ○ **B.** vMotion
   ○ **C.** DRS
   ○ **D.** HA

36. Which RAID level should you incorporate into your vSphere 4 environment if you want to use mirrored arrays?

- ○ **A.** RAID 0
- ○ **B.** RAID 1
- ○ **C.** RAID 4
- ○ **D.** RAID 5

37. You want to come up with a LUN design that works with your vSphere 4 environment. What VMware design schemes are available? (Choose two.)

- ○ **A.** Dynamic
- ○ **B.** Static
- ○ **C.** Adaptive
- ○ **D.** Predictive

38. You want to run the VCB Proxy for your backup solution. On which platform will this utility run?

- ○ **A.** Windows physical machine
- ○ **B.** Windows virtual machine
- ○ **C.** Linux physical machine
- ○ **D.** Linux virtual machine

39. What resources can you monitor on a performance graph of an ESX/ESXi 4 host? (Choose two.)

- ○ **A.** Ports
- ○ **B.** Users
- ○ **C.** CPU
- ○ **D.** RAM

40. You have just installed an ESX 4 host. Which of the following statements is true concerning post installation access to this host?

- ○ **A.** By default, root has full SSH access to the host.
- ○ **B.** By default, root is denied full access to the host using VIC.
- ○ **C.** By default, root is denied full access to the host by means of SSH.
- ○ **D.** By default, root has limited access to the host using VIC.
- ○ **E.** By default, root has limited access to the host using SSH.

41. Where would you find the PermitRootLogin parameter in a vSphere 4 environment?

    ○ **A.** On an ESX 4 host in the /etc/login/login.config file

    ○ **B.** On a vCenter server in the /etc/login/login.config file

    ○ **C.** On an ESX/ESXi 4 host in the /etc/ssh/sshd_config file

    ○ **D.** On a vCenter server in the /etc/ssh/sshd_config file

42. You have just installed an ESX 4 host. What is the default amount of memory allocated to the Service Console?

    ○ **A.** Depends on the hardware used

    ○ **B.** Dynamic, depends on amount of RAM installed but typically between 300MB and 800MB

    ○ **C.** 272MB

    ○ **D.** 300MB

    ○ **E.** 800MB

43. Your ESX/ESXi 4 host physically has two quad-core processors installed in it. You want to license this host on a per processor basis. How many licenses do you need to purchase?

    ○ **A.** 1

    ○ **B.** 2

    ○ **C.** 4

    ○ **D.** 6

    ○ **E.** 8

44. You have three ESX/ESXi 4.1 hosts with four quad-core CPUs in each. Additionally, you want to install vMotion on two of these servers. On a per processor basis, how many licenses do you need to purchase and install to satisfy all licensing requirements?

    ○ **A.** 4

    ○ **B.** 6

    ○ **C.** 8

    ○ **D.** 12

    ○ **E.** 20

45. What is the minimum number of ports an ESX/ESXi 4 vSwitch can have?

    ○ **A.** There is no minimum.

    ○ **B.** 4

    ○ **C.** 8

    ○ **D.** 16

    ○ **E.** 32

46. Which of the following statements correctly reflect similarities between a physical switch and a virtual switch? (Choose two.)

- ○ **A.** They both support STP.
- ○ **B.** Just like physical switches can be connected to one another, virtual switches can be connected to one another.
- ○ **C.** They both forward frames to one or more ports.
- ○ **D.** They both have MAC tables that they maintain.

47. You want to provide communication between virtual machines on a single ESX/ESXi 4 host. You do not want these machines to have access to other networks. Which type of virtual switch configuration should you use to accomplish this?

- ○ **A.** Loopback Virtual Switch
- ○ **B.** Internal Virtual Switch
- ○ **C.** Single Adapter Virtual Switch
- ○ **D.** Multiadapter Virtual Switch

48. You are configuring a virtual switch policy. Which tab should you select if you want to configure the average bandwidth?

- ○ **A.** General
- ○ **B.** Security
- ○ **C.** Traffic Shaping
- ○ **D.** NIC Teaming

49. You have recently deployed several ESX/ESXi 4.1 hosts. Using these hosts, which of the following is a true statement concerning a Fiber Channel SAN?

- ○ **A.** Its maximum transmission rate between two nodes is 1.5GB/sec.
- ○ **B.** Its maximum transmission rate between two nodes is 2GB/sec.
- ○ **C.** Its maximum transmission rate between two nodes is 4GB/sec.
- ○ **D.** Its maximum transmission rate between two nodes is 8GB/sec.

50. Which of the following are considered industry accepted topologies for a Fiber Channel SAN? (Choose two.)

- ○ **A.** Point-to-Point
- ○ **B.** Multipoint-to-Point
- ○ **C.** Multipoint-to-Multipoint
- ○ **D.** Point-to-Multipoint
- ○ **E.** Arbitrated Loop
- ○ **F.** Switched Fabric
- ○ **G.** Mesh Loop

51. You want to install vCenter Server in your vSphere 4 environment. You want to experience the fewest number of glitches possible during the installation. Based on VMware's recommendations, which of the following statements should you follow?

○ **A.** Install the Database Server after the vCenter Server.

○ **B.** Install the vCenter Server after the Database Server.

○ **C.** Install the vSphere Client before any other component.

○ **D.** Install the License Server immediately after the vCenter Server is installed.

52. You are creating a cluster in a vSphere 4 environment. Which of the following are correct statements concerning how you can configure the cluster? (Choose three.)

○ **A.** You can enable it to be Low Availability only.

○ **B.** You can enable it to be High Availability only.

○ **C.** You can enable it to be a Distributed Resource Scheduler only.

○ **D.** You can enable it to be both Low Availability and a Distributed Resource Scheduler resource pool.

○ **E.** You can enable it to be both a Low Availability and a High Availability resource pool.

○ **F.** You can enable it to be both a High Availability and a Distributed Resource Scheduler resource pool.

53. Which of the following is not a type of port group that can be configured on a virtual switch?

○ **A.** Service Console

○ **B.** Root

○ **C.** VMkernel

○ **D.** Virtual machine

54. In a vSphere 4 environment, what is a way to quickly generate similarly configured virtual machines?

○ **A.** Copy

○ **B.** Duplicate

○ **C.** Replica

○ **D.** Template

55. You are interested in installing the VMware Converter in your vSphere 4 environment. Which of the following will not be a good environment for this add-on product?

- ○ **A.** SuSE Linux Enterprise Server 10 SP1 physical machine
- ○ **B.** Windows 2000 Server virtual machine
- ○ **C.** Windows Vista 64-bit virtual machine
- ○ **D.** Windows Server 2008 32-bit physical machine

56. You are interested in installing the VMware Converter in your vSphere 4 environment. Which of the following is not a cloning method used by VMware Converter?

- ○ **A.** Cold cloning
- ○ **B.** Warm cloning
- ○ **C.** Hot cloning
- ○ **D.** Remote cloning
- ○ **E.** Local cloning

57. When you are using vMotion, without EVC enabled on the cluster, which is a true statement concerning CPU requirements?

- ○ **A.** vMotion works across CPU vendors.
- ○ **B.** vMotion works across CPU families.
- ○ **C.** vMotion works across CPUs with different multimedia instructions.
- ○ **D.** vMotion works across CPUs with different numbers of cores.

58. Which of the following statements is true concerning the creation of a virtual machine?

- ○ **A.** You can create a VM with a maximum of 2 SCSI adapters.
- ○ **B.** You can create a VM with a maximum of 60 SCSI hard drives.
- ○ **C.** You can create a VM with a maximum of 4 floppy disks.
- ○ **D.** You can create a VM with a maximum of 4 parallel ports.

59. What is another name for vmmemctl in a vSphere 4 environment?

- ○ **A.** SAN Driver
- ○ **B.** DRS Driver
- ○ **C.** Balloon-Driver
- ○ **D.** vMotion Driver

60. You are installing a new Windows 7 VM in your vSphere 4 environment. You want to install VMware Tools after the VM is installed. Which of the following are benefits of installing VMware Tools? (Choose three.)

    ○ **A.** Improved startup performance

    ○ **B.** Improved video capabilities

    ○ **C.** Improved memory management

    ○ **D.** Improved mouse capabilities

61. You want to create a SuSE Linux virtual machine on your ESX/ESXi 4 host. What is the maximum number of vCPUs that this VM can be assigned?

    ○ **A.** 1

    ○ **B.** 2

    ○ **C.** 4

    ○ **D.** 8

62. You have chosen to use a RAID 5 solution for your vSphere 4 environment. You have four 1TB drives that you want to use for this configuration. In this configuration, how much practical storage space is available?

    ○ **A.** About 1TB

    ○ **B.** About 2TB

    ○ **C.** About 3TB

    ○ **D.** About 4TB

63. Which of the following features are supported if you decide to implement an NFS storage solution in your vSphere 4 environment? (Choose all that apply.)

    ○ **A.** Format VMFS

    ○ **B.** Boot an ESX Server

    ○ **C.** Raw Device Mapping

    ○ **D.** vMotion

    ○ **E.** DRS

    ○ **F.** HA

64. You begin creating a new alarm in vCenter. On the Alarm Settings screen on the General tab, which trigger, by default, is given the highest priority?

    ○ **A.** Red

    ○ **B.** Yellow

    ○ **C.** Green

    ○ **D.** None

65. In the following address, used in a Fiber Channel SAN, what LUN is being accessed?

vmhba0:1:33:2

○ **A.** 0

○ **B.** 1

○ **C.** 2

○ **D.** 33

66. What is another name for the address assigned to the host bus adapter in a Fiber Channel SAN?

○ **A.** Fiber Channel Name

○ **B.** MAC Address

○ **C.** World Wide Name

○ **D.** World Wide MAC

67. What are two types of zoning used in a Fiber Channel SAN? (Choose two.)

○ **A.** Hard

○ **B.** Soft

○ **C.** Static

○ **D.** Dynamic

○ **E.** Defined

○ **F.** Undefined

68. What is the maximum number of vSwitches that an ESX/ESXi 4 host can have?

○ **A.** 32

○ **B.** 64

○ **C.** 127

○ **D.** 248

69. What is the maximum number of LUNs that an ESX/ESXi 4 host will process by default when it is powered on?

○ **A.** 32

○ **B.** 64

○ **C.** 128

○ **D.** 256

70. You want to create a resource pool in vCenter. By default, which of the following roles have the permissions necessary to accomplish this task? (Choose three.)

- ○ **A.** Datacenter Administrator
- ○ **B.** Virtual Machine Administrator
- ○ **C.** Virtual Machine Power User
- ○ **D.** Virtual Machine User
- ○ **E.** Resource Pool Administrator

71. Host failure detection occurs how many seconds after the HA service on a host stopped sending heartbeats to the other hosts in the cluster?

- ○ **A.** 10 seconds
- ○ **B.** 15 seconds
- ○ **C.** 20 seconds
- ○ **D.** 25 seconds

72. What is the maximum number of virtual CPUs per host that an ESX/ESXi 4 can have?

- ○ **A.** 64
- ○ **B.** 128
- ○ **C.** 256
- ○ **D.** 512

73. Which HA cluster component on an ESX/ESXi 4 host keeps a record of the other hosts in the cluster?

- ○ **A.** AAM
- ○ **B.** VMap
- ○ **C.** vpxa
- ○ **D.** IQN

74. You are installing ESX 4.1. What is the default size assigned to the partition used for a core dump?

- ○ **A.** 5GB
- ○ **B.** 544MB
- ○ **C.** 2GB
- ○ **D.** 100MB

75. What are three reasons why a company would elect to deploy a vSphere 4 solution in its enterprise? (Choose three.)

    ○ **A.** Multiple operating systems can be reliably run on a single server device.

    ○ **B.** Increase server utilization.

    ○ **C.** Decrease server utilization.

    ○ **D.** Multiple machines can be managed from a single point.

    ○ **E.** Hardware requirements are increased by a 10:1 ratio.

Answers to VCP4 Practice Exam

1. C
2. A
3. A
4. B, C
5. C
6. D
7. C
8. A
9. C
10. A, C, E
11. B
12. A, D
13. C, D
14. B
15. C
16. C, D
17. A, B
18. A, D
19. B, D
20. D
21. A
22. D
23. D
24. A
25. C, D

26. A
27. D
28. A
29. E
30. C
31. B
32. A
33. C
34. B
35. A, B, C, D
36. B
37. C, D
38. A, B
39. C, D
40. C
41. C
42. B
43. B
44. D
45. C
46. C, D
47. B
48. C
49. D
50. A, F

51. B
52. B, C, F
53. B
54. D
55. A
56. B
57. D
58. B
59. C
60. B, C, D
61. D
62. C
63. D, E, F
64. A
65. D
66. C
67. A, B
68. D
69. D
70. A, B, E
71. B
72. D
73. A
74. D
75. A, B, D

Question 1

C. One of the product features of the vSphere 4 suite is vMotion, which lets you move a virtual machine from one server to another without having to power it off. vMotion is a feature of the ESX/ESXi 4.1 and the vCenter. DRS, the Distributed Resource Scheduler, is a feature of the vSphere 4 suite that provides for the automatic distribution of resources across ESX/ESXi hosts in a cluster. Using the vMotion technique, virtual machines are migrated from an ESX/ESXi host that is low on resources to another ESX/ESXi host that has ample resources. Answer A is incorrect. HA, VMware High Availability, is a feature that enables virtual machines to be automatically restarted during an ESX/ESXi Server failure. VMs that are on a clustered server that fails are rapidly restarted on another host in the cluster. Answer B is incorrect. VCB, VMware Consolidate Backup, is a feature of the vSphere 4 suite that provides a centralized solution for backing up virtual machines using a centralized proxy server. Answer D is incorrect.

Question 2

A. A number of default roles are created during a vCenter installation. These roles provide an administrative way to efficiently assign one or more privileges to a user or group. One of the default roles is a Virtual Machine User. One privilege that a user assigned to the role of Virtual Machine User has by default is Create a Task. The other responses are not default privileges of the Virtual Machine User, so answers B, C, and D are incorrect. They are default privileges of other vCenter roles.

Question 3

A. There are several requirements for setting up an HA cluster in a vSphere 4 environment. One of the key requirements is that DNS resolution of all host-names must be configured. Hosts must be able to resolve other hosts using a configured DNS solution. Hosts cannot have the same IP address or DNS name in a cluster, so answers B and C are incorrect. Answer D is incorrect because it does not take into account that DNS must be configured for resolution.

Question 4

B, C. The ESX Server and the virtual machines that are guests of the server are managed by the Service Console. The Service Console on an ESX Server is the equivalent of a server operating system. Two services provided by the

Service Console are firewall and an Apache Tomcat Web Server. CPU scheduling is managed by the VMkernel, so answer D is incorrect. The VIC, or Virtual Infrastructure Client, allows you to connect to an ESX Server from a Windows station. Answer A is incorrect.

Question 5

C. One of the requirements for installing the vCenter is a 10/100 Network Adapter. That being said, VMware recommends a gigabit adapter for a vCenter implementation. Answers A, B, and D are incorrect because they are not minimum requirements.

Question 6

D. Several key ports that are important when configuring a firewall on an ESX Server include port 3260, which controls transmissions from the iSCSI client. Port 22 controls transmission to the SSH client, so answer A is incorrect. Port 902 controls transmission to the vCenter agent, so answer B is incorrect. Port 8000 controls incoming transmissions from vMotion, so answer C is incorrect.

Question 7

C. Several key ports that are important when configuring a firewall on an ESX Server include port 27000, which controls transmissions from the ESX Server to the license server. Answers A, B, and D are incorrect because they are controlled by ports other than port 27000.

Question 8

A. When creating and configuring a virtual network with standard vSwitches, you need to understand that ESX/ESXi hosts have some limitations. These include the following:

▶ No more than 4096 ports

▶ No more than 1016 active ports per vSwitch

▶ No more than 512 virtual switch port groups

Consequently, answer A is correct and answers B, C, and D are incorrect.

Question 9

C. The default size assigned to the /BOOT partition during an ESX 4.1 installation is 1100MB. Answers A, B, and D are incorrect because they are not the default size assigned.

Question 10

A, C, E. Three benefits of using a VCB solution on an enterprise network are entire virtual machines can be backed up, single VMDK files can be backed up, and single guest files can be backed up using VCB. Answers B, D, and F are incorrect because VCB can be used to back up these three, when integrated with third-party solutions.

Question 11

B. The two major components of the vSphere 4 suite are ESX/ESXi and vCenter. The features that come with the suite are categorized under these two components. One of the features of the ESX/ESXi host is Virtual SMP. The other options are features of vCenter and are incorrect. Answers A, C, and D are incorrect.

Question 12

A, D. When you are installing an ESX/ESXi 4.1 host, you have the option of entering a license key directly on the host, thereby using host-based licensing. You can also use an Evaluation license, or you can add the host to vCenter and assign it a license from the pool of available licenses, thus using Server licensing. There are no options for Network Based or Directory Based licensing of an ESX/ESXi 4.1 host. Answers B and C are incorrect.

Question 13

C, D. When a license is purchased for the vSphere 4 suite, it can be built on either a per processor or per instance basis. In the vSphere 4 suite, there are no per seat or per server licensing options. Answers A and B are incorrect. A license built on the per processor basis activates a feature based on the number of processors on the host. A license built on the per instance basis activates an instance of a feature no matter how many processors are on the host.

Question 14

B. In the vSphere 4 suite, if you are running a license server for backward compatibility with ESX/ESXi 3.x or earlier hosts, there is a 14-day grace period, by default, should a centralized license server fail, during which all ESX/ESXi 3.5 hosts continue to function without interruption. Answers A, C, and D are incorrect because they are not the grace periods as defined by VMware.

Question 15

C. In the vSphere 4 suite, a single instance of vCenter can manage up to 1000 ESX/ESXi 4.1 hosts. Answers A, B, D, and E are incorrect.

Question 16

C, D. In the vSphere 4 suite, if you are running a licenses server for backward compatibility with ESX/ESXi hosts 3.x or earlier, a grace period exists during which all ESX/ESXi 3.x or earlier hosts continue to function without interruption should a centralized license server fail. Certain features are available during this grace period, and some are available after the grace period if you are not able to restore the license server in the allotted time period. Some features that are available after the grace period, if the license server has not been restored in time, include turning on an ESX/ESXi 3.x host and deleting a VM from the inventory. Some features that are not available are powering on a VM and vMotioning a VM between two hosts. Answers A and B are incorrect.

Question 17

A, B. In the vSphere 4 suite, alarms are used when monitoring resource usage and the state of defined systems. These alarms can alert an administrator to a condition that needs attention. Based on the configuration of the alarm, an automated follow-up action can be initialized. When configuring a virtual machine CPU usage alarm, you can configure two options on the Triggers tab. Because this is a usage alarm, those options are Is Above or Is Below. Answers C and D are incorrect; they are not options available for a Usage alarm.

Question 18

A, D. In the vSphere 4 suite, alarms are used when monitoring resource usage and the state of defined systems. These alarms can alert an administrator to a condition that needs attention. Based on the configuration of the alarm, an automated follow-up action can be initialized. One of the tabs that requires configuration when creating an alarm is the Triggers tab. On this tab, you can define the type of trigger, its conditions, and the thresholds for warning and alert. Tolerance and frequency are configured elsewhere when setting up an alarm. Answers B and C are therefore incorrect.

Question 19

B, D. In the vSphere 4 suite, alarms are used when monitoring resource usage and the state of defined systems. These alarms can alert an administrator to a condition that needs attention. Based on the configuration of the alarm, an automated follow-up action can be initialized. When a host is being monitored, such as in this question, a notification email can be sent, a notification trap can be sent, and a script can be run. Answers A and C are incorrect because these are not possible follow-up actions that can be initialized.

Question 20

D. vSphere Client, lets you connect to a vCenter Server or an ESX/ESXi Server from a Windows workstation. One of the product features of the vSphere 4 suite is vMotion, which lets you move a virtual machine from one server to another without having to power it off. VMware High Availability, is a feature that enables virtual machines to be automatically restarted during an ESX/ESXi Server failure. VMs that are on a clustered server that fails are rapidly restarted on another host in the cluster. VCB, VMware Consolidate Backup, is a feature of the vSphere 4 suite that provides a centralized solution for backing up virtual machines using a centralized proxy server. Answers A, B, and C are incorrect.

Question 21

A. A number of default roles are used to secure an ESX/ESXi 4.1 host. These roles provide an administrative way to efficiently assign one or more privileges to a user or group. The default roles available on a host's Service Console are Administrator, No Access, and Read-only. There is no Read-Write role available for an ESX/ESXi 4.1 host. A custom role can be created, but one is not available by default. Answers B, C, and D are default roles and are therefore incorrect.

Question 22

D. The maximum number of ESX/ESXi 4.1 hosts that can be present in a cluster is 32. Answers A, B, and C are incorrect because they do not reflect the correct maximum as documented by VMware.

Question 23

D. In the vSphere 4 suite, alarms are used when monitoring resource usage and the state of defined systems. These alarms can alert an administrator to a condition that needs attention. Based on the configuration of the alarm, an automated follow-up action can be initialized. One of the first configuration steps is to select the type of alarm you are creating. This is done on the General tab. The two options are Monitor a Host for ESX/ESXi 4.1 Hosts and Monitor a Virtual Machine. The correct response is D. Answers A, B, and C are incorrect because they are not options on this tab.

Question 24

A. A resource pool in a vSphere 4 environment is a container created in Hosts and Clusters view used to limit the host CPU and memory utilization for a group of virtual machines. Answers B, C, and D are not the correct definition of a resource pool in a vSphere 4 environment.

Question 25

C, D. A resource pool in a vSphere 4 environment is a container created in Hosts and Clusters view used to limit the host CPU and memory utilization for a group of virtual machines. The attributes of a resource pool that can be configured are Shares, Reservations, Expandable Reservations, and Limits. Answers A and B are not configurable attributes of a resource pool.

Question 26

A. The only user who has full permissions to a newly installed ESX 4 host is the root user. However, when you add this host to vCenter, an additional user account is created on the host and is made a member of the Administrator role on the host. This user is the vpxuser account. This user account provides the vCenter with access to the ESX host. Answers B, C, and D are incorrect; they are not the account created on an ESX host when it joins a vCenter.

Question 27

D. Roles provide an administrative way to efficiently assign one or more privileges to a user or group. When a user is assigned to a role higher in the hierarchy, the permissions he or she receives through the role flow down to objects lower in the hierarchy. Some call this inheritance. If you do not want a user to have permissions to an object lower down in the hierarchy, you can assign the user to another role at that object. In this question, the solution is to assign Alex to the No Access role at the Vista VM. She will keep her permissions above this VM but have no permission at this VM. Answers A, B, and C do not provide a solution that is workable in this situation.

Question 28

A. To access the Web Access interface on a vCenter Server, you need a Windows or Linux computer, an IP address, and a web browser. The required web browsers are IE 6.0 or later on a Windows computer, Netscape Navigator 7.0 or later, Mozilla 1.x or later, and Firefox 1.0.7 or later. The only browser in this question that matches one of these browsers is A. Answers B, C, and D are incorrect because they do not satisfy the requirements.

Question 29

E. The only edition of vSphere 4 that gives the vNetwork Distributed Switch feature is the Enterprise Plus Edition. Answers A, B, C, and D are incorrect because they do not correctly represent the editions on which vDS is available.

Question 30

C. The authentication protocol used by iSCSI in a vSphere 4 environment is the CHAP protocol—the Challenge Handshake Authentication Protocol. This protocol is used by iSCSI initiators and targets. The other protocols are not used for authentication by iSCSI in a vSphere 4 environment. Answers A, B, and D are therefore incorrect.

Question 31

B. In the vSphere 4 suite of products, the ESX/ESXi 4.1 provides the virtualization layer on which virtual machines run. DRS, the Distributed Resource Scheduler, is a feature of the vSphere 4 suite that provides for the automatic distribution of resources across ESX hosts in a cluster. Virtual machines are migrated from an ESX host that is low on resources to another ESX host that has ample resources. Answer A is incorrect. VC, the vCenter, is a Windows-based management tool for managing all enterprise ESX Servers. Answer C is incorrect. SMP, VMware's Virtual Symmetric Multi-Processing, is a VMware solution for providing multiple virtual CPUs to virtual machines. Answer D is incorrect.

Question 32

A. The correct representation of an iSCSI node ID generically is iqn.year-month.<domain name reversed>:<alternate name>. When you use the date supplied in the question, the correct ID is iqn.2008-08.com.pearson:VM1A. The other choices do not follow the naming schema used for an iSCSI node ID. Therefore, Answers B, C, and D are incorrect.

Question 33

C. When creating and configuring a new virtual machine in a vSphere 4 enterprise, you must know both the hardware requirements for a VM and the maximum hardware that you can configure for a VM. If you are using a SCSI disk(s) for a VM, the maximum disk space allowed for a virtual hard drive is 2TB-512 bytes. Answers A, B, and D are incorrect because they do not reflect the correct maximum allowed disk space.

Question 34

B. When a virtual machine is created, a number of files are created that serve specific purposes. They include the file that stores virtual hard disk information and has a .vmdk extension. The other extensions listed represent files that store virtual hard disk information for the VM. Answers A, C, and D are incorrect.

Question 35

A, B, C, D. When a license is purchased for the vSphere 4 suite, it can be built on either a per processor or per instance basis. A license built on the per processor basis activates a feature based on the number of processors on the host. A license built on the per instance basis activates an instance of a feature no matter how many processors are on the host. vSphere 4 products available on a per processor basis are the ESX/ESXi Server, vCenter Agent, vMotion, Storage vMotion, Consolidate Backup, DRS, HA, and DPM. All choices are correct.

Question 36

B. RAID, Redundant Array of Independent (Inexpensive) Disks, is often used in a vSphere 4 environment as the platform from which LUNs are defined. A number of RAID levels are common. One of the most common is RAID 1, which provides disk mirroring (mirrored arrays) and disk duplexing, a type of fault tolerance. The other answers—A, C, and D—do not provide disk mirroring or duplexing.

Question 37

C, D. A logical arrangement of disk space that is allocated from multiple physical disks is a LUN, a Logical Unit Number. VMware uses two schemes: an adaptive scheme and a predictive scheme. VMware does not use the terms dynamic or static for defining a LUN design. Answers A and B are incorrect.

Question 38

A, B. As of VCB 1.2, you can run the VCB Proxy on a Windows physical or virtual machine. Answers C and D are not platforms compatible with the VCB Proxy and are therefore incorrect.

Question 39

C, D. When the Performance tab is selected for a host in vCenter, the resources that you can select are CPU, Disk Space, Memory, Network, and System. There are no options for Ports or Users. Answers A and B are incorrect.

Question 40

C. When an ESX 4 host is initially installed, root has full access to the server using VIC but has no access to the server using SSH. For security reasons, SSH access is denied to root. This access can be changed but should be done so under advisement because of the security issues it raises. Answers A, B, D, and E are incorrect statements of fact.

Question 41

C. The PermitRootLogin is found on an ESX 4 host in the /etc/ssh/sshd_config file. The other answers—A, B, and D—are incorrect because they do not correctly point to the location where you can find the PermitRootLogin parameter.

Question 42

B. The default amount of memory allocated to the Service Console when an ESX 4 host is installed varies between 300MB and 800MB depending on the size of the physical memory installed. For example, if the host has 32GB of memory, the Service Console will get 500MB by default; if the ESX host has 128GB of memory, then the SC will get 700MB by default. Answers A, C, and D are incorrect; they do not reflect the default memory allocated to the Service Console.

Question 43

B. A license built on the per processor basis activates a feature based on the number of processors on the host. According to VMware, a dual-core or quad-core processor counts as a single processor despite the fact that multiple processing units exist on each of these chips. Based on that fact, because two processors are installed, two licenses are required. Answers A, C, D, and E are incorrect because they do not reflect the needed number of licenses.

Question 44

D. A license built on a per processor basis activates a feature based on the number of processors on the host. According to VMware, a dual-core or quad-core processor counts as a single processor despite the fact that multiple processing units exist on each of these chips. In this question, you need 12 licenses just for the ESX/ESXi 4.1 Servers. Answers A, B, C, and E are incorrect.

Question 45

C. The minimum number of ports that an ESX/ESXi 4.1 vSwitch can have is eight. The other responses are not correct. Answers A, B, D, and E are not representative of the minimum number of ports that a vSwitch has.

Question 46

C, D. Physical switches and virtual switches have some characteristics that are similar. For example, they both forward frames to one or more ports, and they both have MAC tables that they maintain. They both do not support STP; you cannot connect vSwitches to one another. Therefore, answers A and B are incorrect.

Question 47

B. In a vSphere 4 environment, the three types of virtual switches are internal, single adapter, and multiadapter types. An internal virtual switch provides communication between virtual machines on a single ESX/ESXi 4.1 host without access to other external networks. There are no loopback switches. Answers A, C, and D are incorrect because they do not accomplish what is called for in the question.

Question 48

C. When you are configuring a virtual switch policy, four tabs are available: General, Security, Traffic Shaping, and NIC Teaming. Average Bandwidth is configured on the Traffic Shaping tab. Answers A, B, and D are incorrect because average bandwidth is not configured on these tabs.

Question 49

D. Fiber Channel SANs are typically rated by their transmission rate. Currently, the highest throughput Fiber Channel SAN is 8GB/sec if you are using ESX/ESXi 4.1 Hosts. Answers A, B, and C are incorrect because they do not reflect the maximum data transmission rate between two nodes.

Question 50

A, F. Two industry-accepted topologies for a Fiber Channel SAN are Point-to-Point and Switched Fabric. The other responses are not Fiber Channel topologies or are not supported by VMware. Answers B, C, D, E, and G are incorrect.

Question 51

B. When you are doing an installation of vCenter in an enterprise, the correct order of component installation is critical if you want to avoid as many issues as possible. The order recommended by VMware is 1-Database Server, 2-License Server (if you plan to have pre-ESX 4 hosts), 3-vCenter Server, and finally 4-vSphere Client. Based on this order, answer B is correct. The vCenter Server should be installed after the Database Server is installed. Answers A, C, and D are incorrect because they do not reflect an order recommended by VMware.

Question 52

B, C, F. When you create a cluster, you can enable it to be High Availability only, Distributed Resource Scheduler only, or both High Availability and Distributed Resource Scheduler. There is no Low Availability option in a vSphere 4 environment. Answers A, D, and E are incorrect.

Question 53

B. Three types of port groups can be configured on a virtual switch in a vSphere 4 environment. They are Service Console, VMkernel, and virtual machine. There is no Root port group on a vSwitch. Answers A, C, and D are incorrect because they are configurable port groups.

Question 54

D. In a vSphere 4 environment, the new and improved way to provision or generate similarly configured virtual machines is to use a template. In some environments, you do this with images, copies, and duplicates, but in vSphere 4, you do this with templates. Answers A, B, and C are incorrect.

Question 55

A. The VMware Converter is a Windows application. It does not run on the Linux platform. It can run on a 32-bit or 64-bit Windows OS as a physical machine or as a virtual machine. This includes Windows 2000 Server and Windows Server 2008.

Question 56

B. The VMware Converter is a Windows application capable of cloning a physical or virtual disk to a new virtual disk. Converter can perform hot cloning, cold cloning, remote cloning, and local cloning. It does not perform warm cloning.

Question 57

D. A main consideration for using vMotion in a vSphere 4 environment, especially if you do not have EVC enabled on the cluster is the CPUs that are in the source and destination hosts. The CPUs in the source and destination hosts must be from the same vendor and family. Also, the CPUs must not have different multimedia instructions. There can be a different number of cores and cache sizes. Answers A, B, and C are incorrect because they violate the CPU requirements for vMotion.

Question 58

B. When creating and configuring a new virtual machine in a vSphere 4 enterprise, you must know both the hardware requirements for a VM and the maximum hardware that you can configure for a VM. A virtual machine in this environment can have a maximum of 3 parallel ports, 4 SCSI adapters with up to 15 devices on each, for a total of 60 devices (hard drives), 2 floppy drives, and 4 serial ports. Answers A, C, and D are incorrect because they exceed the defined maximums.

Question 59

C. Another name for vmmemctl in a vSphere 4 environment is the balloon-driver. Its function is to dynamically reclaim memory in VMs when an ESX system is experiencing physical memory strain. Based on memory needs, the balloon-driver can be inflated or deflated. Answers A, B, and D are not available options.

Question 60

B, C, D. VMware Tools is a software add-on that is installed after a VM's operating system has been installed and is up and running. VMware Tools improves a VM's operability and performance. Some of the benefits of VMware Tools are it improves mouse performance, video capability, and memory management. It does not improve startup performance because the guest OS has to be up and running for the VMware Tools to be active. Answer A is incorrect.

Question 61

D. When creating and configuring a new virtual machine in a vSphere 4 enterprise, you must know both the hardware requirements for a VM and the maximum hardware that you can configure for a VM. A virtual machine in this environment can have a maximum of eight vCPUs. Answers A, B, and C are incorrect because they do not correctly reflect the correct number of vCPUs that a VM can have.

Question 62

C. RAID, Redundant Array of Independent (Inexpensive) Disks, is often used in a vSphere 4 environment as the platform from which LUNs are defined. A number of RAID levels are common. One of the most common is RAID 5, which provides Disk Striping with parity. In a RAID 5 environment, you typically have three or more drives that are in the array. In this environment, data is written across all drives as is parity data. In essence, the practical storage capacity of a RAID 5 array is the equivalent of N-1 drives. In this question, that means you have about 3 TB of practical storage. The equivalent of one drive is written as parity across all drives in the array. Answers A, B, and D are incorrect because they do not accurately reflect the practical storage capacity.

Question 63

D, E, F. In a vSphere 4 suite, an NFS storage solution supports DRS, HA, and vMotion. It does not support Raw Device Mapping, formatting VMFS, or booting an ESX Server. Answers A, B, and C are therefore incorrect.

Question 64

A. In the vSphere 4 suite, alarms are used when monitoring resource usage and the state of defined systems. These alarms can alert an administrator to a condition that needs attention. Based on the configuration of the alarm, an automated follow-up action can be initialized. When you are defining the type of alarm, an available option is to define the trigger priority, the order in which alarms are triggered. Alerts are red, warnings are yellow, and safe/normal operating state is green. The trigger priority can either be defined as red first or green first. The default setting is red, or alerts have top priority. Answers B, C, and D are incorrect because they do not reflect the default trigger priority setting.

Question 65

D. In the address vmhba0:1:33:2, host bus adapter 0 is accessing partition 2 on LUN 33 using storage processor 1. Answers A, B, and C are incorrect.

Question 66

C. Another name for the address assigned to the host bus adapter in a Fiber Channel SAN is the WWN, or World Wide Name. It is also referred to as the World Wide Port Name. Its function is similar to the MAC address assigned to a router port or network adapter. Answers A, B, and D are incorrect.

Question 67

A, B. In a Fiber Channel SAN, zoning is used to create a logical group of physical devices to facilitate communication between them. Two main types of zoning are used in a Fiber Channel SAN: hard and soft. Answers C, D, E, and F are incorrect because they are not types of zones used in an FC SAN.

Question 68

D. An ESX/ESXi 4.1 host can have a maximum of 248 vSwitches. Answers A, B, and C are incorrect. They do not correctly reflect the maximum number of vSwitches that can be configured on an ESX/ESXi 4.1 host.

Question 69

D. When an ESX/ESXi 4.1 host is powered on, it, by default, processes the first 256 LUNs that are present and to which it is given access. Answers A, B, and C are not correct.

Question 70

A, B, E. In a default installation of vCenter, numerous roles are created automatically. Each role has a default set of defined permissions. Based on the task required, some of these roles can accomplish the task, whereas others cannot. The roles that have the default permissions to create a resource pool are the Datacenter Administrator, Virtual Machine Administrator, and a Resource Pool Administrator. Answers C and D are incorrect; they do not have necessary permissions to create a resource pool.

Question 71

B. Host detection Failure occurs after 15 seconds of no heartbeat receipt from the other hosts in the HA cluster. Answers A, C, and D are not correct time-out settings.

Question 72

D. When you are planning an ESX/ESXi 4.1 installation and deployment, it is important to know some of the maximums that you can configure. One important one is the maximum number of virtual CPUs you can have per host. The maximum is 512.

Question 73

A. When an ESX/ESXi host is added to an HA cluster, several components are installed on the host. They include the AAM (Automated Availability Manager), VMap, and the vpxa. AAM is the engine for HA, and the vpxa service manages components of the HA cluster. Communication between the AAM and vpxa is managed by VMap. The AAM keeps a record of the other hosts in the cluster. Answers B and C are incorrect. Answer D is a term associated with iSCSI addressing.

Question 74

D. The default size of the boot partition is 1.25GB, which includes 2 partitions, the /boot with a default size of 1100MB, and the vmkcore partition with a default size of 100MB. Answers A, B, and C are incorrect because they are not the default size assigned.

Question 75

A, B, D. There are a host of benefits for deploying a vSphere 4 enterprise solution that can be delineated, depending on which VMware reference you cite. Three benefits are multiple operating systems can be reliably run on a single server device; server utilization will be increased; and multiple machines, including virtual machines, can be centrally managed. Answers C and E are not benefits of a vSphere 4 solution.

APPENDIX A
Need to Know More?

Atkinson, Brian. http://communities.vmware.com/blogs/vmroyale. Blog.

Epping, Duncan. http://www.yellow-bricks.com/. Blog.

Khnaser, Elias. *VMware vSphere 4 Training Course*. Elias Khnaser. 2010. ISBN 9780981748726. URL: http://www.eliaskhnaser.com.

Lowe, Scott. *Mastering VMware vSphere 4*. Sybex. 2008. ISBN 0470481382.

van Zanten, Gabrie. http://www.gabesvirtualworld.com/. Blog.

Glossary

802.1Q VLAN tagging   VLAN tagging allows you to create several port groups on a single vSwitch and assign them a VLAN ID that corresponds to the VLAN ID configured on the switch. These port groups can then route traffic to the specific VLANs.

A

admission control   This configurable HA option allows you to set a policy to control virtual machine power on tasks. The two valid policies are either to allow or disallow VMs from powering on if they violate availability constraints.

affinity   This DRS rule implies that virtual machines should be on the same ESX host at all times.

alarms   These thresholds are configured on either a host or a virtual machine that is designed to send the administrator a notification that a certain threshold has been reached.

anti-affinity   This DRS rule implies that virtual machines cannot exist on the same ESX/ESXi host at the same time.

available memory   The initial memory that you configure for a virtual machine during its creation.

B

balloon-driver   This guest operating system device driver is installed as part of the VMware Tools installation. When an ESX/ESXi system comes under physical memory strain, the VMkernel selects a virtual machine (after taking into consideration each VM's memory shares and reservations) and inflates the device driver inside the guest operating system and consumes all the available memory that is not being used by the operating system. It then releases this acquired memory to the ESX/ESXi system to ease its memory requirements. When the need for this memory ceases to exist, the device driver is deflated or stopped, and the memory is returned to the guest operating system.

beacon probe   In addition to doing Link Status, this method is similar to a heartbeat; it continuously sends packets between the adapters, and if a heartbeat is missed, it assumes there is an issue and fails over.

block-level transfer   This block of storage is presented to a host as local storage. It is transmitted over the median as a block of data.

C

cluster   This is the implicit collection of CPU and memory resources across ESX/ESXi hosts that are members of this cluster to allow for the creation of VMware Distributed Resource Scheduler (DRS) and VMware High Availability (HA) clusters.

cluster-across-boxes   Implies that the node members of the cluster reside on different ESX/ESXi hosts.

cluster-in-a-box   A type of cluster that implies all the cluster's nodes reside on the same ESX/ESXi host.

cold cloning   The process of cloning a machine while it is powered off.

cold migration   Used to move a virtual machine from one ESX host to another while the machine is powered off.

core services   This is the main module of vCenter, the basic heart of the application that gives way to virtual machine provisioning, Task Scheduler, events logging, and so on.

D

datacenter   This is the logical repository of hosts and virtual machines.

distributed resource scheduler   VMware DRS is an enterprise-level feature that uses vMotion to load-balance an ESX host's CPU and memory resources, thereby maintaining and ensuring that all ESX hosts that are members of this cluster always have a balanced load in terms of CPU and memory.

distributed services   This module gives way to features like vMotion, High Availability, and Distributed Resource Scheduler. This is the place where the features that require a separate license stem from.

E

expandable reservation This option allows child resource pools to tap into the parent resource pool and harness whatever resources are available to satisfy their own shortage.

F

fiber channel This type of SAN is a high-speed transport protocol that moves SCSI commands between two nodes at speeds of up to 8GB.

file-level transfer File-level transfer occurs when the host is presented with a logical pointer to a block of disk; a perfect example of this is a network drive letter in Windows. When transmitting over the network, the data is transferred on a file level.

G

graphical mode Allows you to install ESX using the full-featured graphical interface wizard.

guided consolidation Guided consolidation analyzes systems based on their performance metrics and determines whether they are good candidates for virtualization.

H

hard zoning Implemented at the Fiber Channel Switch level and prevents physical access to any device that is not a member of the zone, thus making this type of zoning a more secure one.

hardware execution context An HEC is a thread that is scheduled on a physical processor. The number of HECs available for scheduling depends on the number of physical cores available in the system.

host isolation ESX/ESXi host isolation occurs when the host stops receiving a heartbeat from the rest of the hosts in the High Availability cluster. When this situation occurs, it is otherwise known as a "split-brain" network phenomenon.

host-based license key This license key is entered into the ESX/ESXi host and can be used only by this particular host.

hot cloning The process of cloning a machine while online without taking it offline or affecting its productivity.

Hyperthreading This Intel Corporation technology allows you to schedule multiple threads on the same processor at the same time.

I

iSCSI Internet Small Computer System Interface is an IP-based storage network that is capable of transmitting SCSI commands over your existing Ethernet infrastructure.

iSCSI software initiator This feature renders a network interface card in an ESX/ESXi server as a multifunction NIC, which can then be used to connect to storage devices using TCP/IP over Ethernet.

L

license server This server is the central repository where license files are stored in a pool and assigned to ESX/ESXi Server hosts as needed. The license server is used for backward compatibility, in cases where you have pre-ESX/ESXi 4 hosts.

limit This is the maximum that a virtual machine can consume in terms of CPU, measured in megahertz (MHz), and physical host memory, measured in megabytes (MB).

link status This method determines if there is a network connection by whether a connection is detected on the port. If a cable is connected to the port, it reports the connection as active; if not, it fails over.

LUN masking This is the process of obscuring or hiding specific LUNs from being visible to hosts.

M

map This is a way of graphically understanding the connection topology of hosts and virtual machines to each other and to networks and storage.

N

NAS Network Attached Storage is a self-sufficient storage system, an entity on its own that can be attached via Ethernet to the traditional network.

NFS Network File System is a network protocol. vSphere 4 supports NFS3 over TCP.

NIC teaming Allows for the grouping of multiple physical NICs on the same vSwitch to provide fault tolerance, redundancy, and load balancing of outgoing IP traffic from the virtual switch.

notify switches This option notifies physical switches of changes such as a physical NIC failover or a new physical NIC addition to a NIC team.

P

per instance A per instance license is based on how many servers in your environment have the software installed on them. Currently, vCenter is the only component that is licensed on a per instance basis.

per processor A per processor license model is constructed based on the number of physical CPU sockets that are available in a system.

permission Assigned to an object in the inventory and grants a user or group the right to perform a certain task that is affiliated with that user's or group's assigned role.

physical-to-virtual cluster In this type of cluster, traditional physical machines and virtual machines make up the cluster's nodes. It is only supported using Microsoft MSCS.

port trunking A trunk port is a port on the physical switch that you configure to be aware of other VLANs that exist on other switches; as such, anything that plugs into this port is able to pass IP communications to all the visible VLANs.

privilege This is an allowed action or function; in other words, a privilege allows a user or group to perform a certain task.

promiscuous mode Promiscuous mode, if set to Accept, would pass all the unicast frames that pass through the virtual switch to a virtual machine connected to that virtual switch. This setting is set to Reject by default to prevent frames destined for a particular VM from being read by other VMs.

R

reservation This is the minimum that a virtual machine needs in terms of CPU and memory resources to function properly.

resource pool Allows for the grouping of virtual machines and applies the same resource policy on them. A resource pool can be created for a single ESX/ESXi host or to a DRS cluster to govern the CPU and memory resources.

role This is a collection of privileges that a user or group is allowed to perform.

root folder This folder is the topmost level of the inventory. It is the highest level, and there is nothing before it.

route based on IP hash When this setting is selected, each packet's source and destination IP addresses are hashed, and an uplink communication link is selected based on that hashing. This would also require the physical switches to be properly configured.

route based on originating port ID This setting configures communications based on the virtual port where the virtual machine is connected on the virtual switch.

route based on source MAC hash This setting configures communications uplinks based on the MAC address of the virtual machine from which the traffic originated. This would also require the physical switches to be properly configured.

S

server-based license file This license file is uploaded on the license server and allows for the licenses to be pooled and, as such, allows any ESX/ESXi hosts that point to this license server to gain licenses as long as licenses are available.

Service Console Used to manage ESX Server, but is also used to help the VMkernel during its boot process. The Service Console operating system is a 64-bit, 2.6 based Linux kernel, compatible with Red Hat Linux Enterprise 5.2, CentOS 5.2, and equivalent Linux systems.

share Identifies the frequency and priority a virtual machine will have in terms of accessing time slices on the physical CPU and memory. All VMs are assigned shares; the more shares a virtual machine is assigned, the more priority it has over physical resources.

snapshot This is a moment-in-time capture of a virtual machine's state, including its virtual machine hardware, memory, and disk states.

soft zoning Soft zoning, which is implemented at the Fiber Channel Switch level, is the method of obscuring ports so that they are not visible to devices outside their native zone.

SSH Secure Shell access allows you to remotely access your ESX Server and configure and manage it from a command line.

T

template Area template is a preconfigured VM whose sole purpose is to allow for the quick and easy provisioning of virtual machines. A template is an image of a VM that you intend to use as the basis for deploying other VMs.

text mode This lightweight installation method has limited graphics, no mouse support, and relies solely on a text-based installation; it is ideal for ESX Server installations over slow networks.

traffic shaping Allows for greater control over the amount of outgoing bandwidth that is available to virtual machines.

transparent page sharing This technique of memory optimization detects virtual machines that are accessing the same memory pages, and instead of allocating different copies of that memory space for each VM, it maps all the VMs that are accessing the same memory space to a single memory space.

U

users and groups Accounts that are allowed to log in to the virtual infrastructure. They are typically based on Active Directory or the local Windows system where vCenter is installed. You are able to create users and groups on ESX/ESXi, but this is strongly discouraged for better manageability.

V

virtual machine A VM is a collection of virtual hardware that collectively presents a framework that allows a guest operating system to be installed and thus allows for the complete functionality of this guest operating system. A VM is made up of software, specifically a collection of files that can be manipulated like any other files.

virtual machine failure monitoring
This technology is disabled by
default. Its function is to monitor
virtual machines, which it queries
every 20 seconds via a heartbeat.

VMFS   Virtual Machine File
System is a VMware-developed file
system designed solely to run virtual
machines. VMFS is a light file system and, as such, does not have all
the overhead that the other file systems have, making it an ideal environment for virtual machines to run
in. The only structures you can create on VMFS volumes are directo-
ries to organize the VM files.

VMkernel   Also known as the
hypervisor, this software is installed
on the bare metal hardware and thus
creates the virtualization layer. The
VMkernel is the regulator that manages access to the physical hardware.

VMkernel swap   The virtual
machine's memory pages are copied
into the swap file to allow the VM
to continue to function and then
relinquish this memory to the
VMkernel. This is a last-resort
measure in case the balloon-driver
cannot allocate enough memory to
satisfy the VMkernel's needs. As
with any other system, when heavy
paging occurs, the VM's performance suffers.

vMotion   This feature allows a running virtual machine to be migrated
without interruption from one host
to another.

**VMware Consolidated Backup
(VCB)**   VCB is an alternative
method of backing up and restoring
virtual machines at the file level or

image level. It is based on snapshots
and is a backup framework that
allows third-party backup software
to plug in and back up VMs in a
centralized fashion.

VMware Converter   This product is
used to extend vCenter capabilities.
Its primary function is to convert
physical or virtual machines into
ESX-compatible virtual machines.

VMware DRS   Distributed
Resource Scheduler is a VMware
cluster technology that allows for
the balancing of ESX host CPU and
memory resources.

VMware HA   High Availability is a
technology that restarts virtual
machines on a different ESX/ESXi
host in the event that the original
ESX/ESXi host should experience a
failure. HA ensures the VMs are
brought back online as quickly as
possible.

VMware SMP   VMware Virtual
Symmetric Multi-Processing is the
VMware-developed technology that
allows virtual machines to have
more than one virtual CPU. SMP
allows VMs to have up to eight
vCPUs.

VMware Tools   This software package is installed after the guest operating system is up and running; it
provides performance and other
enhancements to the virtual
machine's operability.

VMware vSphere 4   A suite of
applications that collectively make
enterprise class virtualization possible.

vpxuser Added to the Administrators group in ESX/ESXi after ESX/ESXi server is joined to vCenter. vCenter uses this user to authenticate itself to the ESX/ESXi host to send preapproved commands.

vSphere client This is the client tool that allows you to administer all aspects of your VMware Infrastructure from a graphical user interface. The vSphere client allows you to create, manage, and monitor your virtual machines and allows you to log in to either your ESX/ESXi hosts directly or to vCenter.

Index

W-X-Y-Z

EXAM CRAM

VCP4

VMware Certified
Professional
VCP-410 Exam

Second Edition

CD FEATURES TEST QUESTIONS

PEARSON   ELIAS KHNASER

 **FREE Online
Edition**

Your purchase of **VCP4 Exam Cram: VMware Certified Professional** includes
access to a free online edition for 45 days through the Safari Books Online
subscription service. Nearly every Exam Cram book is available online through
Safari Books Online, along with more than 5,000 other technical books and
videos from publishers such as Addison-Wesley Professional, Cisco Press,
IBM Press, O'Reilly, Prentice Hall, and Sams.

SAFARI BOOKS ONLINE allows you to search for a specific answer, cut and
paste code, download chapters, and stay current with emerging technologies.

Activate your FREE Online Edition at
www.informit.com/safarifree

> **STEP 1:**   Enter the coupon code: PMVHQVH.

> **STEP 2:**   New Safari users, complete the brief registration form.
>   Safari subscribers, just log in.

If you have difficulty registering on Safari or accessing the online edition,
please e-mail customer-service@safaribooksonline.com

Safari
Books Online

 Addison
Wesley   AdobePress   ALPHA   **Cisco Press**   **FT** Press   **IBM**
Press.   Microsoft
Press   New
Riders

O'REILLY   Peachpit
Press   PRENTICE
HALL   QUE   Redbooks   S/\MS $sas   Sun   WILEY